Social Identities in Revolutionary Russia

Also by Madhavan K. Palat

IDEOLOGICAL CHOICES IN POST-SOVIET RUSSIA

Social Identities in Revolutionary Russia

Edited by

Madhavan K. Palat
Professor of Russian and European History
Jawaharlal Nehru University
New Delhi
India

Lewis

To recall the good old days of 30 years ago, Affectionately Madhavan Nov. 2003

palgrave   in association with
Indira Gandhi National Centre for the Arts

First published 2001 by
PALGRAVE
Houndmills, Basingstoke, Hampshire RG21 6XS and
175 Fifth Avenue, New York, N. Y. 10010
Companies and representatives throughout the world

PALGRAVE is the new global academic imprint of
St. Martin's Press LLC Scholarly and Reference Division and
Palgrave Publishers Ltd (formerly Macmillan Press Ltd).

ISBN 0–333–92947–0

This book is printed on paper suitable for recycling and
made from fully managed and sustained forest sources.

A catalogue record for this book is available
from the British Library.

Library of Congress Cataloging-in-Publication Data
Social identities in revolutionary Russia / edited by
Madhavan K. Palat.
        p. cm.
Includes bibliographical references and index.
ISBN 0–333–92947–0 (cloth)
        1. Russia—History—Nicholas II, 1894–1917. 2. Soviet
Union—History—Revolution, 1917–1921. 3. Nationalism–
–Russia—History. I. Palat, Madhavan K.

DK262 .S53 2001
947.08'3—dc21
                                                    00-054532

10   9   8   7   6   5   4   3   2   1
10   09   08   07   06   05   04   03   02   01

Printed and bound in Great Britain by
Antony Rowe Ltd, Chippenham, Wiltshire

Contents

Acknowledgements

The conference which gave rise to this volume was supported and financed by the Indira Gandhi National Centre for the Arts (IGNCA) in Delhi in 1996 as part of its programme of encouraging academic programmes on the history and culture of Russia and Central Asia. I am most grateful to the participants. Let me also thank the Indian Council for Cultural Relations and the Indian National Trust for Art and Cultural Heritage (INTACH), London, for so generously meeting the international travel costs for Boris Kolonitskii and Judith Pallot respectively; the IGNCA funded both V. V. Serbinenko and A. V. Buganov from Moscow, as well as those who had to travel to Delhi from within India. Gregory Freeze was unfortunately unable to attend, but it is a pleasure to include his substantial contribution. I am especially grateful to Rekha Kamath for translating Dietrich Beyrau's article from the German, and to Hari Vasudevan for translating the three Russian contributions. The conference was held at the India International Centre, which as usual provided the ideal setting for a conference of this sort.

M. K. P.

Glossary

chelobitnaia	a formal address or a humble submission
demokratiia	democracy
gorodskie dumy	municipal councils
guberniia	province
hromady	local committees
iuridicheskoe litso	juridical entity
khokol	pre-national Ukrainian peasant
kraevedenie	regional and local studies
krai	region
kulizhnye	allotment lands
letopisi	medieval chronicles
lubochnaia	literature sold around shrines
meshchane	petty townsmen of the estates hierarchy
murza	member of Tatar gentry
narod	the people
narodnost'	nationality
natsiia	the nation
obrok	quit-rent
obshchestvo	the public or society
obshchina	land commune
opeka	tutelage or guardianship
pochvennichestvo	nativism
pomestnyi sobor	national church council
popechitel'stva	parish guardianships
predaniia	traditions
prikhodskie sovety	parish soviets
prosveshchenie	'enlightenment'
raznochinets	people (usually professionals) who do not belong to any specific estate
sokha	measure of arable land serving as unit of taxation
sotsializm	socialism
sverkhnarodnoe	supranational
svobada	freedom
temnyi narod	ignorant and primitive people
tserkovnyi starosta	church elder
uezd	county

volnodumtsy	freethinking peasants during serfdom
volost'	administrative unit below the *uezd* or county
vsechelovecheskoe bratstvo	universal human brotherhood
vsechelovechnost'	human universalism
zemliachestva	regional associations
zemskii sud	local court
zemstva	elected local self-government institutions
zemtsy	officials of the zemstva

Notes on the Contributors

Dietrich Beyrau is Professor at the Institüt für osteuropäische Geschichte und Landeskunde, University of Tübingen, Germany. He has worked on the military in tsarist Russia and the intelligentsia in the Soviet Union. His publications include *Militär und Gesellschaft im vorrevolutionären Russland* (Cologne, 1984); *Inteligenz und Dissens: die russischen Bildungsschichten in der Sowjetunion, 1917–1985* (Göttingen, 1993).

A. V. Buganov is at the Institute of Ethnology and Anthropology, Russian Academy of Sciences, Moscow. His research interests include Russian peasant folklore and the history of the Church. Among his publications is *Russkaia istoriia v pamiati krest'ian XIX veka i natsional'noe samosoznanie* (Moscow, 1992).

Gregory L. Freeze is the Victor and Gwendolyn Beinfield Professor of History at Brandeis University (USA). He has published a number of monographs and articles on Russian religious and social history, served as editor-in-chief for the Russian Archive Project, and most recently edited *Russia: A History* (Oxford, 1997). He is currently completing the two-volume study *Church, Religion and Society in Modern Russia, 1740–1940*.

Boris Ivanovich Kolonitskii is at the Institute of History, Russian Academy of Sciences, St Petersburg. He has been working on popular political culture in revolutionary Russia, especially on the political culture of 1917. He has frequently travelled to the West and his work has been translated in *Slavic Review*. He has published, jointly with Orlando Figes, *Interpreting the Russian Revolution: The Language and Symbols of 1917* (New Haven and London, 1999). He is currently preparing a new book, *Simvoly gosudarstvennogo perevorota i perevorot v gosudarstvennoi simvoliki*.

Bohdan Krawchenko is Vice-Rector at the Academy of Public Administration, Office of the President of Ukraine. He was formerly in the Department of Slavic and East European Studies, and Director of the Canadian Institute of Ukrainian Studies, University of Alberta, Canada. His major publications include *Social Change and National Consciousness in Twentieth-Century Ukraine* (Basingstoke, 1985).

Madhavan K. Palat is Professor of Russian and European History at the Centre for Historical Studies, Jawaharlal Nehru University, New Delhi. He has worked on labour policy before 1917, the multinational Russian Empire and Soviet Union, the Russian conquest of Central Asia, and Eurasianism. His main publications are *Ideological Choices in Post-Soviet Russia* (New Delhi, 1997), 'Eurasianism as an Ideology for Russia's Future', *Economic and Political Weekly*, vol. 28, no. 51 (18 December 1993), and 'The Russian Conquest of Inner Asia', *Studies in History* (1988) no. 4.

Judith Pallot is a lecturer at the University of Oxford and Official Student of Christ Church, and she is currently researching the history of the Russian peasantry and contemporary problems in post-communist rural society. She is the author of several books on the Russian peasantry, the most recent being *Land Reform in Russia, 1906–1907: Peasant Responses to Stolypin's Project of Rural Transformation* (Oxford, 1999).

Harsha Ram is Assistant Professor in the Department of Slavic Language and Literatures at the University of California, Berkeley. He is currently working on a book tracing the evolution of imperial discourse in Russian poetic and literary culture, from its earliest post-Petrine manifestations in the eighteenth-century victory ode, through the Romantics, Pushkin and Lermontov, up to the revolutionary avant-garde.

V. V. Serbinenko is Professor at the Department of the History of Russian Philosophy of the Russian State University of the Humanities in Moscow. He is also head of the Department of Philosophy of the Moscow Physics-Technical Institute. His research interests include the history of Russian philosophy, the philosophy of history, the oriental theme in Russian culture and philosophy, the West–East–Russia problem and the 'end of history' in contemporary thought. He has published several books, including *Vladimir Soloviev: Zapad, Vostok, i Rossiia* (Moscow, 1994) and *Istoriia russkoi filosofii: Kurs lektsii* (Moscow, 1996).

Hari Vasudevan is Professor at the Department of History, University of Calcutta. He has worked on pre-revolutionary local government reform and the zemstvo in Russia, and is also interested in Russian agrarian structure and the current politics of Russia. His publications include a translation of an important collection of articles by P. I. Liashchenko and A. M. Anfimov on Russian agrarian history, entitled *Commercialization and Agriculture in Late Imperial Russia* (Calcutta, 1997).

Introduction

The conference, which gave rise to this volume, was intended to explore the ways in which identities could be used to understand the revolutionary epoch in the Russian Empire. Ideologies of class and nation, of institution and region, are now sometimes uncharitably regarded as *passé* for analytical purposes; instead, their identities, and constructions of identity, are considered more worthy of attention. Identity is said to provide an individual or a group of any type with strategies of action which the 'objective' circumstance of class, ethnicity or interest by itself would not ensure, and for which the ideologies and mentalities arising from these would be inadequate. It is premised on self-recognition and seeking recognition for itself; its action lies in that process. Earlier, it was assumed that many identities were socially given and that the individual grew into them, be they of citizenship, class, nationhood or of membership in a family or a religion, to cite some of the most obvious. The process of socialization, of growing into that identity, was always recognized as problematic and contested; but the 'difficulties' were regarded as obstacles to be overcome. Now it is increasingly acknowledged that these 'obstacles' are 'differences' which are perhaps to be celebrated. Further, it appears ever more clear that the attempt to arrive at stable self-recognition will remain a pursuit that may not be consummated. Most of all, identity politics and the study of identity reveals the absence, indeed impossibility, of single identities. All too often, the strategy of forging a 'given' identity or studying the process of the formation of one requires the denial of other possible identities or other patterns of their coexistence or combination. In a sense, by making difference the subject matter of politics and therewith of scholarship, it would appear that identities may be created almost arbitrarily and discerned almost randomly. But the effort would seem to be arbitrary and random only to those overly committed in advance to historical processes.

The shifts of emphasis reflect the search for agency in history; and the obsolescence of many familiar ideologies as agency in the world we inhabit today causes us to turn to other possibilities with the hope of fresh insights. It would, of course, always be most useful to have another history of the Russian navy or of the bureaucracy as typical instances of institutional history; and we could do with many more works of class history, for example of capitalists by sector or region. But identity permits us to approach or discern groups, relationships, or forms of action which ideologies of class, nation, region or institution may not have permitted or encouraged. It derives from an awareness that agency is far more diverse than was earlier imagined or, perhaps more accurately, intended in theory. As so often happens, we make a fresh approach to the past with the priorities of our age, but without dismissing the contributions of our predecessors.

The essays here assembled deal with familiar topics but from perspectives that may not always be so familiar. One large group, concerning the identity of region, stretches from Khlebnikov's Eurasia to the liberals' Tver province. The futurist poet saw the identity of Eurasia not in space with its physical constraints, but in time, with its eternal mobility. Harsha Ram suggests how he captured the expansive nature of Russia–Eurasia with its orientation to the future. On the other hand, Serbinenko's contribution on the Russian national idea argues how Dostoevsky and Soloviev did not propose it as a nationalist ideology, which was Uvarov's concern. Instead, they critiqued Western Eurocentrism for its denial of alternative possibilities even as they endorsed the attainments of Western civilization. While Bohdan Krawchenko presents Ukrainian nationalism deriving from the agrarian question, not because 'the human mind is malleable, but because it is conservative', Hari Vasudevan on Tver shows how the regional identity was constructed, not as a local particularism or *kraevedenie*, but as a zemstvo-based liberal regional challenge to centralization.

Another group suggests how the bureaucracy, in different ways, constructed different forms of peasant identity. A. V. Buganov explores Russian nationalism among the Russian peasantry who acquire the same heroes and make the same judgements on them as the bureaucracy itself did during the nineteenth century. Madhavan Palat shows the peasant 'constructing' himself and the autocracy, through the petition which was a form of protest, as the autocracy itself might have dictated or wanted. And Judith Pallot reveals the utopian dreaming of bureaucracy as it constructed the rational peasant idyll and model of modernity in the Stolypin land reform.

The third group examines the intelligentsia and the Church. Thus Dietrich Beyrau exposes the fracturing of the common intelligentsia identity in 1917 into politics and 'enlightenment'. Boris Kolonitskii investigates the multiple identities of the concept 'democracy' during 1917, stretching from Russia as the embodiment of democracy to the masses themselves, then the mentality of a mass cause, the ideology of socialism, and eventually to an authoritarian cult around the democratic hero. Finally, Gregory Freeze presents the supreme irony of the Church being democratized by the Bolsheviks who ensured the empowerment of the parish which liberal reformers had always obstructed for fear of mass involvement at the base.

The formation of identities allows us to examine many familiar processes afresh. The identity of the intelligentsia was fractured and recast, and the democratic revolution was a shifting concept during the revolutionary year itself; there were innumerable ways by which autocracy and peasant defined each other; Tver 'patriotism' was not due to love of the historic region but to the love of parliamentary power; and the elasticity of Russia could be captured only as time. Much more could have been said on these themes, and many more topics deserved such imaginative treatment; we may therefore confidently expect similar and more extended works from these authors in the not too distant future.

Madhavan K. Palat

Indira Gandhi National Centre for the Arts
New Delhi

1
The Russian Idea:
Metaphysics, Ideology and History[1]

V. V. Serbinenko

There are no strict boundaries between the history of ideas and metaphysics on the one hand and ideology on the other. The most complex metaphysical systems are often subjected to ideological interpretation. For example, it might be imagined that Hegelian thought cannot be conveyed in the simplified language of ideology. Yet it has been espoused with extraordinary ease by many radicals and conservatives, both in the West and in Russia, on the basis of their own ideological enthusiasms. I should specify that I use the terms 'philosophy' and 'metaphysics' synonymously. Against the background of positivism and then of Marxism during the nineteenth century, 'metaphysics' acquired a negative connotation: it was set against first 'scientific' and then 'dialectical' philosophy. But the historian of philosophy, even if he partakes of such assessments, cannot ignore the fact that from Aristotle's time the traditional second word for philosophy has been metaphysics. Ideological metamorphoses, which have in this century affected many philosophers (Nietzschean, Marxist, and other), would appear in equal measure to suggest that metaphysics does not provide any security against the ideologization of philosophy.

Such guarantees certainly do not exist. In principle, any cultural form, not merely philosophical ideas, may be deployed as ideological symbols. There are numerous examples of works of art being used ideologically. However, just as ideological art cannot merge into ideology and lose its essence, so also metaphysics proper cannot be reduced to its ideological 'reflection'. The latter is always a distortion of the original and is its simplified schematization. Indeed, it is a case where 'simplicity is worse than theft'. Hegel's *Phenomenology of Mind*, translated into the language of ideology, becomes an altogether different 'text'. Bearing in mind their proper metaphysical content and not their indi-

1

vidual 'motivations', the philosophical investigations of Plato, Hegel and Nietzsche retain their position in the 'eternal' world of Platonic ideas, whatever the ideological elements foisted on them. The ideological orientation of Marxism was obvious enough from the outset; but even so it is not exhausted by the ideology of the Soviet Marxist–Leninist (or any other) variety. Thus whatever the efforts of ideologues, the ontological elements of such doctrines may not be subjected to such 'translation', save at the expense of an obvious vulgarization.

The very concept of the 'Russian idea' and its interpretations emerged and were formulated during the nineteenth century in Russia in the context of just such a Russian and religious metaphysics. The metaphysical level of the notion of the 'Russian idea', which we encounter among so many major Russian thinkers of the nineteenth and then the twentieth centuries, must not be confused with sundry attempts at elaborating a national ideology. Ideology is always functional and the entire meaning of its existence is contained in that purpose. If it appears to be stillborn or ceases to play an active public role, its meaning is dissipated; ideological paradigms sink into obscurity and become of purely antiquarian interest. Their resurrection, naturally in new forms, is entirely possible; even so a new life for an old ideology is determined wholly by the degree of its public influence. The philosophical reflections on the fate of Russia, which occupy such an essential place in nineteenth-century Russian philosophy, did not exert a significant influence on social processes in the country. This was not due to any sort of fragility, debility or abstraction from 'real life' (the standard charges of common sense against 'abstract' metaphysics) but primarily because they were philosophic in nature. Philosophy is always a matter of personal reason. These words belong to Vladimir Soloviev; but many metaphysicians from Plato to Kant proposed as much. Kant declared it the 'sacred duty' of the philosopher to be consistent and to that degree responsible for his ideas. 'Personal reason' of the philosopher is wholly responsible for the results of the search for the truth. They are themselves orientated to another 'personal reason' which may be quite as critical. Metaphysical ideas are founded on understanding (which is impossible without critique), and not on influence, still less of a mass nature. Metaphysics differs from ideology, not by its elite, hermetic or esoteric attributes. The Socratic spirit of European and certainly Russian philosophy (the 'Russian Socrates' G. Skvorod was always ready for 'Socratic disputes' with A. Khomiakov and many others) is profoundly democratic, orientated to any and every person capable and willing to reflect. Esoteric and occult pursuits are essentially anti-philosophical. For example, there is nothing paradoxical in the mystic philosopher Vladimir Soloviev declaring, with doctrines of the occult in mind, that no serious philosophy may be based on that which is hidden. Occultism, in its widest sense, both in the past and now, is a species of ideology which quite effectively acts as much on a narrow circle of the elect as on the masses of the adept.

This is not in the least a critique of ideology as such or in praise of philosophy. Both rise to great heights, and often descend to extreme depths. This is only to note that however these two spheres might have intersected in history (and at times they did so marvellously), they are essentially distinct and answer to distinct human requirements. Ideology and metaphysics may not be appraised in like fashion. Ideology cannot be expected to be consistent and in that sense non-contradictory, as its purpose is certainly not the truth. The thesis that the 'omnipotence' of a doctrine is evidence of its 'truth' captures the nature of ideology; for a socially impotent ideological doctrine is of no use to anyone and is therefore not true. Those interested in the truth of a fact or of a viewpoint turn to science or philosophy, but in any case not to ideology. An ideological doctrine is judged by its effectiveness. It is possible and legitimate, of course, to specify 'bad' and 'good' 'ideologies', 'true' 'elements' of their contents and so on; but in the last resort they are determined by their effectiveness. This is so because first, as is well known, the road to historical hell may be paved with the best of intentions. (It would make no sense to refer to the metaphysical here.) Second, and this is important, any 'ideal', humane ideology is doomed to a speedy and inevitable oblivion if it appears socially ineffective.

The metaphysics of the 'Russian idea', howsoever it be appraised, is in any case a real part of the intellectual culture of Russia in the nineteenth century. The ideology of the 'Russian idea', with its principally nineteenth-century roots, is to this day a ceaseless process of genesis, development and testing of effectiveness (by history naturally) of the most diverse ideological propositions that seek to 'explain' the meaning of the historical existence of the country, state and nation. Turning to the experience of the philosophy of Russian history, we are not secreting ourselves in some isolated 'abstract' world of ideas unrelated to the world of Russian ideology of the last century, with its *Sturm und Drang* of sundry currents of ideas which had aspired to dominate the public. On the contrary, the metaphysics of the 'Russian idea' could help us understand the exceptional drama and ultimately incomplete process of establishing a single ideological system of values in the Russian Empire; for in many respects it conditioned the Empire's inability to survive the domestic and international convulsions of the early twentieth century.

It is symbolic that the very concept, the 'Russian idea', was given literary currency by Dostoevsky. It is difficult to overestimate the significance of the work and ideas of this writer for subsequent Russian religious philosophy. Dostoevsky propounded this when he was dissatisfied not only with Westernism, but also with Slavophilism. He sought to define the new ideal, *pochvennichestvo*. It is symbolic also that from the very beginning the 'Russian idea' was understood by Dostoevsky in a non-ideological sense. It was not a matter of a specific type of national ideology opposed in some sense to other national ideologies such that it would permit Russia to perform certain definite historical tasks, internal and external. When he first used the expression 'Russian idea' in the early 1860s, Dostoevsky proceeded from his own metaphysical intuition of the universalism of the national culture and national character to which he remained faithful to the end. He did so in his renowned Pushkin speech when he called for 'universal human brotherhood' [*vsechelovecheskoe bratstvo*]; and again in the final articles of *The Diary of a Writer* when he spoke of 'Russian Socialism'. His first delineation of the 'Russian idea', in his *Appeal for Subscription to the Journal 'Vremia' for 1861*, was as follows:

> We know we do not shelter ourselves from humanity behind Chinese walls. We can foresee with due respect that the nature of our future activity must properly embrace all of humanity, that the Russian idea would perhaps be the synthesis of all those ideas which, with such resolve and courage, Europe elaborates in its various distinct nationalities; that all that are conflictual in these ideas would probably be reconciled through the further development of Russian nationality [*narodnost'*]. It is not for nothing that we speak all languages, understand all cultures, sympathize with the interest of each European people, and grasp the meaning and rationality of phenomena which are utterly alien to us.[2]

The tone of proposition is significant. Dostoevsky 'knows' that the path of national exclusiveness (Chinese walls) would lead into a cul-de-sac, but he merely 'anticipates' ('perhaps') the probable positive possibilities of Russian (in both senses)[3] 'human universalism' [*vsechelovechnost'*]. Such 'suggestiveness' is entirely out of place in ideological pronouncements. Here everything must be clear and categorical (in words, of course). But in metaphysical discourse it is more than appropriate to proceed through hypotheses. The thinker must be cautious in the extreme so that his metaphysical viewpoint and intuitions could relate to concrete historical prospects.

It is quite clear why Dostoevsky was convinced that the centrifugal forces of a splintering humanity were disastrous. As a Christian thinker he proceeded from the universalism of Christianity without admitting of priority, still less supremacy, to any single national idea. At the same time he did not admit the fact of the alienation of various peoples and traditions as a final and inevitable destiny. The dominion of any single nation aspiring to the role of the 'chosen people' was fundamentally unacceptable from the Christian point of view; but that need not prevent one or another people leaving their special impress on 'Christ's business', or playing an important and possibly even a decisive role in the attainment of the ideal of human universalism or *vsechelovechnost'*. In Russian religious-philosophical thought of the nineteenth century, the question of Christian messianism was posed exceptionally sharply.

Let me make so bold as to affirm as follows: if we were to consider the metaphysical level of the dispute between Slavophiles and Westernisers, and I am convinced that their opposition was founded on metaphysical principles, then the decisive question was not the specific historical fate of Russia and the West, or the relations between the two. Slavophiles and Westernisers (at least the religious Westernisers like Petr Chaadaev and V. Pechorin) disputed about the reality of the Christian path of history, about how far the European peoples and Russia were going down this road and whether it was possible in general. For Dostoevsky the experience of approximating to Christ in history was as justified as for each Christian in personal life. But this was to exclude any form of hegemonism or pretensions to the role of supreme judge and commander. (His negative appraisal of the Catholic idea was related to this position.) Moreover just as the private success of the individual in no way can guarantee his 'success' along the 'narrow path' of Christianity, leading to salvation, so also power acquired by peoples and states in the historical arena is no evidence of having been God's elect. Historical 'pluses' could easily be negated by religious and metaphysical 'minuses'. Ultimately, according to Dostoevsky, the road to power and terrestrial might is the road of the Grand Inquisitor.

The fortitude with which the people bore their tragic historical fate without abandoning their awareness of imperfection and sinfulness is a mark of their having conserved their 'image of Christ'. They did not wish to regard the circumstances and laws of 'this world' as the ultimate truth. Through all the history of Russian thought and literature moves the image of Russia suffering, bearing repeated strokes of misfortune, consuming herself in historic conflagrations, but ever renewing herself like the Phoenix and aspiring to be the true Resurrection. Whatever the historical and intellectual gulf that separates the ancient Russian ideal of 'Holy Russia' and the image of Russia 'crucified' in the revolutions and wars of our epoch, it cannot be denied that they constitute a single perennial theme of the Russian national cultural tradition. In this case there is ground for speaking of a paradigm.

However, the range of ideas within this paradigm was enormous, from total anti-historicism, a radical repudiation of this world, rejection of the historical forms of state and society (including those of the Church), a cultural creativity to the extent of assisting in a holy mission of the Russian state worldwide (the idea of Moscow as the Third Rome), and the sacralization of monarchical power as the sole, true and highest form, not only of political, but also of social life. The first tendency we note in the sphere of religious consciousness, in the Russian schism and in sectarian movements. Finally, such attitudes were found not only outside the Church but even within the Orthodox Church. The continuation of the Russian struggle with history, especially in its most radical forms, may be discerned in the ideas of Tolstoy's later works and in the twentieth century in the works of N. Berdiaev.

The second type of Russian messianism also has its own history. The first was related to the attempt to create a single national ideology during the Muscovite tsardom (most of all I. Volotskii), and then the Russian Empire. These were, however, only the extreme cases of the 'Russian idea'. (As is well known, contradictions were reconciled, and both these types of messianism often in fact coincided, when they acquired strange and even grotesque forms.) In the history of Russian thought the prevailing tendency was to avoid having to choose between the image of Russia and the Russian people on the one hand which, like the legendary city of Kitezh, lay outside history and guarded itself from the world through mystical experiences and moral strivings, and Russia, on the other, the heir to Rome and Byzantium, discerning her historical destiny in the unlimited accumulation of the power of the state. Russian religious ideas of the nineteenth century, and then of the twentieth, faced a dilemma that was not of significance to Russia alone: how, without denying the world and history, to remain faithful to the ideals of Christianity and not submit to the natural course of things, to stand unflinchingly on the well-trodden road of historical struggle for national and state interests? Is the Christian path in history possible in general, or are the wanderings of the hermit and the cell of the monk its sole and true symbols?

In the quest for an answer to this perennial and, I would suggest, agonizing question to Christian thinking, Russian thinkers could not always escape the temptation of utopianism. But it would be totally wrong, in my opinion, to equate the results of their spiritual quest with utopianism, and still less with religious nationalism. Perhaps Dostoevsky alone put his finger on the essence of utopianism when commenting on what numerous forms of utopianism meant for mankind. But Dostoevsky's ideas do not of course exhaust the critical tradition of Russian religious philosophy.[4] His understanding of the 'Russian idea' was definitely directed against nationalist ideology.

He saw Christian messianism as providing for the achievement of two historical objectives. The first was the people defining their place in history and fully expressing their national uniqueness in culture and in all spheres of life; and the second was for them to radically overcome their national exclusiveness through the creative assimilation of other intellectual traditions and the experience of the historical creations of other peoples. Dostoevsky believed that were Russia to choose this, in his opinion truly Christian path, she could not only successfully express her uniqueness and remain true to the historical 'soil' ('to the people's spirit and to the people's principles'), but also demonstrate to mankind the real possibility of coming out of the vicious historical circles of alienation and enmity. In his famous Pushkin speech the writer spoke precisely about this. And, as we know, his main argument was Pushkin's work.

The argument, it must be admitted, was thoroughly metaphysical. From the point of view of common sense and philosophical investigations orientated to both scientific and this same common sense, the effort to present the output of a single – even if great – poet, as the essence of the historical being of the people, would appear not a little absurd. By what criteria can one meaningfully prefer the work of Pushkin, Shakespeare or Tagore to all other facets of the historical life of a nation? The work of an artist is possibly a significant historical fact, but it is just one in an endless series of historical events. Only the metaphysician could admit the possibility of regarding facts 'from the point of view of eternity' and make a selection. In the metaphysical tradition beginning with Plato and following him a Christian

Platonism, Dostoevsky's choice does not in the least seem absurd. In the universe of Plato's eternally paradigm concepts there is a place for the notion of peoples and of their national being. It would be legitimate to seek this first of all through the intellectual life of the people, not the least significant part of which would be their creations of artistic genius. This is exactly what Dostoevsky chose to do by declaring the works of Pushkin a symbol of the 'Russian idea'. The writer spoke about the 'artistic genius' of Pushkin, 'of the capacity for universal empathy and reincarnation through the genius of another nation ...' 'This capacity is entirely a Russian, national capacity and Pushkin merely shares it with all our people; and, like the perfect artist he is, he is the ultimate expression of this capacity ...', affirmed Dostoevsky. 'Our people have the tendency to universal empathy and to total reconciliation ... the Russian spirit ... the genius of the Russian people is perhaps the most capable of all peoples to internalise the idea of the unity of all mankind, of fraternal love, of judicious appraisal, avoiding the inimical, distinguishing between and excusing differences, and eliminating contradiction.'[5]

It is, of course, easy to see in these words only praise for his favourite poet and his own people. It could be regarded also as an expression of national pride. There are any number of outpourings of praise for one's own nation at various times in history. And it is entirely likely that this series would continue. Dostoevsky in fact did speak at Pushkin's jubilee about those traits of his people which he considered the best. It would seem that the writer who, as possibly nobody else in Russian literature, could depict in the most extreme fashion the dark side of Russian life and the national character, had the moral right to speak about what he deemed bright and positive. But that is not the issue either. Having called upon Russia to be true to Pushkin's genius, Dostoevsky formulated an ideal which in his opinion was necessary, not only to his country and people, but to all of mankind. He did not call upon Russia to subjugate other peoples (even if under the sign of the Cross), or to enslave their minds through ideological and cultural expansion. In essence he spoke about the vast moral and historical responsibility of Russia to herself and to mankind. It was a matter of the gift of understanding another style of life, other forms of awareness of the world, which he believed was available to the Russian people but which demanded enormous moral effort. But these efforts were necessary because mankind must have the choice and cannot rest content with an inevitable national alienation, with the law of the jungle which operates both within each people and in international situations.

Dostoevsky repudiated the route of revolutionary socialism as he felt it would inevitably lead to a 'communist anthill'; and when, toward the end of his life, he wrote about 'Russian Socialism', he had in mind that same idea of 'the brotherhood of man'. The writer's critical attitude to civilizational progress of the Western variety was well known. But he did not attack European achievements in culture and civilization; instead he spoke against the historical lack of alternatives asserted by the ideologies of Eurocentrism, which projected the Western path as the high road of human development and all other cultural traditions as peripheral if not marginal. It is not fortuitous that in his final works he reflected on the Eurasian nature of Russia and wrote that her route 'lies in Asia', that it was high time to put an end to the 'servile dread' of acquiring a reputation in Europe as 'Asiatics', and to recognize that the specificity of national character and culture in the existing world was to a substantial degree related to the intellectual experience of the people of the Asiatic continent. These reflections of the later Dostoevsky were close to the ideals of the Eurasianist movement of the twentieth century. Of course it would not be accurate to posit him as a precursor of Eurasianism. Eurasianism was to a significant degree an attempt to create a new type of national ideology based on the specific experience of the 1917 revolution and its aftermath in Russia. Dostoevsky, in his utterances on the universalism of the Russian intellectual tradition, was answering first of all the question of the meaning of history, not merely of that of Russia. The 'Russian idea' to him was the metaphysical principle of the national being of Russia; but this was also the universal ideal of national being in general. The notion of human universalism (*vsechelovechestvo*) could be deemed Russian only to the extent to which Russia could contribute to its attainment in history.

The metaphysical ideas of Dostoevsky did not exercise a serious *ideological* influence on the Russian public. But then this is not in the least surprising. As is well known, the Pushkin speech was received with considerable enthusiasm, though that dissipated fast enough. As both the Russian Western-liberals and conservatives realised, the ideals of Dostoevsky were too remote from their own ideological convictions. Nonetheless the tradition of the metaphysical understanding of the 'Russian idea' was further reinforced. It was just this fundamentally non-ideological strain of Dostoevsky's thought that was espoused by his close friend and great Russian religious philosopher, Vladimir Soloviev. Soloviev's approach to the 'national question' was from the outset metaphysical.

'The idea of the nation is not what she herself thinks of herself in time but what God thinks of her in eternity.' Such was Soloviev's dictum, pronounced in his speech 'The Russian Idea', in Paris in 1888.[6] Soloviev's formulation established with utter clarity the fundamental possibilities and problems of the metaphysics of national life. He always felt that not only the individual and humanity in general, but also the people [*narod*] and the nation [*natsiia*] have a specific metaphysical destiny. Like Dostoevsky, Soloviev appealed to Christian universalism on the grounds that it was incompatible with both nationalism (the ideology of national egoism conflicting with the principle of the metaphysical unity of humanity) and with cosmopolitanism (ideologically diminishing the historical and even more the metaphysical significance of national uniqueness). Soloviev's own theme that 'the ideal of the nation is not what she thinks of herself in time' was directed primarily against the ideology of national exclusiveness.

Like Dostoevsky, the philosopher regarded the real policy of states calling themselves Christian as in no wise Christian. He declared that those who called on Russia to be guided *exclusively* by national and state interests were thrusting her into imitating the worst aspects of European ideology and politics. As he wrote in his work, *Velikii spor i khristianskaia politika* [The Great Dispute and Christian Politics]:

> If we were to posit a national interest [*interes naroda*] ... as lying in wealth and external power, then, whatever the importance of these interests undoubtedly for us, they ought not to constitute the supreme and final purpose of policy, for otherwise they could justify any evil ... In the recent past, patriots of all countries confidently point to the political wickedness of England as an example worthy of imitation. The example is in fact appropriate. Nobody, whether in word or in deed, is so preoccupied with their own national and state interests as the English. Everyone knows how, thanks to their interests, wealthy and powerful Englishmen let the Irish die of hunger, oppress Indians, thrust opium poison on the Chinese, plunder Egypt. ... That this international destruction of humanity [*liudoedstvo*, literally, 'eating of persons'] is despicable, and it is felt even by those who enjoy it the most. The politics of material interest is seldom projected in its pure form. Even Englishmen smugly sucking the blood of the 'lower races' and considering themselves justified in doing so merely because it is of advantage to themselves, often however reassure us that they are conferring thereby a great

blessing on these same lower races by absorbing them into a higher culture. ... As an ideal this is extremely feeble among pragmatically minded Englishmen, but it may be discerned in full force among a nation [*narod*] of thinkers. German idealism and their tendency to high abstraction make such a crude empirical English-style destruction of humanity impossible for Germans. If the Germans swallowed the Wends and Prussians and are about to do the same to the Poles, it is not because it is advantageous to them but because it is their 'calling' as superior races: that by germanising the lower nationalities [*narodnosti*] they should be raised to true culture ... The philosophical excellence of the Germans is evident even in their political destruction of humanity: they direct their absorptive [literally 'swallowing', *poglashchaiushchee*] activity not only at the external worth of a people, but also at their internal essence. One plunders and oppresses people, the other destroys their very nationality.[7]

It would be absurd to discern any anti-English or anti-German attitudes in these utterances by Soloviev. Like Dostoevsky, Soloviev unequivocally condemned just such a politics of 'interests' ('political destruction of humanity') and the nationalist ideology from which it sprang.

What has been said of the politics of Germans and Englishmen does not amount to condemning these peoples. We distinguish *narodnost'* from nationalism by their consequences. The fruits of English *narodnost'* we see in Shakespeare and Byron, in Berkeley and Newton; but those of English nationalism we find in pillage and plunder the world over, in the exploits of a Warren Hastings or a Lord Seymour. The fruits of the great German *narodnost'* are in essence Lessing and Goethe, Kant and Schelling; but the consequences of German nationalism have been the coercive germanization of neighbours from the times of the Teutonic Knights until our day.[8]

National patriotic feeling, according to Soloviev, carries a kernel of truth which may be distorted in nationalism and is negated in a cosmopolitan ideology:

Narodnost' or *natsional' nost'* is a positive force, and every people, according to their special traits, is destined for a special service or duty. Taken to its extreme, nationalism is the undoing of a people and makes of them an enemy of humanity. ... Christianity, by eliminating nationalism, saves peoples, for the supra-national [*sverkhnarodnoe*] is not non-national [*beznarodnoe*]. ... A people wishing to preserve their spirit in a closed and exclusive nationalism loses it [their spirit] and only by committing their entire energy in the supra-national [*sverkhnarodnoe*] universal work of Christ may the people [*narod*] preserve it. ... This purpose urges it on, not toward fake and usurping missions, but to the discharge of a historical obligation, uniting it with all others in a general ecumenical pursuit. ... Raised to this level, patriotism is not contradictory, it is instead personal morality in its fullness.[9]

Like Dostoevsky, Soloviev saw the meaning of the 'Russian idea' in just such an 'ecumenical' duty. Both Russian history and especially Russian national character demonstrated as much. The fundamental ideal of the people [*narod*] is the ideal of Holy Russia, affirmed the philosopher; but 'Holy Russia requires holy action'. However, unlike Dostoevsky, Soloviev felt Russia ought to take the first step to an intellectual reconciliation with the West, starting with the Catholic world. During the 1880s, dreaming about restoring the unity of the Christian world, he saw in it the possibility of overcoming national egoism. But how could the philosopher rely on such an undertaking being feasible (and that not in the remote future), having so clearly acknowledged the power of national tensions to fragment humanity and when even the most developed segments of which, in his own words, explicitly professed not a Christian politics but an international cannibalism?

It should be borne in mind that Soloviev, as a religious thinker, believed in 'the direct action of the beneficence and work of God' in history. Given such metaphysical sustenance, the moral efforts of mankind were undoubtedly capable of success in the struggle with the forces of disruption and alienation. The historical optimism of the philosopher thus drew on his own faith in Russia that she would prove herself capable of such a moral feat and would be able to provide mankind with an example of true Christian politics.

In the struggle to attain his ideal, Soloviev suffered not a few disappointments. He did not escape utopianism. At the end of his life he was obliged to repudiate his concept of 'free theocracy' as unreal and in many senses utopian. His Christian messianism also seemed to falter as it was related to faith in the historic role of Russia. If in the 1880s in his theocratic utopia Soloviev assigned a role to the Russian monarchy and directly to the emperor, then the 1890s opened with a doubt, expressed by the philosopher-poet in his celebrated poem *Svet s Vostoka*:

Oh Rus! With lofty foreknowledge
You engage in proud reflection,
Which kind of Orient shall you be?
That of Xerxes or of Christ?

And gradually the philosopher turned increasingly to a bitter answer, that the Russian monarchy could not attain the ideal of Holy Russia. It should be admitted also that the ideas of Soloviev were not endorsed by the Russian public. In a literal sense he found himself between two hostile camps. In official circles and among conservative traditionalists, his call for reconciliation and rejection of national egoism was adjudged anti-patriotic and hostile to the interests of the Russian nation and the state. To the liberal and radical intelligentsia also, his metaphysics of the 'Russian idea' was utterly alien.

There might be ample ground to treat the ideas of Dostoevsky and Soloviev as unrealistic, even utopian, however humane. Indeed, they did not in any way alter the ideological and political situation in Russia, nor the state of world politics where the practice of the 'international destruction of humanity' continued to flourish and inexorably led humanity to the new and worldwide military conflicts of the twentieth century. However, the problem was that Russian thinkers were neither ideologues who expected (as it happened naïvely) mass and immediate responses to their appeals, nor propagators of abstract humanism reminding mankind how much goodness and peace were to be preferred over alienation and enmity. The 'Christian politics' of Dostoevsky and Soloviev was not an abstract ideal which must erase the variety of history; the latter could not flourish without conflicts and struggles, including ultimately those between national interests. Neither thinker appealed to an anti-historicism. They clearly acknowledged how complex and difficult was the matching of reality to ideal and were convinced that, without such attempts, mankind would lose its sense of its own existence and would find itself in a historical dead end.

Soloviev and Dostoevsky posed to Russia and the West an undoubtedly metaphysical but for all that concrete question: could peoples and states that have declared themselves Christian not only disregard such declared religious and moral principles in their historical actions but also justify the politics of the 'international destruction of humanity' through nationalist ideologies that are absolutely incompatible with Christian faith? And are we right today, on the threshold of the twenty-first century, to regard the meanings of the problems posed by them as abstract and utopian? It seems to me that there can be no question of any utopianism in this case. Dostoevsky and Soloviev were speaking, not of any kind of lapse into 'the beautiful new world', but of the possibility and necessity of efforts to transcend rabid nationalism, to the danger of whose bloody course recent history provides ample testimony. On the other hand, having discerned the meaning of the 'Russian idea' in 'all humanity', neither of them thought in terms of a total syncretism, the repudiation of national uniqueness and of intellectual choice, the mixing of everything in some sort of a worldwide 'melting pot' of nations. Indeed, they tended rather to discern a great danger in such universalism of civilizational progress as remote from the movement to the ideal of 'all humanity'. This last proposed first of all the capacity to understand and respect another cultural experience and other intellectual traditions, the capacity, in Dostoevsky's own words of 'universal responsiveness', 'of sober appraisal, avoiding enmities, distinguishing between and excusing differences, and eliminating contradictions.' Such hopes are scarcely utopian. There is a fundamental distinction between utopian prospects and the public ideal, or, as in this case, an ideal of relations between nations.

The 'Russian idea', as understood by Dostoevsky and Soloviev, and in fact by many other thinkers, did not become the basic national ideology. But that is not because it was too abstract and remote from real life. Metaphysical ideas possess their own worth independent of the degree of their ideological influence. The good shall remain good, and the truth will be the truth even when, apparently, everything originates in neither truth nor goodness. That in any case is how it stands from the point of view of the metaphysics of Christian Platonism, which has played a most important role in the Russian intellectual tradition. And surely Dostoevsky and Soloviev were right when they warned that nationalism is generally a dead end for peoples and states in general and for Russia in particular.

The problem of the necessity of the spiritual unity of Russian society was a perennial and important theme of Russian religious philosophy of the nineteenth and twentieth centuries. Our thinkers reflected on and wrote about the fateful consequences of the Church schism of the seventeenth century for national consciousness; that post-Petrine

Russia was witness to the chasm between the Europeanized upper classes and the people living, as Dostoevsky said, 'in their own way, with each generation more and more intellectually distanced from St. Petersburg', from that most slender layer of Petersburg culture. In the twentieth century G. Fedotov noted it with even greater clarity: 'Russia from Peter's times ceased being comprehensible to the Russian people.'[10] To many it was clear that for the multinational and far from monoreligious Russia, any attempt to formulate a single nationalist ideology through state diktat and penetrating all spheres of public life would be utterly unacceptable and pregnant with future conflict. Those who did not wish great convulsions on their country thought about this and warned against it. As Soloviev wrote:

We accept the current foundations of the state in Russia as unchangeable. But in every political structure, whether republic, monarchy, or Autocracy, the state can and should satisfy, within its limits ... the demands for national, civil, and religious freedom. This is not a matter of political calculation but of the conscience of the state and of the people. And, as long as the system of coercive russianization of the borderlands shall continue in Russia on the basis of hypocritical calculation ... as long as the system of criminal penalties shall prevail over religious convictions, and that of compulsory censorship over religious thought, then in all its activities Russia shall remain morally constrained, spiritually paralysed, and shall know nothing but failure.[11]

The state's effort during the last century to formulate and impose a single ideological system cannot be adjudged as other than a series of failures. The famous Uvarov formula 'Orthodoxy, Autocracy, Nationality' remained to a significant degree an ideological slogan, sanctioning an official ideological surveillance, but not becoming the basis of a system of values capable of uniting various layers of Russian society. Sergei Semenovich Uvarov, president of the Academy of Sciences and Minister of Education, was a person of European education and upbringing (Goethe rated his literary output highly). He does not bring to mind a conservative traditionalist, and still less a nationalist. 'By intellect a universal citizen', was K. Batiushkov's assessment. A typical representative of the Petersburg elite who had undergone a diplomatic apprenticeship, in his ideological purpose Uvarov wanted for Russia the same nationally orientated ideology as was to be found among the other European states, that is, in Soloviev's words, the

ideology of 'national cgoism'. He saw the meaning of the last component of his ideological trinity, that is, nationality (*narodnost'*), as lying
in submission to national and state interests:

> Our *narodnost'* consists in unlimited devotion and submission to
> Autocracy; but the Western Slavs will not excite any sympathy
> among us. They are themselves, we are ourselves. ... They do not
> deserve our sympathy because we constructed our state without
> their assistance, we suffered and blossomed without them; they
> existed in dependence on others without being able to create any-
> thing; and today they have extinguished their historical existence.[12]

The attempt to inject a national ideology from above was unsuccessful. The problem of the psychological unity of Russian society was thus
not solved; and when, at the beginning of the twentieth century,
Russia entered into her phase of worldwide convulsions, ideological
opposition and alienation in society played its fateful role. History
tragically proved Russian thinkers justified in their assertion that ideo-
logized nationalism does not have a future on Russian soil and could
not become a single national ideology. In October 1917, the Bolsheviks
rose to power under the banner of internationalism. And, whatever the
real nationality policy of the regime during these decades, it would be
simply invalid to deny that internationalism was the fundamental
principle of its own ideology. In today's circumstances, there is considerable popularity for the idea that Russia may be transformed only
through a severe authoritarianism which, naturally, could not propose
a return to the practice of ideological diktat, to ideocracy. To many,
such an idea seems both realistic and reasonable. In reality, however,
this is a myth, yet another futile utopia. It was noted long ago that
what was first a historical tragedy would be repeated as a farce. Another
attempt at a dictatorship in Russia, under whatever ideological slogan,
whether of the left or the right, cannot be realized and must become a
farce, although undoubtedly a tragedy for the country and the people.
One does not have to be prophet in order to foresee that over the next
few decades new experimenters would not possess the resources that
history granted the communist regime. In contemporary Russia there is
simply no historical alternative to the formation and development of a
national democracy. The peoples of Russia have come through a
complex (not a mechanical and primitive) organization of state and
social life, a system of spiritual values which would permit a genuine
unity in the multiplicity of cultural–national being. Accomplishing

such tasks cannot be easy or light, if only because we must find our own path, as the mechanical replication of an alien historical experience is simply impossible. But, it appears, this most difficult choice is in fact the most realistic. Our thinkers, having developed their own metaphysics of the 'Russian idea', considered that national unity was impossible without profound understanding and respect for other traditions and other psychological experiences. They believed that Russia could be successful along this path, and it seems to me they were correct.

Notes

1. Translated from the Russian by Hari Vasudevan.
2. F. M. Dostoevskii, *Polnoe Sobranie Sochinenii*, XVIII (Leningrad, 1978) p. 115.
3. Translator's note: The author specifies the distinction between *russkii* denoting the Russian ethnos alone, and *rossiiskii* pertaining to all the inhabitants of the Russian Empire, two words for which there is only one translation, 'Russian', in English.
4. I would select in this context two works: G. Florovskii, 'Metafizicheskie predposylki utopizma', *Voprosy filosofii*, no. 10 (1990); and P. Novgorodtsev, *Ob obshchestvennom ideale* (Moscow, 1991).
5. F. M. Dostoevskii, *Polnoe sobranie sochinenii*, XXVI, pp. 130–1.
6. V. Solov'ev, *Sobranie sochinenii v dvukh tomakh*, II (Moscow, 1989) p. 220.
7. Ibid., II, pp. 60–1.
8. Ibid., II, p. 64.
9. Ibid., II, p. 65.
10. G. Fedotov, *I est' i budet* (Paris, 1933) p. 9.
11. Solov'ev, *Sobranie sochinenii*, II, p. 211.
12. A. V. Nikitenko, *Zapiski i dnevniki*, I (St Petersburg, 1893) p. 488.

2
Agrarian Unrest and the Shaping of a National Identity in Ukraine at the Turn of the Twentieth Century

Bohdan Krawchenko

Before the revolution and for decades after, 'Ukrainian' was synonymous with 'peasant'. This was a fitting description of the Ukrainian population. According to the 1897 census, 81 per cent of the total population of the nine provinces which constituted Ukraine were classified as peasants, and 93 per cent of all Ukrainians belonged to this category. The classification of 'peasant' in tsarist Russia was a juridical one; it did not necessarily denote living in the countryside, or deriving one's living from agriculture. The 1897 census provides data on both these points. Studying the census we find that 97 per cent of all Ukrainian peasants lived in rural areas. In terms of occupation, 74 per cent of the population of the nine provinces derived their livelihood from agriculture. In the case of Ukrainians, 87 per cent supported themselves from agriculture.[1]

It is clear that the peasantry had a crushing weight in the Ukrainian population. Because of this, the 'Ukrainian question' – the national question – was inextricably bound up with the problem of the emancipation of the countryside.

For the overwhelming majority of the Ukrainian peasantry survival – the provision of enough cabbage soup and black bread to fill their stomachs – was not an easy matter. Ukraine, of course, was a territory very suitable for agriculture: 75.6 per cent of its surface could be utilized for agricultural purposes in the narrow sense (crops and animal husbandry). In European Russia, the figure was only 40 per cent.[2] However, despite the propitious agricultural conditions, or more correctly, because of them, the material existence of the Ukrainian peasant was not better and in some respects worse than that of his fellow peasant in Russia.

The Emancipation Act of 1861 'freed' the peasantry but did not provide them with the means for beginning a new independent existence. At first, the peasantry in Ukraine considered the Act to be a fraud, a trick by the landlords, and continued to 'wait for the real Act from the Tsar'.[3] Anticipation soon gave way to open rebellion as Ukraine witnessed scores of uprisings which expressed the peasantry's deep disillusionment.[4]

The Ukrainian peasantry had good cause to be unhappy with the Act. Because of the high productivity of agricultural land in Ukraine (and its consequent high price), it was profitable for the landlords to manage their own estates, using the peasantry as agricultural labour. A reflection of this was the fact that *corvée* or servile labour (*barshchina*), rather than quit-rent or the rent in lieu of labour (*obrok*), was the system of peasant payments in Ukraine: over 99 per cent of peasants in Ukraine had to perform *corvée* obligations prior to the 1861 Act. In discussing the provisions of the impending act, landlords in Ukraine strongly expressed their desire to keep as much land as possible for themselves. The landlords wanted an agricultural labour force, and agreed that the peasantry should receive enough land to be self-sufficient in the most basic of their requirements, but not self-sufficient enough to prohibit their search for work on the estates. The Emancipation Act in its separate provisions for Ukraine reflected the landlords' interests.[5]

To begin with, 220,000 former serfs (over 440,000 souls with the families included) had their land taken away as a result of the break in the personal relationship with the landlord. These former serfs, most of whom had been employed in truck farms or in the households of the landowners, swelled the ranks of a growing agricultural proletariat. The overwhelming majority of peasants – 4,470,000 male peasants – received the so-called 'allotments' or parcels of land.[6]

Following the reform, the extent of peasant holdings was considerably curtailed. Accurate statistics on the loss of land by peasants are difficult to establish because of inadequate data on land usage prior to 1861. It is generally agreed that in the left-bank (eastern provinces) and steppe regions, peasants lost over 30 per cent of the land they previously used. In the right-bank (western) provinces, following the defeat of the Polish uprising of 1863, a new law was passed modifying the provisions of the Act of 1861, which resulted in an increase of peasant holdings by 18 to 25 per cent. All in all, it appears that the average holding in Ukraine per 'revision soul' decreased from 3.2 to 2.8 dessiatines (1 dessiatine equals 1.092 hectares).[7] As a rule, the larger the estate, and the more productive the land, the greater was the peasant loss. For example, in Volyn province, on estates of less than 100 dessiatines, peasants kept 92 per cent of their former land, while on estates of over 10,000 dessiatines, they were deprived of 75 per cent of their former land use.[8]

The redemption price for the 'allotments' which peasants were compelled to pay was high, consuming 70 per cent of their income.[9] In right-bank provinces where peasants had received more land in their allotments, the redemption price in many districts exceeded the income from the land itself. In 1866, for example, in the more prosperous districts of Kiev province, the income from 1 dessiatine of land gave the peasant 1.12 roubles, while the redemption payment stood at 2.60 roubles.[10]

Although between 1877 and 1905 almost 1.5 million dessiatines had been added to the allotment lands, the amount of land was too limited to support the rapidly increasing peasant population. Between 1870 and 1900 the peasant population grew by 8.5 million, and the number of peasant households increased by over one million between 1877 and 1905.[11] As a result, the size of the allotments per 'revision soul' decreased even further as the parcels of land kept being subdivided. Thus in 1861, in the right-bank provinces the Emancipation Act allotment per revision soul was about 3 dessiatines, but by 1900 the average allotment was barely 1.5 dessatines per revision soul. In left-bank Ukraine, the average allotment in the same period declined from 3.3 to 1.7 dessiatines, and in the steppe region from 6.2 to 2.5 dessiatines.[12] Thus in thirty-nine years, the size of allotments had diminished by more than two times per revision soul. In examining the above data one should bear in mind that an allotment of not less than 5 dessiatines per revision soul was needed to make ends meet.[13]

The peasantry clung to the allotments and they remained the main form of peasant landholding. The great land census of 1905 shows that 78 per cent of land owned by peasants, and 67 per cent of land used by them consisted of allotments. In 1905, almost half the peasant households (44 per cent) had plots of less than 5 dessiatines; 40 per cent had plots of between 5 and 10 dessiatines, and 16 per cent of households had allotments over 10 dessiatines. Marked regional differences were to be observed: half of the allotments over 10 dessiatines were to be found in the steppe provinces. The average size of allotments in Ukraine in 1905 was 7 dessiatines, which was almost 3 dessiatines less when compared to 1877.[14]

The possibility of increasing the size of holdings through the purchase of land was open only to the richer and more enterprising peasants. The price of land had increased in a spectacular fashion. For example, the sale price of 1 dessiatine in Poltava province in the 1860s was 20.12 roubles; at the turn of the twentieth century it reached 500 or even 600 roubles per dessiatine.[15] By 1905 'private' lands bought by those classified as peasants amounted to slightly over a quarter of the land held in allotments. Not surprisingly, half the 'private' lands (55.8 per cent) were owned as personal holdings by only a handful of peasants. Only 4 per cent of peasant households owned private land. The other half of private lands were purchased either by associations of peasants (33.5 per cent of private lands), or by the official unit of peasant organization, the commune (10.7 per cent). The size of land owned by the latter was only 12 per cent the amount of land held in allotments, and thus could not really affect the livelihood of the masses of peasants struggling on their plots.[16] At the other end of the scale in the villages were those who owned no land whatsoever. One estimate placed the number of landless households at 17 per cent of the total number of households.[17]

The reform of 1861 increased the differentiation of the peasantry. One contemporary observer was struck by the marked contrast between the 'wealth and joy' of some households and the 'poverty and misery' of others.[18] The more prosperous peasant could be considered one who held allotments of over 10 dessiatines. In Ukraine as a whole one in seven households were in this category; one in eleven in right-bank Ukraine and one in nine in the left-bank.[19] The wealthier peasant augmented his holdings not only by the purchase of land, but also by renting. The sharp increase in the price of rent: from 10 to 12 roubles per dessiatine in the period 1895–8, to 18 to 20 roubles by 1903–4, and 25 to 30 roubles for good land – meant that only the more prosperous peasant could augment his income in this fashion.[20] For the poorer peasantry, they could earn a few roubles by working on the neighbouring farms of the nobles, or travel to the steppe regions to seek work on the great modern estates. But the introduction of modern agricultural machinery and the increasing supply of agricultural labour served to stabilize farm wages. To save themselves, poor peasants from Ukraine emigrated *en masse* to the Caucasus, Siberia and the Far East. Between 1896 and 1914, some two million Ukrainian peasants migrated from Ukraine to the regions.[21]

The holdings of Ukrainian peasants were actually larger than average peasant holdings in countries such as France. In France in 1884 the average peasant had less than 9 acres. The comparable figure in Ukraine for 1905 (all holdings, including allotment and purchased land) was 18 acres.[22] The French peasant, stimulated by a large urban market, made much more productive use of his land. The Ukrainian peasant suffered from primitive agriculture technique. For the mass of Ukrainian peasants, agricultural methods and implements had remained substantially unchanged from medieval times: the wooden plough, the scythe, the three-field system. However, a large proportion of Ukrainian peasants did not possess even medieval implements. In the relatively prosperous province of Katerynoslav, for example, 38 per cent of peasants did not own a wooden plough at the turn of the twentieth century.[23] As for draught animals, in 1891, 43 per cent of households in Ukraine were without a horse; in Kiev province the figure reached 62 per cent.[24] Lack of intelligent state policies promoting infrastructures in agriculture (credit facilities, grain elevators, agricultural schools and the like) compounded the difficulties. As a consequence the yields on peasant lands were low, and the threat of starvation ever present. The per acre yield of wheat in Ukraine was half that of Denmark, Belgium or Germany.[25] In the nineteenth century, under Ukraine's climatic conditions, the peasant could expect to experience pangs of hunger every two or three years when the harvest was poor.[26]

For the peasants who clung to the households of their fathers, real incomes were small. In 1903 the government found a grave discrepancy between the food yielded by allotment lands, and the needs of the people living on them. Using the sum of 640 lb of grain and potatoes as the average amount annually required by each individual, government statisticians found that this average was exceeded by the average income in only two provinces of Ukraine – in the other seven average income fell short of the average requirement by amounts ranging from 35 lb in Kharkiv to 178 lb in Volyn. Although these figures ignored income derived from non-allotment and rented land, from livestock, handicraft production, and from wages for outside labour, they assume considerable significance when set alongside figures on the health of youths called to military service. The proportion of draftees who were rejected or had their service deferred because of unsatisfactory physical conditions ranged from one-seventh to one-quarter of those called. The physical fitness of draftees in five of the Ukrainian provinces was somewhat less than average for European Russia.[27]

The Stolypin reform, which abolished obligatory forms of land communities and redemption payments, alleviated the lot of Ukrainian peasants to some extent. By allowing the consolidation of holdings the reform permitted peasants to show some initiative and improve their farming methods. With technical aid from agricultural cooperatives and zemstvo institutions something was accomplished in this direction. But what the reform did not do was solve the burning problem of land shortage. In the first years of the Stolypin reform, many poor peasants were attracted to the Peasant Bank, hoping to increase their land holdings through the purchase of land from the Bank. However, high land prices and high interest rates on loans for small parcels of land soon brought economic ruin to the small producer.[28] It was only the better-off peasants, who had the means to increase their landholding and to purchase modern implements, who benefited from the reform. On the eve of the 1917 revolution the problem of land hunger remained.

Statistics on peasant landholdings on the eve of the 1917 revolution are somewhat contradictory. The most exhaustive study published to date concluded that peasants with land of up to 3 dessiatines comprised 57 per cent of the total number of rural households (peasant and non-peasant) but owned only 12 per cent of the land; peasants with between 3 and 10 dessiatines represented 30 per cent of households and owned 22 per cent of the land; peasants with 10 dessiatines and over formed 12 per cent of the total rural households and owned 30 per cent of the land, while landlords representing 0.8 per cent of rural households owned 30 per cent of the land. The remaining 6 per cent of land was in the possession of the state and monasteries.[29]

The average peasant farm was approximately 8 dessiatines. A progressive Danish or French farmer could earn a comfortable living on such a farm, but not a Ukrainian peasant. As C. S. Smith, Britain's Consul-General in Odessa, noted in a confidential dispatch to the Foreign Office filed in 1905, 'the peasant class ... as a whole seems to live very near starvation. The peasantry are sure that more land is the cure for their hard lot, and it is on this that their hearts are set.'[30] It is, of course, arguable whether an instant egalitarian redistribution of all of the available 41 million dessiatines of arable land among four million peasant households would have improved the lot of the Ukrainian peasant. Such a redistribution would have increased the size of the average peasant holding by 1.5 dessiatines, with an additional half a horse and half a cow. Under agricultural conditions in Ukraine, this would still be a subsistence farm. However, whatever calculations one could have produced to show the peasantry the economic inadvisability of the solution of the agrarian question by the means of land seizure, there is no doubt that they wanted the upper classes' land. This desire was reinforced by the alien nature of the peasants' immediate economic antagonists, the nobility and merchants.

The nobility owned about a third of all arable land (1905). The average holding of the nobility in the steppe provinces was 733 dessiatines; in right-bank Ukraine, 609 dessiatines, and in the left-bank provinces 136 dessiatines. Merchants owned 16 per cent of the land. The average holding of merchants for the respective regions was 794, 443 and 144 dessiatines. Most of the land held by these upper classes was concentrated in large private estates: 52 per cent of all land privately owned was held by 1.6 per cent of private owners in estates of over 1,000 dessiatines.[31] Although the holding of the nobility slowly decreased because they were not always able to adjust to modern farming, in 1914 there were still 5,000 massive estates with about 1,600 dessiatines.[32]

For the Ukrainian peasant, national antagonism could be added to the problem of land hunger. The nobility, the class owning most of the large estates, were largely non-Ukrainian: 50 per cent were Russian, 20 per cent Polish, and 26 per cent Ukrainian. Almost half the Ukrainian nobility was concentrated in two provinces of the left-bank – Poltava and Chernihiv – where these descendants of the former Cossack officer class formed a layer of small landowners.[33]

The merchants and tradesmen epitomized for the peasant all that was wrong with the economic order. It was they who purchased the peasants' produce at the lowest possible figure, and who sold him manufactured goods at the highest possible prices. In Ukraine, only 13 per cent of all those engaged in trade and commerce were Ukrainian; 62 per cent were Jewish, and 17 per cent Russian. In the impoverished right-bank, only 7 per cent were Ukrainian, 82 per cent Jewish.[34]

Fiscal exploitation by the government was also a source of rural discontent. As Mykola Porsch noted, every year millions of roubles were paid into the Imperial treasury by Ukrainian peasants. These roubles were spent not to raise the economic and cultural level of these lowly taxpayers, but chiefly to maintain the Imperial administrative apparatus and the army, and to subsidize railways and other industries.[35] From these expenditures the Ukrainian peasant could discern no obvious advantage: rather they were personalized for him by corrupt bureaucrats, recruiting officers who dragged off sons into the army and insatiable tax collectors. Russian peasants also poured out taxes and also resented their government, but to the Ukrainian the matter presented another angle: most of officialdom were Russians filled with contempt for the Ukrainian peasant whom they called, derogatorily, *khokhol*. For example, two-thirds of all members of the armed forces garrisoned in Ukraine to maintain order, and whom the peasantry very often had to feed, were non-Ukrainian.[36] For the Ukrainian peasant masses the existing system of economic and administrative subjugation was symbolized by the city. Only 30 per cent of the population of Ukraine's cities and towns was Ukrainian, and in the case of cities with a population of over 50,000 this figure declined to 18 per cent.[37] The Bolshevik V. Skotovstanskii [V. Shakhrai], looking at the ctiy through the eyes of the Ukrainian peasant, wrote:

The city rules the village, and 'foreigners' the city. The city drew all the wealth to itself and gave almost nothing to the village in return. The city drew taxes, which almost never returned to the village in Ukraine ... in the city one had to pay bribes to officials to avoid mockery and red tape. In the city the landowner squandered all the weath gathered in the village. In the city the merchant cheated you when he bought and sold. In the city there are lights, there are schools, theatres and music plays. The city is clean ... dressed as for a holiday, it eats and drinks well, many people promenade. But in the village, apart from poverty, impenetrable darkness and hard work – there is almost nothing. The city is aristocratic, foreign, not ours, not Ukrainian. Russian, Jewish, Polish – only not ours, not Ukrainian.[38]

There was no shortage of grievances for the Ukrainian peasantry. The social conditions were such that on the surface their protest could easily be articulated within the framework of a national demand. However, peasant responsiveness on this score presupposed a certain self-awareness of belonging to a unique cultural community, and this awareness never arises spontaneously. It is the product of social learning which occurs over a long period of time. Neither was there any guarantee that peasant actions would follow an organized purposeful direction. Studies of social movements have shown that infrastructures of pre-existing voluntary associations and resources necessary to sustain organized activity are essential if movements are not to dissipate through lack of focus.[39] We will now examine how much progress had been made prior to the 1917 revolution on both scores.

As Imperial Russia stood on the eve of the twentieth century circumstances were such that it would not be long before the Ukrainian peasantry would rise against its predicament. Behind the Ukrainian peasants stretched a long tradition of direct action. As early as 1902, in the provinces of Poltava and Kharkiv, peasants sacked eighty-two large estates. Piotr Stolypin called these disturbances the worst since the rebellion of Pugachev.[40] Suppressed by the tsarist police and Cossacks, peasant discontent smouldered quietly in 1904, only to erupt still more furiously in 1905 and 1906. Peasant soldiers were dragging themselves home from the Russo-Japanese War with the demand for payment in something besides tarnished glory. Crop failures in the summer and autumn of 1905 sharpened the already chronic pangs of hunger. Then came rumours of rebellion in the streets of Kiev, Kharkiv and Odessa. Rural Ukraine again burst into flames.

At the peak of the agrarian movement, from the autumn of 1905 through the following summer, outbreaks appeared in all of the provinces and most of the districts of Ukraine. Refusing to work or pay rent, peasants demanded higher wages for labour on the large estates, a shorter working day, better living conditions, and the right to rent more land at lower rates. Violent direct action became widespread. The peasants chopped down the landlord's trees, appropriated his crops, pastured their cattle in his meadows, and even attempted to plough his fields. They plundered manor houses. Sometimes they assaulted or even killed resisting landlords. They also turned on the government, refusing to pay taxes and assailing local officials. Troops sent to quell the outbreaks were met with pitchforks, scythes and whatever firearms the peasants could gather.[41]

The 1905 revolution in Ukraine has been characterized as 'unplanned and leaderless'.[42] This was not entirely the case. Parallel to thousands of incidents of direct action, efforts were made to establish organizational structures in the form of peasant unions, popular enlightenment societies and the like. The Ukrainian rural intelligentsia – doctors, apothecaries, school teachers, clerks, veterinarians and zemstvo officials – were groups which played a key role in fostering the growth of peasant-based rural organizations.[43] Isolated village unions grew into *volost* and provincial organizations and finally into an All-Russian Peasant Union, the first congress of which met in Moscow in July 1905. The Russian Social Revolutionaries dominated both the all-Russian organization and the units in Ukraine. Ukrainian Social Revolutionaries had not yet founded their own organization. Social Revolutionary economic and political demands invariably appeared in petitions which the village assemblies addressed to the 'Little Father' in St Petersburg, demanding reforms such as the transfer of land, without compensation, to those who cultivated it, the pardoning of political prisoners and of peasants arrested during the agrarian disturbances, the calling of a constituent assembly to form a government based on universal suffrage, popular education at government expense, and the abolition of the death penalty.[44]

Initially, the national factor did not play a significant role in the peasant upheaval. This was because the peasantry had a poorly developed sense of national awareness, and because the channels transmitting the national message were in their infancy. Tsarist policies towards Ukraine were particularly devastating in this respect.

Mass illiteracy was one of the obstacles standing in the way of the efforts of the Ukrainian national movement. It is true that in the post-reform period, thanks to the efforts of the zemstvo institutions and the intelligentsia's popular enlightenment campaigns, some rudimentary improvement in the level of literacy had been registered.[45] But overall, prior to 1917, the mobilizing potential of literacy was hardly developed. The social and national policies of tsarism had led to a situation, probably unique in European history, where Ukrainians had higher rates of literacy in the mid-eighteenth century than at the turn of the twentieth.[46] In the light of the 1897 census only 13 per cent of Ukrainians were literate – the average for European Russia was 23 per cent. In the village, literacy rates ranged from 9 to 4 per cent depending on the province. Among Ukrainian women only 4 per cent could read. In France, for the sake of comparison, the literacy rate for women in 1848 was 80 per cent.[47]

The literacy rate in Ukraine reflected the state of popular education in the country. The school system throughout Russia was a travesty, but in Ukraine things were worse because national discrimination amplified the debilitating effects of general social and educational policies. From Alexander I's educational reform of 1804 until the time of the 1917 revolution, Ukrainian was banned from schools as a language of instruction and as a subject. The school question, as Otto Bauer noted, is one of the most important of all national questions, for a common national education is one of the strongest bonds of the nation. It is essential for the transmission of the great overarching traditions which give nations unity.[48] This instrument was denied the national movement. Neither could the printed word serve as a means to create a national social opinion. Throughout most of the nineteenth century the printing of newspapers, books and journals in Ukrainian was banned.[49]

The consequence of this situation was that the overwhelming mass of Ukrainian peasants had a poorly developed sense of their national identity. The village, of course, preserved its ethnos, because it was left outside the tide of modernity. The peasant 'stubbornly looked at the world through his ancestors' eyeglasses; he wore his ancestors' clothes, spoke his ancestors' tongue'.[50] S. Goldelman tells us that the national self-identification of the peasants was so low that they were 'hardly aware that the language which they used in their daily life was "Ukrainian"'.[51] An article published at the time of the 1905 revolution entitled 'A voice from the village' characterized the state of national consciousness as follows: 'In our country peasants are only very little conscious when it comes to nationality. They know they are not Muscovites, but Little Russians as they call themselves. But what is a Little Russian? What are his needs and how does he differ from a Muscovite? This they cannot say.'[52]

But this situation would not remain that way forever. The peasant may not have had much of a national instinct, but his sense of economic grievance was acute. Pursuing his economic inclination he had little choice other than to reflect on the political order. When the peasant movement reached the stage of considering wider political issues, the national question emerged. When the agrarian movement evolved from spontaneous action to assume more organized forms, this offered opportunities for the Ukrainian rural intelligentsia to communicate its message. The revolution of 1905 provided the social mobilization essential to the development of national identity and national political demands.

V. H. Bosanquet, the British Vice-Consul in Mykolaiv who toured the southern provinces of Ukraine in September 1905, noted that many had come to understand that 'the peasant question cannot be settled independently of the whole national question with which it is intimately connected'.[53] As Leon Trotsky wrote, the 'political awakening of the peasantry, could not have taken place otherwise ... than through their native language – with all the consequences ensuring to regard to schools, courts and self-administration'.[54] The agrarian revolt roused the peasant masses from their age-old slumber.

The Poltava peasantry, which rebelled as early as 1902, began to incorporate in its petitions to authorities demands for the 'Ukrainian language school, and the granting of political autonomy for Ukraine' only towards the end of 1905.[55] A study of peasant activity throughout the entire 1905 agrarian upheaval shows similar trends.[56] Plans were made for an all-Ukrainian peasant congress that would strive for 'civil and national equality and autonomy for Ukraine'.[57] The Ukrainian rural intelligentsia which had been active among the Russian Social Revolutionaries gradually broke away and formed their own national organization. The Ukrainian Party of Social Revolutionaries was founded in 1906.[58] Disillusionment which followed the collapse of the all-Russian agrarian movement strengthened the claim for autonomy.

All the petitions, peasant unions and congresses had resulted only in the cancellation of the 'redemption dues' for the allotments, a step which brought but little more bread to the peasant's table. Nor was the Stolypin Reform, which the government inaugurated after the 1905 revolution, more helpful, since it aimed to consolidate the landholdings of the more prosperous peasants. The entire sequence of events had made the Ukrainian peasant more receptive to the idea of escaping from the imperial yoke through the establishment of some system of Ukrainian autonomy. All-Russian peasant socialism gave way to a Ukrainian variant.[59]

In 1917, events in the Ukrainian countryside moved at 'fast forward' speed. An analysis of peasant actions from March 1917 to March 1918 shows that out of 500 cases reported, 41 per cent involved the seizure and free distribution of land. A comparable analysis for the rest of the Russian Empire (1,400 cases) shows that only 28 per cent of peasant action was directed at the seizure of land in this period. In the case of Ukraine, 90 per cent of land seized belonged to landlords, the Church or the state, and only 10 per cent involved taking land from homesteaders who established separate farms under the Stolypin reforms. By the end of September 1917 the peasantry, organized into local committees (*hromady*) had already redistributed about one-third of all non-peasant lands.[60] The point is that the agrarian revolution was well on the way to being settled before the Red Army established the Bolshevik regime in Kharkiv the end of December 1917.

The extent of the self-organization of village society in 1917 took even seasoned political observers by surprise. By the end of that year, the Ukrainian Peasants' Union (*Selianska spilka*), allied to the Ukrainian Party of Social Revolutionaries, had branches in the villages of most provinces and a membership that ran into the millions. It is estimated that in 1917 one in four Ukrainian rural adult males belonged either to the Union or to the Ukrainian Social Revolutionaries. (The Bolsheviks, for the sake of comparison, had 8,000 members in Ukraine.) The Union's newspaper, *Narodnia volia*, by May 1917 reached an astonishing circulation of 200,000. Scores of new cooperatives were founded.[61] The development of these infrastructures of national life permitted the national idea to penetrate the masses. The speed with which this happened was to be measured not in months, but in weeks and days. In peasant conferences and meetings the outlines of a national consensus were emerging: land to the peasants, a Ukrainization of the army, schools and administration, self-government for Ukraine in a loose confederation with Russia.[62]

The rise of national consciousness in the countryside was not because the human mind is malleable, but because it is conservative. The masses had always spoken the 'simple language' and sung 'the simple songs';[63] during the revolution, these age-old facts of their existence became politicized. The rural intelligentsia took the lead in this process. But in and of themselves, they would not have been able to accomplish this enormous task had they not been reinforced by tens of thousands of fresh cadres which the war and the army supplied.

Hundreds of thousands of young Ukrainian peasants – the most dynamic element in the countryside – were placed in uniform, where they learnt the effectiveness of organization. While serving the tsar they also experienced in a thousand different ways – from the taunts and insults of reactionary Russian officers to encounters with nationalistic Poles – the social contrast which is the yeast of national self-awareness. There too they met the heart and soul of the Ukrainian national movement, the village teachers, thousands of whom had been drafted as subalterns, and who became instrumental in transforming the young peasant recruits' new experiences and awareness into a national ideology. The national movement in 1917 as a mass phenomenon began in the barracks, often in urban garrisons, with discussions, concerts, clubs and congresses. The movement developed to such an extent that the 2,500 delegates attending the Second Military Congress in Kiev (July 1917) held mandates from over a million and a half troops.[64] When the soldiers returned home (or deserted), they greatly expanded the existing organizational forces of the Ukrainian movement in the countryside.

The national awakening of the Ukrainian peasantry was tied to the agrarian question. If the peasantry supported *en masse* the idea of Ukrainian autonomy in 1917, which they understood to mean full equality with Russia, it was because experience had taught them not to trust any agrarian reforms originating from the north. They were convinced that only a Ukrainian government 'run by "our people" ... who know what "our people" in Ukraine need' would give them the agrarian order they desired.[65] When the peasantry cornered members of the Central Rada (Ukraine's Provisional Government) and 'pounded' them with the demand to 'take power' immediately, this was an expression of their socio-economic realism.[66] In the spring of 1917 seizures of land had begun. Peasants needed a guarantee that their title to this land would be backed up by the power of a state from which they could expect a sympathetic hearing. Moreover, Ukrainian peasants were fearful of the prospect of having to share their land with Russian immigrants. It is not surprising that peasants were in the forefront of criticism of the Central Rada for its lack of resolve in obtaining autonomy from Petrograd. Delegates to the First All-Ukrainian Peasants' Congress (10–15 June 1917) could not understand why the Rada 'requested' autonomy and did not 'demand it'.[67]

If before the revolution most commentators agreed that the peasantry had a weak sense of national identity, after the revolution this evaluation changed. Speaking of the Ukrainian peasantry, Trotsky in 1923 noted, 'National ideology for peasantry is a factor of great significance. National psychology ... is an explosive force of immense proportions.'[68] When the Ukrainian peasant masses gave Ukrainian parties an impressive victory in the Russian Constituent Assembly elections (two months after the October revolution) there could be no doubt that the national movement had secured a popular base.[69]

Notes

1. *Pervia vseobshchaia perepis' naseleniia Rossiiskoi imperii 1897 goda*, 89 vols (St Petersburg, 1857–1905). Hereafter cited as *Perepis' 1897*; volumes 8, 13, 16, 32, 33, 41, 46, 47, 48 provide data for the Ukrainian provinces. Notes will refer to table numbers, which are identical in all volumes, and not to pages, which vary. See Tables XXI, XXII, XXIII, XXIV.
2. Mykola Porsh, 'Iz statystyky Ukrainy', *Ukraina*, III (1907) p. 42.
3. Mykhailo Drahomanov, *Novi ukrainski pisni pro hromadsi spravy (1764–1880)* (Geneva, 1881) p. 66.
4. See A. Z. Popelnitski, 'Pervyie shagi krestianskoi reformy', in *Velikaia reforma*, vol. 5 (Moscow, 1991) pp. 184–94.
5. M. Iavorskyi, *Ukraina v epokhu kapitalizmu: Na shliakhu kapitalistychnoi akumuliatsii* (Kharkiv, 1925) pp. 28–30.
6. Porsh, 'Iz statystyky', 42, and *Istoriia selianstva Ukrainskoi RSR*, vol. 1 (Kiev, 1967) p. 384.
7. V. P. Teplytsky, *Reform 1861 roku i ahrarni vidnosyny na Ukraini* (Kiev, 1959) pp. 106–9.
8. P. Maslov, *Razvitie zemledeleniia v Rossii* (Moscow, 1912) p. 129.
9. *Istoriia selianstva*, vol. 1, p. 387.
10. Iu. Ianson, *Opyt statisticheskogo issledovaniia o krestianskikh nadelakh i platezhakh* (St Petersburg, 1881).
11. M. Porsch, 'Statystyka zemlevolodinnia v 1905 r. i mobilizatsiia zemel'noi vlasnosty na Ukraini vid 1877 r po 1905 r.', *Ukraina*, IV (1907) pp. 166, 176.

12. *Istoriia selianstva*, vol. 1, p. 392.
13. Ianson, *Opyt*, p. 66.
14. *Statistika zemlevladeniia 1905 g. Svod dannykh pp 50-ti goberniiam evropeiskoi Rossii*, (St Petersburg, 1906–7) pp. xxxiv, xxxv, xxxvi, 11, 24, 25.
15. *Istoriia selianstva*, vol. 1, p. 387.
16. *Statistika zemlevladeniia*, pp. 12–13, 56–63, 68–9.
17. Iavorskyi, *Ukraina*, pp. 41–2.
18. L. Kotelianskii, 'Ocherki podvornoi Rossii', *Otechestvennye zapiski*, no. 2, pt 2 (1878) p. 133.
19. *Statistika zemlevladeniia*, pp. xxxv, xxxvi, 11.
20. N. Mirza-Avakiants, *Selianski rozrukhy na Ukraini 1905–1907* (Kharkiv, 1925) p. 6.
21. P. P. Telychuk, *Ekonomichni osnovy ahrarnoi revoliutsii na Ukraini* (Kiev, 1973) p. 174.
22. *Statistika zemlevladeniia*, pp. xxxv, xxxvi, 11, and G. T. Robinson, *Rural Russia under the Old Regime* (New York, 1932) p. 97.
23. *Istoriia selianstva*, vol. 1, p. 395.
24. 'Vysochaishe uchrezhdennaia 16 noiabria 1901 g. komissiia po issledovaniiu voprosa o dvizhenii s 1861 po 1901 g. blagosostoianiia selskogo naseleniia srednezemledelcheskikh gubernii sravnitel'no s drugimi mestnostiami Evropeiskoi Rossii', *Materialy*, vol. 1 (St Petersburg, 1903) pp. 204–5, 208–9.
25. Isidor Shafarenki, *The Natural Resources, Industry, Exports and Imports of the Ukraine* (London, 1920) p. 3.
26. *Istoriia selianstva*, vol. 1, p. 482.
27. 'Vysochaishe uchrezhdennaia', vol. 1, pp. 28–33, 88–9.
28. F. Ie. Los and O. H. Mukhaliuk, *Klasova borotba v ukrainskomu seli, 1907–1914 rr.* (Kiev, 1976) pp. 31–8.
29. I. K. Rybalko and F. H. Turchenko, 'Sotsialno-klassova struktura naselennia Ukrainy naperedodni Zhovtnevoi revoliutsii', *Ukrainskyi istorychnyi zhurnal*, no. 11 (1981) p. 24.
30. Public Record Office, FO 65, 1712, ERD/7108, 3 October 1905, no. 108, p. 1. Hereafter cited as PRO.
31. *Statistika zemlevladeniia*, pp. 12–15, 56–63, 68–79, 72–3.
32. *Podgotovka velikoi oktiabrskoi sotsialisticheskoi revoliutsii na Ukraine, Sbornik dokumentov i materialov* (Kiev, 1955) p. 9.
33. *Perepis' 1897*, Table xxiv.
34. Ibid., Table xxi.
35. Mykola Porsch, *Ukraina i Rossiia na robitnychomu rynku* (Kiev, 1918) pp. 32–5.
36. *Perepis' 1897*, Table xxi.
37. Ibid., Table xxii.
38. V. Skotovstanskii [V. Shakhrai], *Revoliutsiia na Ukraine* (Saratov, 1919) pp. 7–8.
39. Michael Hechter and Margaret Levi, 'The Comparative Analysis of Ethnoregional Movements', *Ethnic and Racial Studies*, no. 3 (1979) p. 266.
40. Sir John Maynard, *Russia in Flux before October* (New York, 1962) p. 62.
41. Pavlo Khrystiuk, *1905 rik na Ukraini* (Kharkiv, 1925) pp. 160–5.
42. P. N. Pershin, *Narysy ahrarnoi revoliutsii v Rossii* (Kiev, 1959) p. 157.

43. PRO, 26 September 1905, no. 58, p. 3.
44. Khrystiuk, *1905*, pp. 97–100
45. *Narysy istorii ukrainskoi intelihentsii (persha polovyna XX st.)* Knyha, I (Kiev, 1994) pp. 44–8.
46. A. Ia. Efimenko, *Istoriia ukrainskogo naroda* (St Petersburg, 1906) p. 325.
47. *Perepis' 1897*, Table xv; Paul Johnson, *The Birth of the Modern* (London, 1992) p. 482.
48. Otto Bauer, *Die Nationalitätenfrage und die Sozialdemokratie* (Vienna, 1924) pp. 215–17.
49. See *Narysy istorii ukrainskoi intelihentsii*, pp. 44–9.
50. St V., 'Ukrainska polityka', *Dzvin*. *Zbrnyk*, vol. 1 (Kiev, 1907) p. 239.
51. Solomon I. Goldelman, *Jewish National Autonomy in Ukraine, 1917–1920* (Chicago, 1968) p. 19.
52. *Rade*, 17 September 1916.
53. PRO, 26 September 1905, no. 58, p. 4.
54. Leon Trotsky, *The History of the Russian Revolution*, vol. 3 (London, 1967) p. 32.
55. *Istoriia selianstva*, vol. 1, p. 446.
56. Khrystiuk, *1905*, pp. 101, 106.
57. N. Mirza-Avakiants, *Selianski rozrukhy na Ukraini 1905–1907 r.* (Kharkiv, 1925) pp. 41–8.
58. A Zhyvotko, 'Do istorii Ukrainskoi partii sotsialistiv revoliutsioneriv', *Vilna spilka*, no. 3 (1927) pp. 128–32.
59. Konstantyn Kononenko, *Ukraine and Russia: A History of the Economic Relations between Ukraine and Russia (1654–1917)* (Milwaukee, 1958) pp. 95–9.
60. Vsevolod Holubnychy, 'The 1917 Agrarian Revolution in Ukraine', in I. S. Koropeckyj (ed.), *Soviet Regional Economics: Selected Works of Vsevolod Holubnychy* (Edmonton, 1982) pp. 10, 12, 57.
61. Pavlo Khrystiuk, *Ukrainska revoliutsiia. Zamitky i materiialy do istorii ukrainskoi revoliutsii, 1917–1920 rr.*, vol. 1 [reprint] (New York, 1969) pp. 24–5, 45–6; P. L. Varhatiuk, 'Bilshovytski orhanizatsii Ukrainy v liutnevi revoliutsii', *Ukrainskyi istorychnyi zhurnal*, no. 2 (1967) pp. 39, 44; B. I. Marochko, *Ukrainska selianska Kooperatsiia* (Kiev, 1995) pp. 46–63.
62. For example, see *Robitnycha hazeta* (12 April, 11 May, 10 June, 24 August and 31 August 1917).
63. Volodymyr Vynnychenko, *Vidrodzhennia natsii*, vol. 1 (Vienna and Kiev, 1920) p. 176.
64. Khrystiuk, *Ukrainska revoliutsiia*, vol. 1, pp. 22–3.
65. Ibid., p. 177.
66. Volodymyr Vynnychenko, *Shchodennyk. tom pershyi, 1911–1920* (Edmonton, 1980) p. 273.
67. Khrystiuk, *Ukrainska revoliutsiia*, vol. 1, pp. 65–6.
68. L. Trotskyi, 'Natsionalna sprava', *Nova kultura*, no. 1 (1923) p. 34.
69. O. H. Radkey, *The Elections to the Russian Constituent Assembly of 1917* (Cambridge, MA, 1950) pp. 78–9.

3
Identity and Politics in Provincial Russia: Tver, 1889–1905

Hari Vasudevan

In recent times, where identity has been associated with 'a mode of being' and 'claims to a capacity for action or change', the distinction between what exists and what might provide legitimacy to action is clearly crucial to the point at issue.[1] This is especially so in the case of 'regional identity' in Russia; for it has been the dissociation of 'claims to a capacity for action or change' here from the connotations of the region in terms of historical and social attributes (except in the Ukraine, Siberia and the Lower Volga), that has left the identity of the locality unattended except as a focus of *kraevedenie*, that is, the study of an area for its own sake. Otherwise, regional and national identity in Russia has been dealt with in standard terms: that is 'construction' (intellectual and social)[2] and with regard to religion ethnicity, sensibility and political economy. In such cases, identity is linked directly to territorial and political claims, and a clear interconnection is apparent in the very rhetoric which accompanies 'claims'.

With an eye to such literature, this essay examines 'claims' for unencumbered local self-government in the *uezd* (county) and the *guberniia* (province) in European Russia at the turn of the century; it indicates the implications for such claims of regional identity in this area at this time, with specific attention to local government affairs in Tver province of the Central Industrial Region. The assertion of claims took place at the time of the 'liberal' defence of country and provincial local self-government, in the 'zemstvo movement', against the background of the 'counter-reforms' and other legislation of 1889–1904. The argument of the essay is that the construction of the identity of a region, in terms of history, cartography, statistics, folklore and so on, set the contours of the locality at this time; and a network of interests, which were linked to the region, underpinned 'liberal' mobilization in the zemstvo movement around claims for local self-government. Here the 'construction' certainly cannot *directly* be associated with the formation of 'claims'. For much of that 'construction' was parochial or transregional, in that it acknowledged 'province', 'district' and region, but celebrated the village, town and locality, or the nation and Tsar. 'Interest' networks in a locality were crucial to liberal mobilization, but these were held together by ties of sociability, and professional, institutional and economic compulsions, which were linked to broader all-Russian concerns and multiregional associations, even if they had a specific regional focus on occasion. 'Community' here was weak and, for example, professionals in a province had a local focus, but their terms of reference were set by societies such as the (All-Russian) Pirogov Medical Association. Again, in the instance of the provincial gentry, compulsions of estate management demanded a focus on the locality, but local groups had extensive connections with the bureaucracy and they frequently possessed substantial interest in a variety of provinces.

Central to 'claims' for local self-government bodies, undoubtedly, was liberal *coordination* of various interest groups (the agrarian interest among the gentry, and medical professionals for instance) around a powerful argument for devolution and decentralization within a locality and outside it. The argument was stated in liberal journals such as *Vestnik Evropy* and *Russkaia Mysl'*, in the course of meetings of the government committees on the needs of agriculture (1904) and in other forums. It derived its strength from the debates and convictions of the liberal and socialist intelligentsia, whose prime identity was with 'society' or the 'public' (*obshchestvo*), rather than specific regional sensibilities. The importance of the arguments, and the ubiquitous character of the assumptions from which they were derived, is indicated by the regard that 'centralizing' officials of the 'counter-reform' showed for the position in their formulation of policy. They either made outright concessions on occasion (as in the case of the Hospital Statute of 1894), or adjustments to make room for local variations (through giving 'discretionary authority' to officials in the provinces). In Tver province, it will be clear, this was undoubtedly the pattern to be seen in 'claims' against officials who intervened decisively in the affairs of local government in 1890, 1894 and 1898. The coordinating centre here was a group of liberal zemstvo representatives from Torzhok and Ves'egonsk counties (I. I. Petrunkevich, A. A. Bakunin, P. A. Korsakov, and so on).

Aspects of this presentation, however, modify its general thrust. Due attention is paid to how regions were 'constructed' and 'imagined', and how regional sociability was established, in order to indicate contemporary definitions of the county and the province and the space with which they were associated. This background cannot be discounted from the statement of claims for local self-government, and the provincial politics of its defence. It must be regarded as significant though not decisive in formulation and assertion of 'claims.' Equally, it is implied that attention should be paid to the contribution of claims and political mobilization to regional sensibilities – given the political and social authority of liberal activists at the time – although the language of identity hardly reflects the significance of 'claims'. Undoubtedly, attribution of significance to provincial identity in such a manner does not seriously undermine current reading of the origins of the zemstvo movement and the Revolution of 1905 (to which it contributed), although it must alter that reading. It does, however, imply a distant lineage to 'claims' of Russian provinces today:[3] a lineage implied in current polemic, where the example of the zemstvo movement, and 'construction' of the *zemstva* is certainly at the core of the assertion today of 'claims' in Russia's localities. This, in turn, requires renewed attention to what the nature of the original mobilization was, to indicate where the present situation differs or compares.

Here in sections I and II, this essay draws out the markers of the county and province and discusses liberal 'claims' for the locality, pointing out that they were linked to a critique of bureaucracy, and an assertion of the value of administrative devolution and the importance for government of elected authority. Such a statement was pitted against public policy which assumed that while the specificity of local problems required recognition, rigorous coordination of authority, through officials, was essential for good government; that, in arrangements to deal with the distinctive problems of the locality, preference for the 'loyal' noble 'estate' deserved attention, as much as principles of election, representation and publicity. In section III, the essay focuses on Tver province and the liberal initiatives against official measures regarding the local self-government bodies of the locality. The essay draws on prevailing literature[4] on the zemstvo movement, together with a range of archival sources.

'The region' and the counter-reforms of 1889–1904

Identity and the region in 1889

In 1889, when officials undertook the first 'counter-reform' of provincial institutions, the 'county' (*uezd*) and 'province' (*guberniia*) – that is, the primary administrative–territorial units associated with the region – were identified most readily in terms of history, statistics and cartography.[5] Scholars and officials active in 'service', the Academy of Sciences, or learned societies constituted and reconstituted local history from monastic chronicles (*letopisi*).[6] Historians also drew on the evidence of 'lays', which often played on regional sentiment,[7] chronicles[8] and tales.[9] Outside the Ukraine, such literature was of special significance in the case of the counties and provinces around Moscow; but there was also a run of these accounts for a later time (the seventeenth century, for instance), for the south of the country.[10] Cartographical and statistical work was normally carried out by the Army and provincial statistical committees; and after the local government reform of 1864, provincial statistical bureaux of the *zemstva* extended the work. Historical research developed later in the century in archival commissions and regional museums,[11] as well as in the universities, learned societies, and so on. The connotations of the county and the province were further established in folklore and the *lubochnaia* literature sold around shrines,[12] where specific towns were renowned for the presence of an icon, or of relics; and associations with a particular county or province were the organizing point of student and worker *zemliachestva* (regional associations) in metropolitan areas. Invariably folklore and regional associations had some renown in the hinterland of major metropolises and in provinces and counties themselves, although the local significance of *zemliachestva* was limited; and folklore was of a scattered character, placing no proper boundaries to the 'region' mentioned, and frequently becoming wholly particularist.

Here, and in the case of scholarly investigation, officials discouraged discussions of the region in terms of 'traditions' (*predaniia*), if this led to more broad-ranging political conclusions. This was the case in the early work of A. L. Shchapov, who called for a location of authority in communities which, he argued (far from convincingly), had been formed by patterns of settlement, determined by 'land and water'. Officials sponsored research in local 'lore', which sought the essence of Russianness (*narodnost'*) in local legends and sayings; and most of the literary studies of the time stressed that the 'regional' themes of old Russian literature had given way to a reverence for the emergence of Muscovy as the focus of the realm.[13] The efforts of civil servants, however, only limited the accumulation of 'lore' around a county or province marginally. Localities acquired a status in memory, public reference and academic endeavour, even as powerful interests coalesced in counties, provinces and regions (the more indistinct *krai*) around economic issues and leading families. These features of local life persisted although legitimate administrative authority in the *uezd* and the *guberniia* lay with the governor and his chancellery, and the police officials of a locality, who were directly subordinate to ministries in St Petersburg.

Institutions, claims and the region in 1889

Political and institutional claims of any significance, however, were seldom made with reference to such 'identity' except in Siberia and the Ukraine. In counties and provinces a variety of public bodies, drawn from inhabitants of the locality, worked in a position wholly subordinate to that of official agencies of central government without specific reference to the past of the region and its distinct rights. This was the case of parish boards, where members of an orthodox congregation undertook philanthropic actions and helped to maintain places of worship; and a variety of institutions (of the gentry, the *kupechestvo*, the *meshchanstvo*, and sections of the peasantry),[14] who were associated with the 'estates' (*sosloviia*) which denoted the divisions of society for administrative and legal purposes. This behaviour on the part of these bodies has been explained in terms of the creation by the autocracy of such 'estates' and the failure of other processes to create regional affinities. In the case of peasant institutions, the sensibilities of their members were particularist; while in the case of the nobility, many possessed land in a number of regions and families were rarely associated with a specific province or county.

All-class elected local self-government institutions (*zemstva*) were not an exception here. These were bodies whose decisions could only be challenged in accordance with their legality even if their independence was curtailed by their reliance on officials for the implementation of their decisions.[15] The self-government bodies existed in thirty-four provinces of European Russia, where the bases of the institutions were county and provincial zemstvo assemblies (*uezdnye* and *gurbernskie sobraniia*), elected (by ballot) by landowners, taxpayers and peasant allotment holders, on the basis of a property franchise. Together with municipal corporations (*gorodskie dumy*), they involved a measure of public initiative in the definition of the character and requirements of a locality and in assistance towards its governance. *Zemstva* and *gorodskie dumy* worked closely with *volost* bodies of the peasant estate, civil servants and 'estate' officials (such as the Marshals of the Nobility); they elected the members of various local boards and institutions of regional importance (the Peasant Land Bank and so on). The institutions spawned a number of organs to deal with public health, elementary education, insurance against fire, and veterinary assistance, while they also assumed responsibility for the distribution of taxation and the maintenance of the local grain reserve.

Certain claims were made for the *zemstva* well before 1890 and the emergence of the zemstvo movement of 1904–05. In some regions, the zemstvo was a straightforward assembly of leading figures from various social groups, where, despite the work of serious professionals, the primary concern was self-aggrandizement and local status; here, the 'claims' were tantamount to an assertion of the rights of the zemstvo, in a specific case, over those of the bureaucracy. In other areas, the bodies were the focus of conservative, liberal and populist networks, of which liberals, although varied in opinion, agreed to make of *zemstva* a 'school for self-government', and they sought to assure the 'independence' and 'rights' of *zemstva* in order to ensure the development of a capacity for self-government. Liberals also sought to find representation for the *zemstva* in the major consultative councils of the Empire (the Senate and the State Council), to 'crown the edifice' of self-governing bodies, in order to strengthen the principle of self-government in Russian government. In the localities, liberals sought both to devise schemes for public welfare, to improve systems of taxation, and to refine systems for interaction between constituents and the *zemstva*. By and large, 'liberal' gentry were influenced by their interest in parliamentarism and self-government, albeit from differing points of view. Among liberal leaders, Boris Chicherin wished to involve broad sections of the public in the practice of government, with the proviso that a strong state should be retained as this involvement grew, that the tasks of government should be few and that problems of welfare should be left to private action and the dictates of conscience and morality. I. I. Petrunkevich was wholly committed to 'four-tail' parliamentarism (universal, equal, secret and direct suffrage), was uninterested in the strong state, and insistent on limited welfare functions; 'Slavophils' such as D. N. Shipov were interested in both representation and welfare, provided that forms did not necessarily follow the 'four-tail' path set by liberalism in France, Germany and elsewhere.

In all this, members of *zemstva* were concerned with ideology or religion rather than regional and parochial sentiment; and the politics of *zemstva* and other institutions drew on local patterns of sociability, centred on broad professional or transregional associations (the Imperial Russian Free Economic Society, the Pirogov Society and so on). Their perception of their problems was established within a framework that transcended the locality. Such affiliations and sociability, though, crystallized often around powerful noble and non-noble families and noble and merchant assemblies of a locality. Local bodies also acted as a specifically local forum for interests which had broader transregional associations. Although members of the institutions made few claims for the region, they provided the space where residents gathered. Other bodies (agricultural societies, fire-fighting societies, cooperatives and so on) served the same function. All in all, the groupings gave authority to local institutions and often directed the course of their activites. Local alliances and associations, like the 'constitution' of the region in literature and sceintific accounts, lay significantly in the background of local bodies and their 'claims' – though they seldom became fundamental to the character of such claims.

The 'counter-reform' and subsequent legislation, 1889–1904

The scope of legislation

In these circumstances, local institutions were subjected to extensive reorganization from 1889. In the 'counter-reforms' of that year, officials abolished the position of Justice of the Peace, elected from the *zemstva*, and established the salaried post of land captain (*zemskii nachal'nik*), appointed by the governor to deal with local legal and administrative problems. In the local government law of 1890, officials extended the authority of governors over *zemstva*, permitting them to halt local government actions if they felt that these contravened the interests of the locality, while, in 1894 and 1900, the powers of civil servants over zemstvo finance were reinforced.[16] In measures of 1892, 1894 and 1896, the *zemstva*'s jurisdiction over elementary schools was reduced;[17] and zemstvo insurance, together with large zemstvo hospitals, were brought under the Ministry of Internal Affairs in 1894.[18] In November 1894, the Ministry of Agriculture increased the regulation of zemstvo measures to assist agriculture;[19] legislation of 1902 removed coordinating powers over district grain reserves from the *zemstva* and established close official controls over zemstvo veterinary projects.

Finally, reorganization of local government, and plans for development of social policy, increased the authority of officials in the localities. Hence, the decision to rework the principles of election to zemstvo assemblies, to determine their composition by 'estates' rather than according to the interest of property owners, led to nomination of peasant representatives by the provincial governor (albeit from a list provided by estate bodies); and in 1894, when the Grot Commission discussed the introduction of public assistance for the destitute in Russia, members suggested distribution of assistance through provincial, county and cantonal committees, under the supervision of officials.[20]

Official concerns: discretionary authority and budgetary imperatives

'Counter-reform', however, did not merely reorder provincial institutions and establish the ascendancy of officials and 'estates' in a manner adequate to the reinforcement of St Petersburg's authority. Its protagonists extended, or sought to extend, institutional flexibility to officials, to enable them to take proper account of local circumstances. Regard for such circumstances is evident not only in the modulation by a major official, K. Pobedonostsev (Procuror of the Holy Synod), of his support for 'counter-reform', with insistence on 'a measure of freedom' for local institutions. Functionaries and 'conservative' *zemtsy* worked to confer exceptional powers on 'official agents': to make them independent of statistical assessments and legal precedent in coping with immediate issues. In this, protagonists of the counter-reform expressed a preference for gentry resident in this region, with considerably less regard for education, nit-picking legal argument and university ideas. The land captains (who were created in 1889) were distinguished by their 'middle' or 'lower' education and their residence in a locality. Officials and supportive publicists sought to provide them and members of the imperial bureaucracy with 'discretionary authority' independent of the guidelines of officials, the injunctions of government circulars, and the letter of the law, giving them the capacity to adapt to local requirements.

Support for 'discretionary authority' (*diskretsionnaia vlast'*) was noticeable in the course of the famine of 1891–2, when gubernatorial circulars stressed that land captains should ignore official injunctions and the letter of the law in emergencies; later the *Moskovskie Vedomosti* made it clear that this was a principle that it supported without qualification. Clearly, however, 'discretionary authority' was not to be provided to officials of local self-government; nor was it guaranteed to independent individual initiative (such as philanthropic activity) in times of hardship; this exclusion vouchsafed 'discretionary authority' to those designated by functionaries and the locality's noble corporate structures.[21]

Elsewhere, in the case of the reform of local government finances, Finance Minister Witte provided local authorities with the wherewithal to make demands for exceptional requirements,[22] even as he tightened his department's control over them. Pobedonostsev and Witte took 'counter-reform' fiscal measures in the course of their search for greater restraint in public spending. They considered the financial and fiscal powers of *zemstva* excessive and their supporters argued that practices of self-government lent a random element to budgetary arrangements; and the influential Procuror of the Holy Synod was certain that the 'measure of freedom' he desired for local initiative did not require the right that local self-government possessed to levy rates with mere reference to the 'income and value' of property (the standard for zemstvo rating). Pobedonostsev noted that such powers impaired, '... the indispensable fixedness and capacity for regulation of economic affairs'.

Witte, meanwhile, sought to regulate monetary policy, while he contended with the reports of three major commissions that taxation was insupportable, given peasant incomes; and he attempted desperately to effect a reallocation of redemption dues to deal with peasant tax arrears. He also complained of recent high expenditure by the *zemstva*, in 1897, setting out a clear criticism of the financial system that permitted it. Other officials took a similar view, and were alarmed over the state of zemstvo finances.[23] In such circumstances, Witte introduced new administrative controls over zemstvo funds and powers of 1891, 1894 and 1900, which limited the self-governing capacity of county and provincial bodies. He was clear that only through official regulation could problems of local government be solved without prejudice to industrial investment, and to the availability of larger resources to central government institutions and projects.

However, Witte felt bound to make arrangements for the exceptional demands of individual regions; and he set up a system with the Ministry of Internal Affairs to receive petitions and provide permssion in all cases where the appeal was justified.

Disputing the counter-reforms and Russian liberalism

Liberal politics and the counter-reforms

It was in these circumstances that, in a number of zemstvo assemblies, liberals passed petitions against official measures, and found support from assembly members. Liberals required a position for elected local bodies that was regulated primarily by law, arguing that the region was best governed through elected local self-government. Liberal activists hotly disputed the application of 'discretionary authority' in everyday circumstances, and deplored the reinforcement of *zemstva* to official bodies and functionaries. In 1894 and 1895, zemstvo liberals agreed to meet in Moscow to coordinate petitions against counter-reform legislation. K. K. Arsenev (St Petersburg), I. I. Petrunkevich, F. I. Rodichev (Tver) and D. I. Shakhovskoi (Iaroslav) arranged these gatherings and they persuaded zemstvo men from Tula, Kursk, Moscow, Chernigov, Tambov, Tver and St Petersburg to attend.

The leaders of this movement were seldom prominent provincial gentlemen whose prime commitment was to their estate, or to a particular region. The case of Petrunkevich, whose brief biography is given in the account of the Tver zemstvo below, is not untypical. Those concerned were social activists (*obshchestvennye deiateli*), whose commitment to the cause of devolution was part of a broader concern with democratization and socialization; it rarely coincided with a profound interest in the affairs of any one region. Among such activists themselves, distinctions of 'metropolitan and 'provincial' undoubtedly existed – as revealed in the notes kept by F. I. Rodichev's daughter of the distance between the metropolitan publicist, Arsenev, and her father, who had spent much of his life in provincial work. These sentiments were not the resentment on the part of a *tverianin* against the cosmopolitan: they were the upshot of problems of family status, social position and wealth.[24] Such sentiments were fellow-travellers of provincialism and provincial sensibility, but could not be directly linked to it.

To achieve their ends, consequently, liberals faced difficulties in various provinces, for assembly members were far from committed to liberal principles generally; and this proved a major limitation when liberals themselves were divided in their views, varying from the vague, to the Slavophile (Shipov), and to the constitutionalist (Petrunkevich). Hence, in Iaroslav, A. P. Kryllov and D. I. Shakhovskoi had to deal with a variety of 'interests' in the assembly, while they held their own in the provincial town and the major entrepot of Rybinsk. In Kursk, despite the personal influence of K. P. Arnoldi, P. P. Dolgorukov, V. E. Iakushkin and others, zemstvo decisions had to receive the approval of that prominent local nobleman N. F. Kasatkin-Rostovskii; in Orel, M. A. Stakhovich had his own inclinations, and in Voronezh, although a number of professionals were influential in the *zemstva*, certain families required to be satisfied (the Lisanevichs, Levchenkos, Teviashevs and so on). Similar patterns can be traced in Kherson, Simbirsk, Novgorod and elsewhere; and few *zemstva* had strong liberal parties such as those that existed in the case of Tver, Smolensk, Moscow and

Khar'kov. Relentless lobbying, and resort to personal influence, was essential; and it became a part of the liberal style of functioning in provincial bodies during these years.

The consequence of such action was seen most clearly in 1894 and 1902, during campaigns against the Hospital Statute and the Veterinary Statute. Liberals were able to mobilize a run of petitions against the statutes and made it clear that proper implementation of the laws would be difficult. Officials thereupon suspended implementation of the statutes pending further consideration. Elsewhere, during meetings of the Agricultural Committees (1902), where liberal zemstvo leaders were well represented, liberal assumptions regarding the character of the locality and how it should best be governed were indicated clearly: a Khar'kov committee deplored 'the narrow margin of bureaucratic regimentation' in which *zemstva* had to work, and Orel, Poltava, Moscow and Kostroma committees complained of government restrictions and a lack of trust from officials. A Chernigov committee argued that functionaries must recognize that if *zemstva* were to work effectively, they had to have greater freedom from supervision by state departments.

Committee members stressed that economic and social reform was best achieved in country areas by elected bodies: that an indispensable condition for the success of reform was that implementation of measures should not depend on 'persons not having any interest in the results of the measure, who are not concerned with their speedy and proper realization, who look upon them as merely one more of the tasks allotted to them in the course of service, and who do not have any moral responsibility, before society, for their fulfilment, their failure or success'. *Zemstva* were said to have an advantage over official bodies in policy implementation in that their self-sufficiency and independence from other agencies was greater. Election, it was said, ensured the institutions were 'in the closest control of the local population', and represented 'the gamut of minor local interests'.[25]

As they took up various aspects of public policy for criticism, zemstvo influential 'liberals' took issue with the 'limited amount of independence, which the law of 1890 left to the *zemstva*';[26] and they pointed to appalling problems of the government's initiatives relating to the noble estate and discretionary authority. Hence, reports in *Vestnik Evropy* were harsh in the coverage of the V. A. Protopopov affair (a Khar'kov scandal of 1894, where a *zemskii nachal'nik* (or land captain) abused his authority).[27]

There was little dispute that broad-ranging public policy on crucial issues, initiated by central authorities, was not *per se* objectionable; that, rather, it was crucial 'to contend with the greed and lack of foresight of those living', and to enable the state 'to fulfil the role of champion of the national interest, to serve generations as yet unborn'. But liberal publicists questioned the nature of the state that was to undertake the intervention: it was stressed that representative government and 'self-government' were the best basis for good government. Criticism of partiality to the noble estate was couched in the broadest terms. In 1889, a contributor to the liberal *Russkaia Mysl'* pointed out that the *zemstva*'s achievement in social welfare was no tribute to the gentry who had only made something of the institution because they had to work within the competitive atmosphere of electoral politics. Claims of a long history of service were rejected, as was the notion of the nobility as a source of stability. Even at its highest reaches, the commentator pointed out, the 'estate' was severely divided. Hence, there was a clear difference between Cherkasskiis, Vorotynskys, Trubetskois and Golitsyns (whose names were among those of boyars, but not among those of *okol'nichi*) and Kurakins, Pozharskiis, Baryatinskiis and Pushkins (whose names occurred in both). In existing circumstances, a preoccupation with estate (*soslovnost'*) led to exclusivity (*iskliuchitel'nost'*) and introversion (*zamknutost'*), which did not help in the work of local government.

Support for the liberal critique in Zemstvo circles: provincialism – more and less

In zemstvo assemblies most liberals, even while they represented themselves as 'intelligentsia', were members of the very estate to whom officials appealed in the 'counter-reform' legislation, that is the nobility, which had hitherto dominated zemstvo assemblies; and their supporters came from the same 'caste'. The latter were *glasnye* from the landowning gentry, who looked on *zemstva* as 'a string of jobs' they could dispense, who had their portraits put up in public places and were accustomed to speeches and biographies in their honour. Patrons of temperance societies, agricultural associations, minor periodicals, consumer societies and fire-fighting associations,[28] these gentlemen had been able to call on zemstvo funds to assist their 'clients' when their own resources did not permit them to help; and in the new dispensation, their freedom was circumscribed.[29] Their social ambit was the 'noble club' of the province, and the 'circles' of country society.

Support for liberals in zemstvo assemblies came from others like P. D. Dolgorukov, M. V. Chelnokov, N. A. Karyshev and 'liberal' *zemtsy* who attended the agricultural conferences of 1895 and 1901, and criticized government agricultural policy (or the lack of it). This appealed to those incensed by official failure to do anything about falling grain prices in general and, later, Witte's revaluation of the currency and the consequent increase in import prices of agricultural machinery and fertilizer. 'Conservative' remedies, through revision of State Bank and Noble Bank statutes, proved abortive, given the inability of the Minister of Agriculture to assert his plans for the development of advanced farming and the scepticism of Witte.[30]

Here, liberals attracted the support of a variety of squires who often came together in inter-regional associations and pressure groups, such as the Imperial Agricultural Society of South Russia. Specific local pressures, though, determined the predilections of such gentry. In Orel, Tambov, Penza and Simbirsk there were those who lost income after trading agents began operation from stations and points on the railways, bringing to an end the gentleman's control over the long-distance trade in cereals. In the southern black-earth areas, and the lacustrine and Moscow area, many profited from this development, but had problems with agricultural labour, agricultural machinery and so on.[31] Several landowners in both these regions benefited from the government's economic measures (in the case of sugar beet producers and sugar manufacturers, for instance), while others were only marginally affected by such problems, since they preferred to share crop or rent, and received additional income from urban real estate, industrial investments, positions in the civil service, or professions and so on. But such benefits hardly dealt with the problems of agricultural dislocation at this time which affected rent payments; and, in such circumstances, liberals found support for their position on the government's economic policies, making 'unholy' alliances with 'conservative' squires in Kursk and elsewhere, often touching on the specific animosities of a locality, such as anti-semitism. Liberal activists established their critique of official economic policy both in zemstvo assemblies and in the major forums to which proprietors belonged, whether such forums were local or transregional.

Meanwhile, absenteeism at zemstvo electoral assemblies was high and peasant participation uneven and erratic; hence liberals returned from the assemblies and spoke more for a large network of connections which gave them public standing[32] than for an undifferentiated provincial community or public. The circumstances of their presence in the zemstvo assemblies, and in provincial society, however, detracts from the significance of this distinction. 'Liberals' were associated with the formation of special commissions to improve the elementary education network, doctors' conferences, teachers' conferences, statistical analyses to add rigour to professional social work, schemes to improve professionals' conditions of work through provident funds and so on. Liberal commitment to major 'causes' such as the abolition of corporal punishment for the peasantry, universal education and commutation of dues in kind, were well known; and they were often powerful individuals who used invective and style picked up in acute observation of electoral and parliamentary technique in France, England, Germany and the United States.[33] Hence, they were nodal members of 'kruzhki' of professionals and peasants. And they were patrons of teachers who were the leading influence in peasant brotherhoods in Saratov and other provinces of the lower Volga.

The social distance between 'gentleman' representative and professional, taxpayer and zemstvo employee, vitiated relationships, but liberals had personal links with a variety of professionals with broad-ranging connections, such as the Nizhnii physician Mitskeevich, who had an extensive network of acquaintances among peasants and factory workers through the Social Democratic Party, for which he spread literature. They were consequently able to call upon the support of physicians and other professionals when they organized zemstvo campaigns against official policy.[34] Hence, in 1895, D. N. Zhbankov (of the Smolensk zemstvo medical statistical office) and Dr F. F. Erisman of Moscow (both well known to Petrunkevich and his circle) exhorted physicians to assist those zemstvo members who campaigned against the Hospital Statute of 1895. Zhbankov's letter to this effect was published in the influential *Physician*, while Erisman made his point at the Pirogov Society Conference in Moscow. Zhbankov argued the point that 'the new statute introduces difficulties for the successful development of zemstvo medicine ...' and tends 'to squeeze zemstvo medicine into narrow confines and hinder its further development'. Zhbankov expressed sympathy with the view of the Kostroma zemstvo that the statute was contrary to public interest, while Erisman asserted that 'it would be quite unfortunate to remove [public health] from the self-governments and to transfer it to the administration ...'.[35]

The liberal critique in the public domain

Prominent scholars and publicists expressed views hostile to official measures and supported liberals in the *zemstva*. The terms of the 1890 statute went against the spirit of Rudolph Gneist's injunctions for the development of healthy local self-government (injunctions which were given publicity in the liberal journals *Russkaia Mysl'* and *Vestnik Evropy*). And the provisions of the statute, consequently, earned the antagonism of those who were sympathetic to Gneist's precepts.[36] In a lecture in Paris at the Kovalevskii School, the noted economist A. I. Chuprov indicated his antagonism to official policy when he argued for decentralization and self-government to deal with the dissemination of know-how among small-scale proprietors, stressing that it could not be done from 'one centre' but required efforts from 'countless points' in the country. Here, Chuprov echoed the views of I. I. Ianzhul, I. Kh. Ozerov and other leading economists.

T. I. Osadchii and V. I. Gessen meanwhile voiced liberal prejudices in their writing on effective government. Osadchii argued that officials were incapable of providing any genuine solutions to social problems since they were exceptionally well provided for and hardly affected by industrial crises or famine and want. Naturally, 'an indifferent attitude to the fate of society' developed in such a parasitic class, which 'lived on the produce manufactured by other classes with whom it hardly has any contact'. Naturally, again, 'in the class of functionaries, the abilities of an individual to garner, to manufacture, and generally, to produce and create, atrophies significantly', and they 'lose their capacity to imagine with clarity a situation as it actually is'.[37]

Tver province, 1889–1905

The province and the *zemstva*

It was in Tver province, a centre of liberal activity, that many of these issues concerning self-government for the county and province were underscored in the course of a prolonged crisis in *zemstva* affairs from 1890 to 1905. The province and its counties were a well-known area of the Upper Volga region; and they were singled out for pilgrimage and for curiosity by virtue of their role in the conflicts of the fourteenth century (when Tver was a major principality) and for mention of the area in a number of old chronicles and 'lives' (such as the *Eulogy of the Pious and Great Prince Boris Alexandrovich*, the *Book of Generations*, and so on) which were published in various forms during the mid-century. Distinctive features of the province's landscape (the flora and fauna of the Lake Seliger region, for instance), aspects of the history of the area (such as details associated with the churches of Tver, and the former principality), attracted attention in the various exhibits in the provincial museum. In the metropolitan press, and in major geographical and statisitical accounts of the country, the region was distinguished from others by its history, its places of worship and its lore.[38] Finally as V. N. Lind was to point out in his memoirs, the county gentry were tightly knit, and followed cults of respect for various families;[39] a substantial interest in the landscape and wildlife of the area was not uncommon, though much of this was finally expressed in the form of contributions to 'national' journals.

The *zemstva* were known for the active participation of the eccentric Bakunin family of Novotorzhok and for the 'liberal' demands of its gentry representatives in 1860. In the local government bodies of this province, Petrunkevich, A. A. Bakunin, Rodichev and other liberals were prominent in provincial and district assemblies and councils. During the period 1889–1904, the county *zemstva* of Ostashkov, Kashin, Kaliazin and Vyshne-Volots were peaceful, while conflict between officials and liberals marked provincial and metropolitan discussions of government policy. Criticism, however, of public policy was aired, with severe repercussions, in the county assemblies of Tver, Novotorzhok, Ves'egonsk and Staritsa, and in the provincial zemstvo, which had a record in 1890 of regular confrontation with officials.

The contours of conflict

Until 1891, much of the tension that developed around incidents of conflict between *zemstva* and officials was kept in check by the pliant attitudes of N. D. Somov (governor of Tver until 1889) and the Ministers of Education during 1881–9. After the passage of the 'counter-reform' legislation of 1889 and 1890, relations between officials and *zemtsy* rapidly deteriorated, a direct consequence of the attitude among officials towards local self-government and their determination to contain 'liberalism' and the criticism of official institutions. In 1890, Minister of Internal Affairs I. N. Durnovo nominated the Moscow conservative, P. D. Akhlestyshev, governor of the province, in order to establish control over liberal influence in local institutions; in this, he was guided by the significance of the appointments that had to be made to positions of land captain under the 1889 statute, and reports of N. D. Somov's lackadaisical attitudes towards liberal influence in the *zemstva*. The measures Akhlestyshev adopted, with firm support from St Petersburg, and the governor's excessive zeal in the implementation of such measures, was the major source of conflict between *zemstva* and official bodies. In January 1891, in the provincial zemstvo, after the election of Rodichev and B. B. Kostylev as council president and council member respectively, Akhlestyshev refused to confirm these 'liberals' and nominated B. V. Shturmer to chair the Council. In December 1894, after S. D. Kvashin-Samarin, A. A. Dem'ianov and Kostylev were elected to the provincial council, he intervened again and nominated A. S. Paskin, F. N. von Ott and P. M. Kariakin. The governor thereby undermined liberal control over provincial zemstvo departments and services. His nominees for positions on the provincial council were conservatives who had an alternative programme for local government work. And Akhlestyshev himself attempted to regulate the work of schools and other zemstvo institutions. Akhlestychev's successor, Prince N. D. Golitsyn, followed the same course. In January 1898, he refused to confirm elected 'liberal' council members A. P. Apostol and L. A. Miasnikov. And in January 1899, Prince Golitsyn extended the area of conflict with the provincial and the county *zemstva* when, backed by St Petersburg officials, he stopped increases in rates in 1899 and 1900, arguing that these exceeded the paying capacity of the local population.

Liberal representatives in the provincial assembly comprised a formidable group: I. I. Petrunkevich, M. I. Petrunkevich, F. Rodichev, P. Korsakov, A. B. Vrasskii, A. Apostol, N. Lodyzhenskii, A. A. Dem'ianov, B. B. Kostylev, S. D. Kvashin-Samarin, A. S. Medvedev and D. Romanov. They considered that Akhlestyshev's (and later Golitsyn's) measures were the 'arbitrary' assertion by governors of their own preferences above those of the zemstvo assembly – an echo of initiatives elsewhere at the time. A number of zemstvo initiatives were clearly at stake, initiatives which had taken shape under a dispensation of elected local self-government. Such initiatives included the work of various bodies under the provincial zemstvo: the Burashev Colony for the Mentally Insane (the first major such zemstvo institution in the country, whose statute had been drafted by A. B. Vrasskii and which had been directed from its inception by the 'liberal' P. M. Litvinov); the P. P. Maksimovich Teachers' Training Academy (which had been formed with the assistance of P. A. Korsakov and A. A. Bakunin and which was intended to provide local schools with teaching personnel); the Provincial Hospital (whose facilities had been developed by M. I. Petrunkevich to ensure the locality had sophisticated services and equipment); and the zemstvo Insurance Department, which ran the insurance schemes developed by P. A. Korsakov and V. N. Lind (the compulsory and voluntary fire insurance schemes, and the new scheme for insurance of movable property).[40] The state of affairs in the provincial zemstvo council affected appointments and funds in all such bodies. It also affected the allocation of grants for school projects and public health schemes to *zemstva* in Novotorzhok, Tver, Rzhev and Ves'egonsk, where liberals were powerful, and where the scope of such projects was large.

Of county zemstvo services, schools attracted the attention of peasant proprietors. Returns from agriculture in most counties (especially Vyshne-Volots and Ostashkov) were poor. Yields were low; and such a situation, at a time of falling prices for agricultural products, compelled peasants to look for work away from the commune. Between 1880 and 1891, 40 per cent of commune allotments were surrendered in the province. In conditions where most districts were within easy reach by river and by rail of the main industrial centres of the province (Kimry, Vyshne-Volots and Tver) or St Petersburg and Moscow, the local population supplied the workforce of local industrial centres and the metropolises (as is clear from the large number of passports issued by peasant bodies at this time). But a smattering of literacy was required for such travel, and zemstvo schools were consequently of importance, as were those who ran them.

Liberal members of county and provincial zemstvo assemblies were local gentry who were aware of much of this. Although many such squires had sold off sections of their estates, a number continued to cultivate (in over 50 per cent of cases[41]), and rented out land extensively, the majority of *zemtsy* living on their estates. Such liberal squires knew of local demands and requirements. Liberal *zemtsy* were concerned personally with the fate of professionals in zemstvo bodies, many of whom they had recruited. P. A. Korsakov's position was not untypical. After an extensive connection with the zemstvo insurance system and with the P. P. Maksimovich Teachers' Training Academy, his influence was of great imporance in these institutions. When insurance agents met, they sent a telegram of greeting to Korsakov, and at the Maksimovich Academy, the appointment of a new Head to the Academy took place with Korsakov's close participation. He still hosted social gatherings for the zemstvo 'third element' in his country home in Ves'egonsk.

Liberalism and its supporters in Tver province[42]

A number of ideological and personal differences divided Tver liberals. Some were professionals, some were country squires; individually, in social and educational background, they had as much in common with 'conservatives' and officials as among themselves. Liberals disagreed on fundamental issues. The Bakunin brothers were sharply at odds on philosophical matters. Pavel and Alexander were strongly opposed to positivism and the ideas of Sechenov, while Alexei was disinclined to fall in with their idealism. V. N. Lind thought of himself a democrat and regarded the Bakunin claim to a similar title with scepticism. Commitment to 'liberal' politics also varied. As I. I. Petrunkevich, the activist from Chernigov, noted, among Tver *zemtsy*, A. P. Apostol 'was a little inclined to opportunism', Evgenii de Roberti was a 'pseudo-liberal', and A. B. Vrasskii was so preoccupied with practical matters that he gave little attention to issues of principle. Liberals worked closely with S. D. Kvashin-Samarin, who, according to I. I. Petrunkevich, although he 'became accustomed to us, his ideological opponents ...', reacted to the ideas of the Pazukhins and Khvostovs 'as if to law, and on no occasion disputed them ...' I. I. Petrunkevich himself contrasted sharply with such *zemtsy*; a 'social activist', he had been exiled in 1879 from Chernigov for his zemstvo activities. This ban lasted from 1879 to 1886; and from that time until 1905, he was forbidden to return to his place of birth or to reside in the Ukraine.

Liberals, however, always peppered their language with similar phrases: 'the extirpation of estate and national inequality', the necessity for 'broad ranging self-government from the highest to the lowest levels of administration', 'the destruction of autocracy and of the bureaucratic system of government;' and they had common cause on a number of occasions in zemstvo work, attracting the ire of officials.[43] They spoke of the same books: Mill on representation, Sumner on US government, and a variety of texts on the factory question, women's emancipation and the shortcomings of official economic policy;[44] and they now approached official policy from a common perspective. Here, a formidable social cement held them together. For V. N. Lind and M. I. Petrunkevich, the atmosphere of the Bakunin house at Priamukhino in Novotorzhok was an important memory which linked them to the family (as did their marriages), even if they differed with the Bakunin brothers on ideological issues. Lind remembered the Bakunin women with great feeling, as well as the small mansion above the Osuga, with its large forest and trysting places, where Barbara Bakunin had held her country parties, where Stankevich, Belinskii and Pushkin had stayed, where the Bakunin brothers held open house for local squires (Lvovs, Poltoratskiis, Diakovs and so on), and from where visitors went on to spend time at the neighbouring estates of Zaitsevo and Luganovo. The latter, Lind later reminisced, was 'a paradise', where in 'the gardens and the park adjacent to them (both covering an area of a hundred dessiatines) ... one could live in the lap of nature ... walk, bathe, read, play the piano and feel oneself completely free and uninhibited'. In Ves'egonsk, Korsakov's country house and Rodichev's estate held a similar place in the memories of young *zemtsy* and local government professionals.

It was through common ties of education and social interaction, meanwhile, whose character is easily established from a quick glance at the families of I. I. and M. I. Petrunkevich or S. V. and E. V. de Roberti,[45] that liberals were able to appeal to a broader spectrum of gentry within the *zemstva* as much as through similar ideological preferences. Here, in the provincial assembly, forty-seven of seventy-three assembly members in 1897–1900 were county nobles who owned between 200 and 250 dessiatin and more (twenty-seven over 500 dessiatin), with few liberal credentials to their name; and, setting aside peasant representation, the situation was true of county assembly members, especially in Vyshne-Volots, Kaliazin, Zubtsov, Staritsa, Rzhev and Ostashkov counties.[46] Few here were integrated into the Ves'egonsk and Torzhok county coteries, but the majority, like a number of liberal leaders, led the lives of retired squires, with limited property, who were educated in elite establishments and had a number of connections within the civil service and elsewhere. There is the odd instance of the 'great' man: Prince Pavel Arsenevich Putiatin, husband of Olga Chabelskaia (formerly a Lady of Honour at Court), with a brother at Court, uncles in the army and navy (in senior rank) and a son at the Corps of Pages – very much a grand squire with interests in archaeology, genealogy and good food, with good personal connections at court. Of the rest, many were of good name: Saltykovs, Potemkins, Svistunovs, Tolstois, Kuzmin-Karavaevs, Nevedomskiis, Trubnikovs, Ushakovs, Obolenskiis, Zakreevskiis, Meshcherskiis, Ladyzhenskiis and so on; and, on occasion, they had a full range of celebrities related to them somewhere in the past.[47] But the squires concerned were themselves rarely distinguished, and there were many in the assemblies, like the liberals here, who had no associations whatever with the very eminent, even if they had connections with the 'elite' education, civil and military institutions of the time, that is the Imperial School of Law, the Corps of Pages, the Alexander Lycée and so on, as well as the Guards regiments.[48] Professionals, career civil servants and military men, among zemstvo assembly members, were limited to a few, like the odd S. B. Meshcherskii (an officer in the army).[49] The common 'type' was M. L. Ushakov, a landowner who had done little with his life, following in the footsteps of an unpretentious and unambitious father, with reasonable connections.[50]

Liberals against official policy in the locality

It was therefore with great personal commitment, and also with substantial social backing among the county gentry, that 'liberals' took up cudgels with official policy in Tver, even as I. I. Petrunkevich and F. I. Rodichev actively participated in the campaigns against counter-reform in Moscow and St Petersburg. Liberal *zemtsy* vigorously defended 'self-government' in the locality in their actions and measures; and they quickly abandoned compromise, once their moves in this direction proved pointless after the resignation of the nominated president of 1891–4, B. V. Shturmer. With the total breakdown of compromise politics during 1894–7, A. A. Bakunin and I. I. Petrunkevich pressed assembly members, in 1899, to boycott council activities and to reject the nominated council's request for extension of local government commitments to education. The matter came to centre on the appointment of additional personnel for the Pedagogic Bureau which had, since 1893, collected statistics on schools and pupils, and which required more staff to undertake a universal literacy programme.

Bakunin and Petrunkevich were adamant that the state of the council made grants impossible. They contended that the *uprava* lacked the 'confidence' of the assembly, hence no new initiatives could be entrusted to it. According to A. A. Bakunin, 'private' or 'institutional' concerns, such as how statistics for future planning of education might be gathered, were not the only concern of the assembly. Equally important in local self-government was 'social benefit' and 'social meaning', and these were based on 'spiritual principles' or 'moral principles', which were to be found in 'attempts to unite society, to give a general direction, to give its activity genuine meaning'. According to A. A. Bakunin, the process of election and the practice of representative government was the best means of achieving this end: the element of choice given to citizens and representatives was crucial to the establishment of public involvement and public confidence in institutions, and this was in turn also the best index of social requirements and preferences. When bodies such as the *zemstva* ceased to follow such principles, they were incapable of achieving the ends set for them.[51]

Such a position came to be further defined during disputes over zemsvo rates in 1899–1900. Here, conflict stemmed from the assembly's outright rejection of the governor's demand that increases in county zemstvo rates should not be permitted, and that zemstvo expenditure should be frozen. The assembly's editorial commission found no legal or material basis for the demand and the assembly voted to ignore the governor's suggestion. Rather, the provincial zemstvo increased its budget outlay. P. D. Akhlestyshev had raised such issues earlier in 1894, with B. V. Shturmer, demanding that zemstvo finances be put in order and objecting to debit financing, the incessant resort to loans for provincial zemstvo outlays, and to increases in rates. Shturmer, in keeping with his agreement with liberal representatives in the assembly, had played for time; and he resorted to outright subterfuge when he supplied incorrect information concerning zemstvo finances to the governor's office. These manoeuvres, together with guarantees supplied by 'influential deputies' had taken the zemstvo through the crisis at the time, but the issues raised remained on record and attracted Golitsyn's attention in 1898, when he appealed to the provincial assembly to take steps to deal with the situation, as it was empowered to do. Finding that the assembly refused to take any measures to reduce rates, Golitsyn turned to the Minister of Internal Affairs and received permission to halt rate increases and zemstvo expenditure.

Conflict over rates occurred again in the following year (1900). Ignoring what had taken place, county *zemstva*, with the exception of the Vyshne-Volots zemstvo, increased taxes and expenditure for 1900. Prince Golitsyn took up the matter again with the provincial zemstvo which, though it accepted a few points in the governor's note, refused to accept his reading of the situation. He therefore took the matter up with the Provincial Board and placed a halt on rate increases. In response, the assembly's Commission argued that zemstvo services:

> have as their aim better organization of the popular schools, of medical assistance, of social relief, agricultural enterprises, of satisfying the requirements of the provincial administration itself or of placing capital in funds with special purposes and thus closed to loans. Not one of the ... credits can be considered as blatantly disrupting the interests of the population, since no one other than the very same population benefit from people's schools, hospitals and the care of orphans and castaways.[52]

The Commission took issue with the governor's view that the *zemstva* were private organizations and that the central administration belonged to a different institutional order. They consequently disputed the implication of the governor's arguments that since the material condition of the population was difficult and the state's needs were supreme, the *zemstva* should decrease its fiscal demands on the population in order that St Petersburg's requirements could be met:

> If the private interests of some Peter or Ivan are satisfied by the medical assistance given to them, by instruction at school, by the distribution of good seed for sowing, or they are compensated for buildings which have been burnt, then issues affecting a number of Peters and Ivans, issues of public health, education, insurance and so on are not private but important state interests, without whose correct organization changes in the conditions of the economic life of the population, of whose far from idyllic nature the Governor speaks are unimaginable. ...

Local government politics

In asserting their position, 'liberals' had to contend with a powerful official initiative to establish a new dispensation in the province around the 'counter-reforms'. In district zemstvo assemblies, Akhlestyshev and Golitsyn relied on the support of representatives of the peasant 'estate' for assistance in containing the influence of liberals. Many such peasant *glasnye* were officials in peasant self-administration bodies, nominated to their positions by the administration and appointed to the district assemblies by the governor. Both Akhlestyshev and Golitsyn also called upon members of *gorodskie dumy* for help, since these *kuptsy* (businessmen in the estates hierarchy) were rarely connected with the district and provincial *zemstva* or with liberal *zemtsy*.

Officials mobilized 'conservatives' who were sympathetic to their prejudices and were council members in Bezhets (B. V. Shturmer, A. S. Paskin, A. N. Tatishchev, L. A. Ushakov). Those who supported the governor's measures were to be found in a number of counties: in Vyshne-Volots county, S. A. Putiatin, O. P. Medvedev, P. N. Malygin, A. A. Shirinskii-Shikhmatov were pre-eminent, with the assistance of a tightly knit group of gentry (Volkovs, Konshins, Kharlamovs and Medvedevs). In Kaliazin, S. I. Golikov controlled the council with the Vonsiatskii brothers. In the county councils of Kashin,[53] Ostashkov[54] and Korchev[55] 'conservative' squires held important positions. Liberal *zemtsy*, V. D. Kuz'min-Karavaev and A. A. Dem'ianov (in Bezhets), A. P. Apostol and V. I. Pokrovskii (in Ostashkov) and B. D. von Derwiz, A. A. Golovachev and P. A. Korsakov (in Korchev) attempted to gain a foothold in local government affairs in these counties – though with little success. 'Conservative' squires held all the main positions of land captain, e.g., Marshal of the Nobility, Head of the Reserve, and so on.

In the circumstances, 'liberals' resorted to vicious invective, poison letters, commission manoeuvres and assembly intrigue to hold their own; and their tactics hardly reflected well on the principles of 'self-government' that they defended. Assembly sessions of 1896, 1899 and 1900 were replete with pandemonium, walk-outs and appeals to the governor. The uproar of these occasions is evident in A. S. Paskin's intervention in December 1895 in the provincial assembly, when he expressed his outrage at the statements made by I. I. Petrunkevich in 'such language that the assembly had never heard before and at which he would either have to remain silent or to leave the assembly'.[56] Such invective combined with resignations from service of doctors, teachers, statisticians and insurance workers in 1896 and 1899[57] to render zemstvo affairs so strained that officials resorted to negotiations time and time again with 'liberal' leaders; 'liberal' use of the press and the reluctance of 'conservatives' to hold zemstvo positions in such turbulent circumstances was noted in gubernatorial reports. Invective and manoeuvre were clearly a part of the political practices of local self-government; and they were used with effect in its defence in Tver province.

Conclusion

This course of events in the Tver zemstvo at the time of the counter-reform reflects much that has been said concerning the character of 'claims' for local government at the time of the counter-reforms more generally. Despite close links between landlords and other provincial inhabitants, as a consequence of prolonged residence in the area, the 'claims' were the product of liberal activists in the zemstvo assembly, and did not indicate any intentions of speaking for a broader provincial population. Officials, in fact, successfully countered liberal influence in the *zemstva* by calling upon the assistance of various groups in local society who were not directly affiliated to liberal circles. Again, the terms of the liberal 'claims' did not refer to the attributes of the province, or the province's sense of uniqueness: they stressed the importance of the work of local government and the worth of the conventions of *zemstva*. Certainly, these terms stressed far from purely institutional interests; rather, the claims centred on the character of provincial problems and the government that was best for the province. But liberals did not speak of the rights of the province at a time when the connotations of the designation *tverianin*, like that of *moskvich* and so on, remained strictly apolitical; and the implications of local history that could be traced to Novgorod or the Grand Princes of Vladimir and Suzdal remained marginal to the claims that liberals advanced.

It is worth pointing out, however, that while the relation between identity and 'claims' was fragile, the significance of a regional identity, so clear in the historical self-awareness of the time, acted as the background to the formulation of claims; and the link betwen 'claim' and locality was reinforced by the existence of various forms of regional sociability, where the link between liberals was one. In Tver, the importance of social background in holding liberals together and winning them support within the local squirearchy is self-evident. The literature and folklore of this period, meanwhile, and the terms of government reports, undoubtedly drew attention to the history and characterstics of a region. Although it did not draw political conclusions from such descriptions, the literature enjoyed a substantial readership, and the sources of folklore were broad-ranging. Hence, while in a comparison of 'claims' in provincial Russia and those voiced in Siberia or the Ukraine, the importance of 'identity' in the former can be easily discounted, the link cannot wholly be ignored. In fact, perhaps, the political 'claims' of regions today can be connected to this subtle link which has survived centralization and social change thereafter. There are certainly some grounds, however frail, for the suspicion that political regionalism has a longer lineage in Russia than is suggested in the standard histories of the province in recent times.

Notes

1. A. Touraine, *Return of the Actor: Social Theory in Post-Industrial Society* (Minnesota, 1988) p. 81.
2. 'Construction' of regional and national identity has been best dealt with in E. Hobsbawm and T. Ranger (eds), *The Invention of Tradition* (Cambridge, 1983), and Benedict Anderson, *Imagined Communities* (London, 1983); more standard approaches to identity are discussed in E. Hobsbawm, *Nations and Nationalism since 1780* (Cambridge, 1990). By politics, here, the sense intended is the more comprehensive image provided in R. Rémond, *Pour une nouvelle historie politique* (Paris, 1988).

3. Political rhetoric in the Russian Federation during the last decade has repeatedly stressed the importance of the 'subjects' of the Federation, i.e., not only constituent republics and autonomous regions, but 'regions' (*oblast*'s), themselves. 'Claims' here refer to zemstvo experience, which, for instance, was a focus of attention during the discussion of a 1992 conference on decentralization and self-government (which envisaged a permanent workshop on the subject in the Mari Republic). The significance of a region-focus, from other points of view, are to be found in essays by V. Kaganskii, '*Sovetskoe prostranstvo: konstrukstiia i destruktsiia*', and A. Filippov, '*Smysl imperii: K sotsiologii politicheskogo prostranstva*', in S. B. Chemyshev (ed.), *Inoe. Khrestomatiia novogo rossiikogosamosoznaniia* (Moscow, 1995).

4. V. V. Leontiev, *Istoriia liberalizma v Rossii, 1762–1914* (Paris, 1980); B. B. Veselovskii, *Istoriia zemstva za sorok let* (St Petersburg, 1909–11); N. M. Pirumova, *Zemsko-liberali'noe dvizhenie* (Moscow, 1977).

5. The limited and scholarly appeal and use of such literature, at the time of its publication, is discussed in Vladimir Kuskov, *A History of Old Russian Literature* (Moscow, 1980). Statistical enquiries and their character in the mid-nineteenth century, are discussed in N. A. Svavitskii, *Zemskie podvornye perepisi* (Moscow, 1961). An impression of folklore is to be found in M. G. Rabinovich, 'Otvety na programmu Russkogo geograficheskogo obshchestva kak istochnik dlia izucheniia ethnografii goroda', in *Ocherki istorii russkoi ethnografii, fol'kloristiki, i antropologii*, vol. 5 (Moscow, 1971). Notes of traditions of folklore were made in statistical collections of the 1860s (such as *Materialy po geografii i statistike Riazanskoi gubernii*, Riazan, 1860), and they figure in booklets in private collections, such as that of I. V. Vereshchagin, see M. M. Gromyko, *Mir russkoi derevni* (Moscow, 1992).

6. A number of these came to be published from the eighteenth century, starting with the extensive *Biblioteka* series put out by Nikolai Novikov (1773–4 and 1788–91), and Kuskov, *A History*, p. 37ff.

7. The *Pskovskoe vziatie* (1510), is a case in point, see Kuskov, *A History*, p. 205ff.

8. A good example is the *Stepennaia Kniga* which deals with Tver of the same period, see Kuskov, *A History*, p. 208ff.

9. This includes moral tales such as *The Tale of Peter and Fevronia*, which deals with Murom and Riazan in the thirteenth century (see Kuskov, *A History*, p. 210ff.).

10. These touched on the defences and campaigns against the Turks, as for instance, in the case of *The Tale of the Defence of Azov by the Don Cossacks* (see Kuskov, *A History*, p. 281).

11. For the large number of such institutions, see the relevant articles, e.g. 'Muzei' in *Entsiklopedicheskii Slovar'* (St Petersburg, 1890–1904).

12. For the character of *lubochnaia* literature, see J. Brooks, *When Russia Learned to Read* (Princeton, NJ, 1985).

13. See Rabinovitch, 'Otvety na programmu Russkogo'; S. F. Starr, *Decentralization and Self-Government in Tsarist Russia* (Princeton, NJ, 1972); A. S. Madzharov, *Afanasii Shchapov* (Irkutsk, 1992).

14. For the structure of pre-1864 institutions, see I. P. Eroshkin, *Istoriia gosudarstvennykh uchrezhdenii dorevoliutsionnoi Rossii* (Moscow, 1968), and Starr,

Decentralization; P. N. Zyrianov, 'Sotsial'naia struktura mestnogo upravleniia kapitalisticheskoi Rossii, 1861–1914', in *Istoricheskie Zapiski*, 1982.

15. The best references for local government are Veselovskii, *Istoriia*; T. Emmonns and W. Vucinich, *The Zemstvo: An Experiment in Local Self Government* (Cambridge, 1981); and V. A. Narodova, *Gorodskoe samoupravlenie v Rossii* (Moscow, 1984).

16. This (in the case of the law of 1894) was through the formation of provincial statistical committees; and, in 1900, officials restricted increases in local government budgets to 3 per cent over that of the previous year; see Veselovskii, *Istoriia*, vol. 1: 'Zemskie finansy'.

17. Elementary schools were transferred to the jurisdiction of the Church in 1892. In 1894 and 1896 the influence of the elected local authorities in school councils was reduced (Veselovskii, *Istoriia*, vol. 1: 'Narodnoe obrazovanie').

18. Veselovskii, *Istoriia*, vol. 2; *Vestnik Evropy* (October, 1894); N. Frieden, *Russian Physicians in an Era of Reform and Revolution* (Princeton, NJ, 1982).

19. *Russkaia Mysl'*, no. 6 (1891). Peasants were also permitted to use special funds for agricultural improvements independent of the *zemstva* (6 May 1896), following processing of their applications by local officials, *Russkaia Mysl'*, no. 6 (1891).

20. 'Vnutrennoe Obozrenie', *Vestnik Evropy* (August/September, 1893).

21. See N. M. Korkunov, *Iuridicheskii Letopis'*, no. 12; *Moskovskie Vedomosti*, no. 356 (1891); *Vestnik Evropy* (February, 1891) pp. 855–62 and (January, 1892) pp. 381–7.

22. *Ob"iasneniia Ministerstv Vnutrennykh Del i Finansov po povodu zamechanii Ministra Zemledeliia i Gosudarsvennykh Imushchestv i Gosudarstvennogo Kontrolera na zakonoproekta ob ustanovlenii predel'nosti zemskogo oblozheniia i osvobozhdeniia zemskikh uchrezhdenii ot nekotorykh raskhodov* (St Petersburg, 1899).

23. For official alarm over zemstvo finances, see House of Commons, *Bills and Reports* (1894) p. 24.

24. F. I. Rodichev Papers, Bakhmateff Archive, Columbia University.

25. For further complaints of the treatment of *zemstva* see reports of the Moscow, Chernigov, Khar'kov, Orel and Poltava committees, in *Vysochaishe uchrezhdennoe Osoboe Soveshchane o nuzhdakh sel'skhoziaistvennoi promyshlennosti. Svod trudov mestnykh komittetov. Zemstvo* (St Petersburg, 1904).

26. They also pointed out that this independence itself was 'being eroded little by little, by later legislation'; and they inveighed against the cumbersome machinery that was involved in official projects, and the consequent obfuscation of public initiative (as in the case of the Grot Commission's recommendations). They replied to official criticism of zemstvo work, arguing that it was only because government failed to supply *zemstva* with proper infrastructure that their performance in the past had been slipshod; see *Vestnik Evropy* (1895).

27. The commentator dismissed the defence counsel's demand for leniency and his statement that a recently constituted system based on *popechitel'stvo* or 'trusteeship' (rather than the artificiality of legal rights) was in its formative stage and required protection. The journal's commentator countered that 'trusteeship' of this sort did not reduce administrative confusion. It was

'trusteeship' when one 'estate' had been given powers over another, where, consequently, the trust between classes which underlay genuine 'trusteeship' (only to be achieved by equal representation of all classes in the political process) was wholly lacking. What was at issue in the Protopopov case, it was argued, was merely the arrogance of power, to which the new institutionalization gave free rein, *Russkaia Mysl'*, no. 4 (1893); 'Vnutrennoe Obozrenie', in *Vestnik Evropy* (December 1892).

28. The various associations that existed in provincial life have yet to be charted. The range of societies is clear from the variety of *obshchestva* mentioned in the *Entsiklopedicheskii Slovar'* (Brokgauz and Efron); but this is far from comprehensive and does not include zemstvo societies such as fire-fighting societies, which are mentioned in Veselovskii, *Istoriia*. Agricultural societies are dealt with in A. F. Devrien, *Polnaia entsiklopediia russkogo sel'skogo khoziaistva i soprikasiushchikhsia s nim nauk*, vol. 6 (St Petersburg, 1905) p. 47. A. M. Anfimov mentions the significance of these bodies in *Krupnoe pomeshchich'e khoziaistvo* (Moscow, 1967).

29. This would clearly apply to the likes of *zemtsy* such as the Orel Marshal of the Nobility, Sheremet'ev, who obtained a railway concession for the zemstvo and was responsible for placing it in the hands of the railway constructor, P. I. Gubonin, with substantial profit to himself. It would also apply to the dreamers and profiteers of the Saratov gentry who had almost ruined the local government bodies of the province through the construction of the Saratov–Khar'kov railway, and who were importunate concerning the construction of a rail-link between Saratov and Delhi – see B. N. Chicherin, *Vospominaniia, Zemstvo i Moskovskaia Duma* (Moscow, 1934) p. 46, and Veselovskii, *Istoriia*, vol. 4, 'Saratov'.

30. V. S. Diakin, 'Den'gi dlia sel'skogo khoziaistva', *Istoriia SSSR*, no. 3 (1991) p. 73ff.

31. P. I. Liashchenko, 'Khlebnaia torgovlia', in A. F. Devrien's *Polnaia entsiklopedia*, vol. 9, and his *Russkoe zernovoe khoziaistvo v sisteme mirovogo khoziaistva* (Moscow, 1927).

32. For the suspicion with which *zemstva* were viewed among the peasantry, see A. Smirnov, 'Krestiane i zemstvo', in *Ekonomicheskaia Gazeta* (1 May 1905). The class bias of the *zemstva* is clear in *Svod svedenii o lichnom sostave zemskikh uchrezhdenii po dannym na 1900–1903*; see also Pirumova, *Zemsko-liberali'noe dvizhenie*, p. 76, and B. B. Veselovskii, *K voprosu o klassovykh interesakh v zemstve* (St Petersburg, 1915).

33. Liberal journals and newspapers were replete with observations on the electoral process elsewhere. During travel, liberal activists took an avid interest in the process; see, for instance, Gosudarstvennyi Arkhiv Rossiiskoi Federatsii (GARF), *fond* 5102 (A. A. Kornilov), *delo* 147, *zapisnaia kniga* for 1889, for the author's detailed observations on the French elections.

34. Pirumova, *Zemsko-liberal'noe dvizhenie*, and *Zemskaia intelligentsiia* (Moscow, 1986).

35. Frieden, *Russian Physicians*, pp. 167–76.

36. Gneist was hostile to 'the control of local matters by bodies elected to represent local interests', which he associated with the consequences of broad franchise and party tyranny; and he stressed that proper self-government involved 'the organization of the whole community for the service of the

state, so arranged that the classes most capable by their wealth and position for government bore the burdens and administered the affairs of their neighbourhood'. Gneist's own interpretation of this was spelt out in the Prussian laws of 1873–83, and publicized in his writing of 1886, where he defined 'classes most capable' according to rates paid rather than legal status. The Prussian laws also gave broad powers over police to elected representatives. Gneist argued, in his general consideration of self-government, that without 'confidence' from higher authorities, the healthy development of self-government was impossible, and a harmonious state structure unattainable (see A. Lawrence Lowell, *Governments and Parties in Continental Europe* (London, 1904), and 'Les Réformes Administratives en Prusse', in *Revue Generale du Droit et des Sciences Politiques*, 1 October 1886).

37. *Nuzhdy derevni* (1904) p. 287ff.
38. S. I. Nosovich's travelogues in *Istoricheskoe Obozrenie*, no. 10 (1899), and no. 11 (1901); N. M. Oglobin, 'Na verkhnei Volgi', in *Istoricheskii Vestnik* (1900) pp. 81–7; L. F. Tiumenev, 'Na srednem plese', ibid., 95 (January 1904) pp. 209–57, (March 1904) pp. 679–720; 'B verkhov'iakh Volgi', ibid., 56 (April 1894) pp. 128–60; ibid., 56 (May 1894) pp. 435–61; ibid., 56 (June 1894) pp. 679–707; and *Niva*, no. 25 (1895); and later N. N. Reikhel't, 'Poezdka v Kashin', in *Istoricheskii Vestnik* (1909) pp. 117–18; S. S. Okreits, 'Iz skitani po belu svetu', ibid. (1910) pp. 121–7. See also V. P. Semenov (ed.), *Rossiia: Pol'noe geograficheskoe opisanie nashego otechestva* (St Petersburg, 1899–1913) which includes many folklore details of the localities of the Upper Volga and of Tver.
39. V. N. Lind, 'Pervye shagi Tverskogo zemstva', in *Zemskoe Delo*, nos 2–4 (1910) and 'Vospominaniia o moiei zhizni', in *Russkaia Mysl'*, nos 7–8 (1911) and nos 6–7 (1916).
40. All information regarding zemstvo bodies is from B. B. Veselovskii, *Istoricheskii ocherk deiatel'nosti zemskikh uchrezhdenii Tverskoi gubernii* (Tver, 1914).
41. *Gosudarstvenni Istoricheskii Arkhiv* (GIA), *fond* 1287, *opis'* 27, *delo* 402.
42. Unless otherwise mentioned, these impressions of Tver liberalism have been pieced together from V. N. Lind's memoirs in *Russkaia Mysl'*, I. I. Petrunkevich, 'Iz zapisok obshchestvennogo deiatel'ia', in *Arkhiv Russkoi Revoliustsii* (22), and the family information in N. Ikonnikov, *Noblesse de la Russie*, 2nd edn (Paris, 1958–66).
43. The Tver address of 1894 was the best known of these occasions at the time. I. P. Belokonskii, 'Zemskoe Dvizhenie', in *Byloe* (1907); B. B. Veselovskii, 'Tver', in *Istoriia*, vol. 4.
44. GIA, *fond* 1284, *opis'* 223, *delo* 23 B, mentioned in the Governor's Report for 1896.
45. The father of I. I. and M. I. Petrunkevich had been Vice-Governor and Acting Governor of Chernigov province; both brothers had been to the exclusive Kiev Cadet Corps and later St Petersburg University. Sergei Valentinovich and Evgenii Valentinovich de Roberti belonged to a recently ennobled family, where the father, Valentin Karlovich, had received noble status for his services in the army. Evgenii Valentinovich was a distinguished academic in St Petersburg and owned a sizeable estate in Tver, having been educated at the Imperial Alexander Lycée. Of his brothers, Petr

Valentinovich graduated from the Imperial School of Law and became a JP in Warsaw, Alexander Valentinovich embarked upon a military career, Sergei, Nikolai and Valentin all spent periods in the army. Of the sisters, Ekaterina married Reonskii, who eventually attained high position in the bureaucracy (rank 2); Elizaveta married a fairly successful military man; and Elena married Miller, who later became the Head of the Warsaw Municipal Administration. See Ikonnikov, *Noblesse de la Russiie*, entries under 'de Roberti', 'Petrunkevich', 'Korsakov'.

46. The provincial assembly members reflect the situation in the counties. Hence, 3–5 Kashin members owned 200–250 dessiatin; 3–7 Korchev members, 3–6 Tver members, 4–5 Ostashkov members, all 6 Vyshne-Volots members, 3–7 Ve'segonsk members, 4–6 Rzhev members, 4–5 Zubstov members, 4–6 Staritsa members, 5–6 Kaliazin members. The exception was in Bezhets (2–9) and Torzhok (1–5), *Tverskie Gubernskie Vedomosti* (April, 1897).

47. M. E. Saltykov, the famous Vice-Governor of Riazan and Tver, for instance, was the uncle of E. D. Saltykov, assembly member. E. D. Saltykov's aunt, Nadezhda, had been educated at the Catherine Institute, while his uncles Sergei and Ilia had been at the Imperial Naval School and with the Chevalier Guards respectively. His own brother was Director of Indirect Taxation in Vitebsk in 1900. V. I. Zakreevskii (Staritsa) retired from the civil service after attaining tenth rank, but his uncle had been Count Arsenii Andreevich Zakreevskii, who had risen from the elite Probrazhenskii regiment to become Governor-General of Finland, Minister of Internal Affairs (1823–31), Governor-General of Moscow and a member of the State Council. Konstantin Nevedomskii was a local nobleman, but his sister Anna was married to M. I. Khil'kov, Minister of Communications, and his other sisters, Olga and Alexandra, were married to other members of the Khil'kov family.

48. The cases of V. P. Svistunov, V. A. and N. A. Tolstoi and A. N. Trubnikov, is indicative of the straightforward squire, as is the case of L. A. Ushakov (below). Vladimir Pavlovich Svistunov was the son of a local landowner who had served briefly and none too significantly in the army (reaching the post of sub-lieutenant). Vladimir and his brothers Mikhail and Ivan were landowners (the brothers having served for a little time in the army). The sisters of the family married noblemen, but nothing is known of them, as is the case of other members. The father of Vladimir and Nikolai Tolstoi, Alexei Andreevich, was a lower civil servant. Their uncle, Vladimir Andreevich, was a Guards officer (1835, General-Major). The father of Nikanor Arsenevich Trubnikov was a provincial landowner and a respectably placed army officer. Nikanor Arsenevich's uncle, Nikolai, was a middle-ranking officer in the army and later held a similar position in the civil service; he married Daria, the daughter of Artillery General Vassilii Dimitrevich Korsakov, who had a sizeable estate in Bezhets county. Another uncle, Ivan, was also a middle-ranking army officer and Nikanor Arsenevich only served in the bureaucracy in a minor position (rank 14); the sisters appear to have made undistinguished matches and other family members were obscure. See Ikonnikov, *Noblesse de la Russie*, entries under 'Svistounov', 'Troubnikov', 'Tolstoi'.

49. A military man, with brothers in the civil service (Alexander, a professional engineer, Boris, a graduate of the Imperial School of Law) and sisters who had been Maids of Honour at Court and married to persons in the Judicial and Civil Service.

50. Ushakov's connections were comparable to other well-established gentry. His uncle Valerian was in the civil service and married Princess Maria, the daughter of Prince Alexander Putiatin. Another uncle, Nikolai, had served briefly as an army officer. His sister, Varvara, married Alexander Kluppgel, who had been at the Corps of Pages and who was an officer in the Guards.

51. '... only moral principles – spiritual principles – serve society [as a whole]. They are to be found in attempts to unite society, to give society a genuine direction, to give its activity genuine strength and meaning ... take away, gentlemen, this moral side [to social activity] and all social activity crumbles. We are left with only private interests. There is no reason for us to meet to deal with such private interests, since this kind of assembly in the absence of genuine social benefit, social meaning, would be merely a superfluous, empty expense (*Stenographicheskie otchety gubernskogo zemskogo sobraniia 1898-ogo g.*, (Tver, 1899) p. 118ff.).

52. *Zhurnaly Tverskogo gubernskogo zemskogo sobraniia sessii 1899g.* (Tver, 1900) p. 88ff.

53. V. P. Kislovskii, P. P. Kislovskii and D. N. Dubasov, see B. B. Veselovskii, 'Tver', in *Istoriia*, vol. 4.

54. A. V. Gruzinov and A. A. Kushelev, ibid.

55. Here P. A. Azanchevskii and A. L. Kegel' were dependent on the funds of the *podriadchik* Fruktov (ibid.).

56. A supporter of the 'conservative' council of the time proceeded: '... as an individual, I might smile at this Bobchinsky–Dobchinsky method of quarrel ("you whistle through your teeth", etc.). But as a *glasnyi* I have to respond. The tactic of attacking, insulting, confusing one's opponent is old, especially here in the Tver zemstvo assembly, but according to me, it does not yield results. I have seen much of this type of antagonist and, in regard to this 'style', in my opinion, the dignity of *glasnyi*, the dignity of the assembly and the importance of issues at hand demand dignified methods of dispute – not individual insults or insinuations' (Gosudarsvennyi Arkhiv Rossiiskoi Federatsii, *fond DP* 102, III *deloproizvodstvo*, 1895, *delo* 1719, *ch.* 2, *l.* 222).

57. *Saratovskaia Zemskaia Nedel'ia*, no. 30 (1898); Gosudarsvennyi Arkhiv Rossiiskoi Federatsii, *fond* 102, 1895, *delo* 1719, *ch.* 2

4
Historical Views of the Russian Peasantry: National Consciousness in the Nineteenth Century[1]

A. V. Buganov

A sense of a common historical past is essential to the formation and development of national consciousness. This relation is established in two ways. First, a historical memory is in itself evidence of a certain degree of ethnic self-awareness. A common knowledge of the past is one of the elements of ethnic and, at a certain stage, national consciousness. Second, historical judgements serve as a source for the study of different aspects of national consciousness. Such sources permit us to identify the historical events and individuals that are committed to collective memory, the reasons for such, various ethnonyms, and so on. We may also discern the degree of national awareness in particular epochs, and the social classes and strata which had made national causes their very own, and so on.

The inadequacy of source material for the study of national consciousness is a basic problem. Sources of peasant origin, especially those that might reveal their ideas and mentality, practically do not exist. (According to the last Russian census of 1897, the rural population was 86.6 per cent of the total). The most thoroughly studied have been, for example, slogans and demands during the peasant wars, peasant community decisions, or petitions – all those which permit an initial survey of class consciousness among the peasantry. But sources that might substantially reflect peasant awareness of national interests are seldom found.

Let us examine these last in somewhat greater detail. First, there is historical folklore – songs, traditions, legends and lays. Most of it was produced in the peasant milieu, and it subsisted among the peasantry for an extended period, down to the nineteenth century. Bereft, to a certain degree, of precise information on historical events, folklore sources generally provide instead popular appraisals and reflections on those events. In this context, genres of historical folklore like songs and legends are most useful.

The sources most abundant in information are war songs. They concentrated throughout on foreign political history and especially on wars, that is on those periods when the defence of the Fatherland and of national interests were of paramount concern. Songs also tended to generalize about historical events and persons. Compared with legends or traditions, for instance, events were much less related to locality, and the personal receded into the background.

The events of legend generally occurred in the very places where the tale was composed. The researcher may use historical folklore to examine the relation between local and national traditions, and thereby the relation between the regional and the more generally national in peasant consciousness. Legends are most illuminating in the study of social and religious consciousness. Among national themes, traditions of conflict with external enemies are of primary interest. However, only a few legends with this subject matter have been preserved among the Russians. These are most often fragmented general references to alien peoples, such as the 'Tatars', 'Pans' or 'Lithuanians' who invaded at some time, and who plundered and slaughtered the local population. In such cases it would be preferable of course to use legends found all over the country.

Surveys conducted by academic bodies during the nineteenth century are another source. The archives of the Russian Geographical Society contain material collected in mid-century, while the manuscript collections of Prince Viacheslav Nicholaevich Tenishev's Ethnographic Office are significant for the end of the century. Official papers, memoir literature etc. as a possible category should also be noted. A supple use of these sources, bearing in mind their peculiar features and provenance, would provide an adequately objective picture of such aspects of peasant consciousness as are being studied.

One should say a few words about how peasants received historical information and how they arrived at historical concepts. The historical and national consciousness of the Russians developed over time through oral tradition. With the growth of literacy, books came to play a major role in the acquisition of knowledge about the world and about the past. Manuscripts and printed literature circulated among the peasantry with growing vigour during the nineteenth century. Books, and later newspapers, transformed peasant thinking and erased barriers between the countryside and 'educated society'.[2]

Books appeared in the countryside in many different ways. In the 1860s and 1870s, the book trade was carried on primarily by itinerant peddlers, by basket vendors [*ofeni, korobeiniki*]. Besides books, they carried also *lubok* pictures depicting religious subjects and historical events. The *ofeni* were prominent in Vladimir, Kostroma, Moscow, Tula and Iaroslav provinces. While buying books in the bazaar from a passing hawker, peasants took them 'for reading' to the local intelligentsia – teachers, clergy, medical staff, agronomists, and so on. However, the influence of books on peasants radiated chiefly from schools and rural libraries.

As recent research reveals, both the organization and construction of schools, and everything concerning the education of peasant children, were in the province of the peasant *obshchina*. Thus peasant communities allotted land for school buildings and financed lighting for schools, and they often took the initiative for opening both ordinary and high schools.

Besides parish, zemstvo and high schools, literacy spread in other ways which cannot be captured in statistics. Peasants sent their children to literate persons in the neighbourhood. The so-called literacy schools, which had mushroomed before the 1864 reform, quickly spread. Unlike other elementary schools, they did not belong to the school network, and the peasant *obshchina* (or land commune) paid for such teachers. These teachers generally were parish priests, peasants who had completed their schooling, retired soldiers, and so on. About 36 per cent of the population who had become literate were the products of these unregistered (voluntary) schools.

The opening of free libraries in villages and *volosts* (the administrative units above villages) also contributed to popular education. Books now reached the peasantry by a shorter route. During the 1890s, *volost* assemblies energetically supported the opening of library reading rooms. Peasants generally responded actively and with interest, allotting and constructing buildings, providing book grants from community resources, and so on. Private libraries also existed. Research has shown that some of the private libraries of *serfs* contained up to 2,000 volumes.

The coming of libraries to villages substantially augmented peasant access to books and thereby reduced the demand for peddlers. Libraries also served as insulation against so-called secondary illiteracy. As is well known, peasants at times had no further use for their newly acquired skills and knowledge, which then tended to atrophy. But it would be unwise to attempt a direct correlation between reading and literacy figures since the practice of reading aloud was widespread among the peasantry. The love of reading was absorbed, not only by school pupils, but also by illiterates listening to the literate.

Between 1895 and 1900, so-called public readings for the people, usually conducted by school teachers in village schools, became quite common. As V. Rachinin, correspondent of the Ethnographic Office, reported about Saransk *uezd* of Penza province in 1899, 'peasants wait for public readings impatiently and listen attentively ... in our village. ... They have acquired a reputation as avid readers and lovers of book knowledge and they fill every inch of place available in spacious halls.'[3] All correspondents of the Office reported in this manner on the popularity of readings.

Peddlers of books, builders of libraries, and organizers of public readings catered to tastes and popular reading preferences that had already been established. Of what sort were these?

In the first place, peasants preferred books with a spiritual, historical or agricultural content. During a survey conducted by the Vladimir zemstvo council at the turn of the century, the question about what kind of books 'the rural population find useful' returned the following: 'godly' books – 60.8 per cent; agricultural – 17.9 per cent; historical – 11.5 per cent; novels and stories – 3.5 per cent; fairy tales and proverbs – 2.2 per cent; craft – 1.1 per cent; textbooks – 1.1 per cent; others – 1.8 per cent.

Analyses of readers' demands in village schools and public libraries yielded additional information. Demands for books of a religious and moral character constituted 31 per cent of the total, literary subjects 46.5 per cent, biography and history together 15 per cent, and natural sciences and traditional economy 7 per cent. It is interesting that in all peasant communities the demand for scientific subjects fluctuated between 21 per cent and 36.3 per cent, and religious between 16 per cent and 56 per cent; in urban areas, however, the respective ranges were 8–10 per cent and 1–13 per cent. The majority of correspondents of the Ethnographic Office also identified religious-moral and historical themes as of fundamental interest to the peasant readership. Here, the preference for the Scriptures and other 'godly' books tended to grow with age.

In fact, religious literature was most widespread and popular. The enormous interest in spiritual books is only to be expected among believing Russian peasants, to whom salvation, church construction, and leading the 'godly life' were always of paramount concern. Ever since Kievan times hagiographies had been popular throughout

Russian society, including the peasantry. (According to the zemstvo statisticians of Vladimir, 58.8 per cent of the books in peasant collections were of religious and moral content; of these about a quarter were the lives of saints).

The influence of spiritual literature on reader and listener was not confined to the religious and moral sphere. Hagiographies and Apocrypha furnished peasants with abundant historical information and knowledge of the past. With the advent of Christianity, Russian historical individuals – political and church figures, or pious ones – became the objects of religious reverence, and their lives and careers entered the written record.

Certainly, the interest in history was satisfied also by secular publications. Thus Russian historical essays, short stories and novels predominated among the *lubok* distributed during the 1870s among peasants of Porechsk *volost*, Mozhaisk *uezd*, Moscow province – for example, *How Our Slavic Ancestors Lived, Dmitrii Ivanovich Donskoi, A Short Russian History, Essays of 1812*, and so on.

In the nineteenth century, peasants read not only printed but also handcopied books. The tradition of reading manuscript books dated to pre-Petrine times, and was especially common in the northern provinces of Vologda, Arkhangel and Olonets. The copying of books of the seventeenth and eighteenth centuries along with their artistic format continued. Peasants as a rule left their comments and inscriptions in handcopied books. They permit us to establish the fact of the possession of a book, how it reached the owner, and often the peasant's active reading of it.

Besides books, newspapers and journals often found their way to the peasantry. Interest in them mounted substantially if they dealt with themes of peasant interest. Thus, those who visited the country at the end of the 1850s and the beginning of the 1860s, when the 'peasant question' was being widely discussed in the press, noted a growing peasant inclination to read. 'Crowds of illiterate peasants surrounded persons who read newspapers and who discussed what they read.'[4]

Newspapers enlightened peasants on the course of the last Russo-Turkish War in 1878–9. Essentially it was the rural intelligentsia and priests who subscribed to newspapers. But gradually peasants also began to do so. There are reports from the 1870s that wealthy peasants in many places received newspapers, which 'circulated by hand and were read before large throngs ... and during the war, newspaper subscriptions shot up' (information from Novoladozhsk *uezd*, St Petersburg province). The poorer peasants sometimes jointly subscribed to some inexpensive newspaper or flysheet and had group readings at meetings or in taverns.

Thus literacy spread rapidly in rural Russia during the second half of the nineteenth century. Having read books and newspapers, peasants could compare their newly gleaned information with oral traditions. The interaction between book knowledge and the age-old oral tradition enriched their historical memory and fortified their national consciousness.

The selective nature of the historical component of national consciousness is one of its important features. The historical events and persons that were the most significant to the peasant have been emphasized and conserved in the popular consciousness. This took place at two levels. First, peasant historical accounts marked out the distinct historical epochs in their general temporal sequence. These were, for example, the founding of the Russian state, the Tatar–Mongol conquest, the Time of Troubles, and the reigns of the most powerful monarchs – Ivan the Terrible, Peter the Great, the Empress Catherine II. Second, the collective memory identified the most salient events of these segments of history. In either case, the facts were clustered around specific figures like tsars, military commanders, popular heroes and leaders of insurrections. Peasants formed their own notions of chronology at both these levels. The peasant historical memory suffered from neither chronological confusion nor substitution with respect to the major epochs. But their historical awareness of the transition phases between epochs was often confused and the general chronological sequence was broken. This phenomenon may be ascribed as much to the peasants' inadequate grasp of the course of history as much as to their particular manner of understanding the historical process.

Of the tsars before Peter, Ivan the Terrible has left the most significant impress on popular memory. Popular judgements of Ivan IV distinctly evolved from the sixteenth to the nineteenth century. During his lifetime itself he was cast as the one who beat off boyar treachery. Boyars and the people were set in opposition to each other, and the tsar routinely appeared as the champion of the latter.

The first tsar, Ivan Vasilievich

> ... did not help out treason in stone-walled Moscow,
> And here the tsar's heart became inflamed with passion
> Worse than fire, worse than the griddle,
> He looked on the boyars with unfriendly eyes,

And they concealed themselves, these boyars, the younger behind
the elder,
They concealed themselves these boyars, the elder behind the
younger.[5]

At the height of the *oprichnina* during the 1560s and 1570s, a certain
critique of Ivan the Terrible prevailed. It said the tsar had deceived
God, who had appeared in the form of an old man, and that this was a
betrayal of Rus which could not now be undone. However, the popular
idealization of the tsar had begun by the beginning of the seventeenth
century. The privations of the Time of Troubles diverted attention
from the arbitrary and lawless conduct of the *oprichnina* (see Glossary).
The tsar's reign was now depicted as prosperous, and he himself was
represented as a fighter against untruth. Peasant imagination had made
of him 'the just ruler'; and legend now claimed that he had been
'elected tsar from among the poor by command of the Almighty.' This
tradition was widespread in the nineteenth century.

Popular views of Ivan the Terrible varied from region to region in
addition to the changes over time. This could be ascribed to the particular history of each region. Legends of the terrible tsar, with generally
flattering appraisals of his reign, were to be found especially in the
Nizhnii-Novgorod country through which his armies had marched to
Kazan in 1564. In the middle of the nineteenth century P. I. Mel'nikov,
the writer and ethnographer, travelled along Ivan's route and identified
the traditions that had been preserved. It is remarkable that the songs
and legends about the events of the sixteenth century were well known
in practically every village along the route of the tsar's Kazan campaign.
It is quite as significant that local tradition, in its essential factual detail,
agreed with the accounts in the chronicles, with, for example, peasant
folklore surprisingly accurately pinpointing each royal camp.

However, as distinct from the oral tradition of the Volga, the folklore
of Pskov and Novgorod presents a negative image of Ivan. The
favoured themes here are related to the *oprichnina*, and the sacking of
Novgorod the Great. In the Novgorod tradition, massacres of innocent
people drew the wrath of God; the tsar repented and built the
Khutynsk monastery. (In fact the Khutynsk monastery was founded by
Varlamei Khutynskii at the end of the twelfth century, but a refectory
and church were constructed within it in Ivan's time.) Themes of this
sort, with Ivan acknowledging his sins, or being made to see reason by
some holy servitor or through one of God's miracles, recurred often in
Novgorod and Pskov folklore.

Some publicists today seek to derive the Stalin cult from the faith of 'the peasant masses' in the benevolent tsar. In fact, the peasantry never endorsed the cruelty and tyranny of rulers. Folklore speaks only of Ivan IV's *oprichniki* as 'sons of bitches' who 'rode around with their mongrel heads'. According to one of the correspondents of the Ethnographic Office, Ivan's *oprichnina* 'evokes an image of oppression among the common people'.

The idealization of Ivan IV in popular consciousness may be ascribed as much to religion as to the specific social and political circumstances of peasant thinking. After Ivan's coronation as Tsar and the symbolic derivation of authority from Byzantine emperors, service under the tsar acquired a special theocratic connotation. The authority of the monarch was officially sanctified, and he stood before his subjects as 'the chosen of God'. In popular monarchism now, the tsar was the anointed of God. Those who are given to historical analogy ignore this decisive issue when attempting to discover the roots of the cults of communist leaders in 'essential' [*spetsificheskie*] popular traits.

However, religion did not by itself determine attitudes to the tsar. The popular cult of the tsar rested on the wholly pragmatic concerns and calculations of the peasantry, and these lay in the social sphere. Peasant consciousness perennially reproduced hopes for a just social order; and these determined their relation to a tsar who was supreme and cared for the peasant. This was in tune with the peasant's notion of the state, which differed from the views of the ruling classes. Most of the nobility conceived the state as a structure of estates and hierarchy which secured to them substantial privileges, but among the people it was thought of as the domain of social justice free of undeserved or illegal privilege. Attitudes to the tsar varied accordingly. To the ruling caste, the tsar was the first nobleman of the country; in the eyes of the peasantry, he was the defender of the people's interests against the 'internal' enemy of evil boyars and landlords. And in fact it was to the tsar, as the chosen of God and the foremost figure of state, that the hopes and expectations of the lower orders turned.

Popular responses to the epoch of Peter the Great were also varied. Memories of 'the first emperor' and his achievements were widespread throughout the eighteenth and nineteenth centuries. To Russian historical folklore from the beginning of the eighteenth century, Peter I's greatness lay in his military leadership and royal status, unsullied by estate prejudices. But in popular tradition Peter was a changeling, not the legitimate (*prirodnyi*) tsar; and it threw at him the legend of the 'genuine' tsarevich Aleksei to the point of regarding him as the

Antichrist. Two legends about Peter flourished among Old Believers down to the nineteenth century, one as 'the changeling Tsar' and the other as 'Peter the Antichrist'. Oppositional stances in Old Believer interpretations, especially in the north, were determined by confessional positions.

The most radical Old Believer convictions notwithstanding, the attitude of the majority of Russians to Peter could not be described as negative. He is recalled more vividly in idealized form. Soldiers gloried in recalling the victorious captain of war and tsar, the 'first emperor'. In popular memory, Peter was invariably the Russian Orthodox tsar ('and thus spake our little father, the Orthodox Tsar of All Russia, Petr Alekseevich ...').

The tradition of Peter I as the 'peasant Tsar' evidently belongs to the north. Peter had marched with four thousand troops from Arkhangel to Petrozavodsk, in the autumn of 1702, through the Kemsk and Povenetsk *uezd*s in Arkhangel and Olonets provinces respectively. Those who had observed and worked on the construction of the 'royal road' in these regions handed down to their children impressions of their direct encounters with the worker-tsar, how he stayed the night and christened the daughter of his host, of his extraordinary physical strength as he chopped wood, and so on.

At the end of the nineteenth century, peasants in the Belozersk *uezd* of Novgorod province were convinced that Peter 'certainly knew how to do everything'. The common people 'peasantized' the tsar – as a result no doubt of his frequent sojourns in the north, where 'he roamed through bogs and marshes ... appearing among the people with an axe in his belt and a sickle in his hands'.

The tradition of depicting Peter as the worker-tsar was found in other regions also. D. N. Sadovnikov, the collector of folklore, took down the following tradition of Peter I in Samara province: 'During his breaks from office work, he would visit the taverns, seek out master craftsmen and enquire about their trade; he wished to learn everything from everyone.'[6]

There was a popular memory of the tsar's stay near Briansk in Orel province at a wharf built by himself on the river Desna. In Bolkhovsk *uezd* of this province, peasants remember him as one who 'knew all the trades and even learnt how to weave bast, though he cursed this trade for not providing the worker with enough to eat and drink.'

Different aspects of Peter's work may have been idealized and his image among the people may have been 'peasantized', but peasants never linked his name to their hopes of emancipation from serfdom.

His name does not appear in the list of 'liberator tsars' in the peasant social utopias of the eighteenth and nineteenth centuries.

The further the times of Ivan and Peter receded into the past, the more these rulers were revered among the people. There were nonetheless certain differences of image in the idealization of these monarchs. Gromyko dates them to the beginning of the eighteenth century: 'To the peasant of the eighteenth century Ivan IV primarily meant an abstract image of a harsh sovereign, but Peter ... was endowed with lively human qualities.'[7] Nineteenth-century negative assessments of these tsars were due either to the particularism of a region (as in the case of Ivan the Terrible) or to religion (the repudiation of Peter in the Old Believer tradition).

The idealization of Ivan and Peter was determined also by the peculiar nature of the development of the peasantry's public awareness during the nineteenth century. The euphoria of victory in the Patriotic War of 1812 and the gradual growth of peasant consciousness led to concepts of 'rights and freedoms' that went beyond the customary (for example, hopes for the abolition of serfdom 'as a reward' for the liberation of the Fatherland). They also stimulated more critical appraisals of the tsars of the nineteenth century. Peasants inevitably compared them with the tsars of 'the glorious past' and, in the comparison, the latter-day tsars were the losers.

In songs about the Patriotic War of 1812, Alexander I, like his predecessors, stands out as a symbol of national worth:

> They all stood, so they say
> That power there might be behind the Tsar

However, this was now not 'Our Sovereign-Tsar', 'Our Sovereign the Little Father' (as Peter I was called in folklore), who, with his 'beloved soldier offspring' prepared to attack the Swedish king. The depiction of Alexander was more of a tribute to tradition than a recognition of the real services of the tsar and of his role in the defence of the Fatherland; moreover, following threats from Napoleon, 'our Orthodox Tsar fell deep in thought ... and he vacillated'.

A number of rumours circulated among the people about Alexander I and the mysterious circumstances of his death in Taganrog in 1825. Talk that the emperor was alive and that somebody else had been laid in his tomb became, during the 1830s and 1840s, the legend of Fedor Kuz'mich. The names of two persons were thus conflated: that of the Russian emperor who saved Europe from Napoleon, and that of an unknown Siberian monk. The legend was widely current in Russia both among the common people and even in high places, with the historian N. K. Shil'der conceding the possibility of Alexander's faked death.

Let us set aside this mystery and ask the question why the image of Alexander should have troubled and agitated his contemporaries and successors for so long. Once again by all counts the answer is to be sought in the religious consciousness of the Russian. When V. G. Korolenko was prosecuted for publishing L. N. Tolstoy's work *The Last Notes of Fedor Kuz'mich*, his counsel spoke thus:

> It is a great, entirely Russian legend. ... The people wished to believe and fervently believed that the most powerful of tsars and the most powerless of his powerless subjects came to be united in one form. ... Fedor Kuz'mich embodied the idea of a sovereign's atonement for that great sin for which no one may be pardoned, the sin of murder or of complicity in the murder [that is, the assassination of the Emperor Paul I]. This legend of humility and repentance belongs so essentially to the Russian conscience and mind.

These words explain much about the aura of martyr that envelops the memory of Alexander I. The Christian notion of atoning for sin, entrenched for so long in the Russian world-view, was intercalated into the known circumstances of the life and death of the emperor and gave rise to the legend about him.

Discussions about the death (or withdrawal from the 'world') of Alexander, the interregnum and the Decembrist rising bring us to the last of the major utopian legends of the 'deliverers' – to the legends about Constantine. According to the legend, Constantine, the brother of Alexander I, wished to grant freedom to peasants, for which the nobility removed him from the throne. The peasantry were negative to the Decembrist rising.

It should be said that the traditional popular idealization of the tsar often coexisted with the utopia of an ideal desired sovereign as opposed to the real one. K. V. Chistov has noted the tenacity of legends about 'deliverers' from the beginning of the seventeenth century to the middle of the nineteenth. He showed that the origin of legends of 'deliverers' were independent of similar legends in the past; and this was evidence that utopian expectations were perennial among the people. It is not surprising that the serf emancipation of 19 February 1861 became a memorable landmark to the public and that the peasantry should have venerated the name of Alexander II. At the end of the nineteenth century in Saransk *uezd* of Penza province, peasants 'know the years, month, and day when they were freed, and they know which tsar did it'. Memories about how the 'Sovereign-Emperor Aleksandr Nikolaevich granted freedom' were established by correspondents of the Ethnographic Office in Vologda and Novgorod provinces also. At the end of the century, in the southern *volosts* of Peshekhovsk *uezd* of Iaroslav province, peasants celebrated 19 February, the day of the Emancipation. In some localities, the collective memory directly linked the Emancipation with the assassination of Alexander II: 'they killed him because of us, because he gave us freedom; God bless him.'

In the ceaseless reproduction of peasant utopian dreams, most of the new legends were composed during interregnums, especially 'when the ruling tsar was not of directly royal "origin"' (Boris Godunov, Vasilii Shuiskii and Catherine II). The image of the deliverer in peasant construction was initially as blurred as that of the ideal monarch. His contours became sharper generally with the apperance of the Pretender. At the end of the eighteenth century and during the first half of the nineteenth, the Pretender phenomenon atrophied and ceased to be the symbol of protest. But the faith in the 'good tsar' persisted for long. Pretenders were replaced by faith in the distant Promised Land where truth and freedom prevailed.

The popular masses assigned the defence of the state and national interests and the establishment of social justice not only to the leader of the state, the tsar, but also to distinguished public figures, military commanders and popular heroes. Peasant collective memory for long cherished the names of the defenders of the Russian Land, of Alexander Nevskii, Sergii Radonezhskii, Dmitrii Donskoi, and so on.

Peasant folklore of the nineteenth century contained not a few compositions devoted to the Time of Troubles and the historical actors of the time, to Koz'ma Minin, D. M. Pozharskii, Prokopii Liapunov and M. V. Skopin-Shuiskii. In 1859, the correspondent of the Ethnographic Office reported from Gzhatsk *uezd* of Smolensk province: 'The renown of Minin and generally the whole scene of the donation [money for troops] ... moves the common people and arouses their patriotism. The people love to read about those who sacrificed for Russia.' (Evidently, the Minin image played a definitive role in promoting a sense of 'sacrifice' during the Patriotic War against Napoleon. It is understandable that in the circumstances of the voluntary contributions and patriotic wave of 1812, the figure of Minin became ever more known and attractive to peasants.

Social motifs accompanied the obvious patriotism of folklore about the Time of Troubles. Prince Pozharskii was cast not only as the saviour of the Fatherland (the traditional representation in both popular official discourse of the nineteenth century and in peasant folklore), but also as the chosen of the common people: 'our dear young soldiers, our young cohorts, chose this daring chief', Pozharskii. One of the songs takes liberties with history to speak of the election of Prince Pozharskii as tsar. Indeed, Pozharskii's name was proposed at the Zemskii Sobor of January–February 1613, but Mikhail Romanov was elected tsar. In the song, Pozharskii declined in favour of Mikhail:

And so spake Prince Pozharskii to the boyars
Oh you lord boyars and voevody of Moscow ...
Now take unto yourselves a Christian Tsar
From the famed and wealthy house of Romanov
Mikhail, the son of Fedorovich
And they chose as their Tsar, Mikhail, son of Fedorovich.[8]

Such a treatment of events suggests not only a peculiar refraction of collective memory about the struggle between the various candidates for the throne, but also attitudes to the 'saviour' of Rus, Prince Pozharskii, and popular views on the comportment of a Christian tsar.

The historical songs devote much attention to the *voevod* (the governor), Prince Shopin-Shuiskii. His victories over the Poles and the Second False Dmitrii ensured his heroic image. The songs make him the 'preserver of the Christian world and of all our holy Russian Land'. Often Shopin-Shuiskii and Prokopii Liapunov are set in opposition to the 'traitor-boyars'. For example, the song 'Liapunov and Guzhmund' stresses that as then 'many Russian boyars ignobly retreated and deserted the Christian faith', the thoughful *voevod* Prokopii Liapunov 'stoutly defended the faith ... and put the traitors to flight'.

In the songs about Peter's campaigns, the commanders stand out: B. P. Sheremet'ev, 'the great boyar of the tsars, the general and the cavalier', and the ataman (cossack leader), I. M. Krasnoshchekov. This tradition may be further traced through the images of P. A. Rumiantsev, Z. G. Chernyshev and others. In folklore about the defence of the Fatherland, the focus shifts steadily from the tsar to military leaders beloved of the people. Indeed, they are often contrasted with royal favourites, 'traitor-generals' and even the tsar himself.

The folklore references to A. V. Suvorov are innumerable. Soldiers found no problem too great when they were with him:

O with you, lord Prince Suvorov
Dear Commander and leader ours
The might of the foe is not terribe to us
The might of the foe, the evil Turk.

The archives of the learned societies of the nineteenth century contain much that reveal the peasant view of Suvorov's personality. In Dorogobuzhsk *uezd* of Smolensk province, 'there are enduring accounts among the people of how Suvorov "knew God's Ways" and therefore always triumphed over his enemies ...' Similar explanations for his victories may be found in the correspondence from Tarusskii *uezd* of Kaluga province where Suvorov, along with Kutuzov and Skobelev, 'are regarded the chosen of God'.

While popular opinion acknowledged Suvorov's military and leadership qualities, it remembered him also for his proximity to the common soldier. In the 1840s in Olonets province there is a legend of his visit to the Aleksandrovskii cannon foundry. In this, Suvorov 'always turned up before he was expected, he arrived in Petrozavodsk on a cart clad in a soldier's wrap ...'. In 1899 the correspondent of the Ethnographic Office reported from Saransk *uezd* that the peasants 'know ... about Suvorov, how he dressed as a common soldier, arrived in camp, and was welcomed by everyone as an ordinary soldier, and how he ordered his soldiers to respond when asked something'.

Similar stress on his simplicity of taste and habits, and his readiness to share the burden and privation of campaigning are also typical of the historical songs and legends of the Suvorov cycle. In fact, this combination of unsurpassed military ability and innately democratic demeanour in Suvorov, 'the chosen of God', created in the popular imagination the ultimate image of the national hero and commander, and it accounts for the prolonged historical memory of the man.

M. I. Kutuzov and M. I. Platov have secured a place in the peasant historical imagination after the war of 1812. They now appeared as the people's representatives and protectors of their interest. After Suvorov, Kutuzov was certainly the most popular among Russian soldiers. According to F. I. Glinka's memoirs, Kutuzov's journey from St Petersburg to the army resembled a triumph: 'Not finding any other way of expressing their simple heartfelt sentiments, the people resorted to the old sentimental custom ... they unharnessed the horse and bore the carriage themselves. ...'

The historical actors who won a place for themselves in the popular mind after the Russo-Turkish War of 1877–8 are obvious enough. They were M. G. Cherniaev, M. D. Skobelev, I. V. Gurko and F. F. Radetskii. The name of Skobelev was the best known. When listing the military commanders most favoured among the general public, informants for the Ethnographic Office placed the 'White General' alongside Suvorov and Kutuzov; and like his illustrious predecessors, he was invariably victorious in battle. As they would say, 'If it were not for him, it would have gone badly with us.' In Borisoglebsk *uezd* of Iaroslav province, 'more stories of General Skobelev are to be encountered than any other. ...' In Dorogobuzhsk *uezd*, 'Skobelev and the times of his heroic exploits are immensely popular.'

Naturally enough, Skobelev's military victories on behalf of Russia and his defence of 'Orthodox Christians from the heathen', were central to the peasant appraisal of his personality. But the social side to the image is quite as evident. Like Kutuzov and Platov, Skobelev was contrasted with the ruling class and the 'traitor-generals'. In the village of Vassa in Shchelkanovsk *volost* in Kaluga province, some peasants

> praised our generals, others excoriated them, for they were the traitors and the tsar does not trust them. It further became known that at Plevna our men were beaten because our generals betrayed them. Skobelev alone was a hero and ordered his men to shoot their commanders should they be afraid of the Turk or turn traitor.

Besides the social, the religious factor also determined the memory of the leaders of the peasant risings. Stepan Razin and Emel'ian Pugachev were not merely deliverers who avenged the sufferings of the people. In many Volga legends, Razin was a great sinner whom the earth would not receive. The anathematized leader of the insurgents narrated his sufferings to the people: 'I will suffer until the end of the world if the Russian people shall not see the light.' In those legends, when Razin was depicted as the future deliverer, the link with Christian views were less visible. But even in them he promised to come and punish the people for their sins and falsehood.

In the memoirs about Pugachev, the typical and repetitive themes of justice meted out to noble landowners tended to predominate. The severity of the Pugachevites did not excite sympathy, but it was often enough accepted as vengeance for all that they had endured.

In the nineteenth century, as before, Russians clearly acknowledged their belonging to the Orthodox faith. This was expressed both in peacetime, when the normal form of address at village assemblies was 'Orthodox Christians', and especially in war and during armed conflict.

At such moments identification by confession was still more evident. The confessional term [confessionym or *konfessionim*] defined Russians ethnically and completely; opponents, even if Christian, were deemed 'non-Christian'.

The victories of Russian forces and the exploits of military chiefs were directly related in the popular mind with the grace of God, and defeat was regarded as punishment for sin. Many old peasants, veterans of the Crimean War of 1853–6 which Russia lost, declared in conversation with K. M. Staniukovich that 'Sebastopol fell because of sin', dissolute conduct and the cruelty of the commanders. Peasant servitude, traditionally regarded by them as a violation of divine justice, was also one of the causes of military defeat: if 'peasants are not granted freedom ... then Mother Russia shall collapse and all shall prevail over her'.

In military matters, exceptional significance attached to Church blessing. At the end of the nineteenth century, in the Maloarkhangel'skii *uezd* of Orlov province, local peasants narrated how, before the battle of Kulikovo field, Dmitrii Donskoi was blessed by Saint Sergii of Radonezh. According to the recollections of many soldiers, officers and generals, and veterans of the Russo-Turkish War of 1828, all those who had paid a visit to the monk Serafim Sarovskii, received his blessings, and had recited with faith 'Lord have mercy and pray for the starets Serafim', came through unscathed, 'even from situations of extreme danger and certain death'.

At the end of the nineteenth century, E. V. Barsov noted down a legend that Peter the Great disobeyed the Patriarch and therefore lost the battle of Narva. Only after he had 'attended divine service and been blessed by the Patriarch' did Peter win. Such an intertwining of memories of defeat at Narva and of the battle of Poltava (in Barsov's opinion, these are the two events in question) appears to be the logical consequence of popular views about 'Peter the Great's attitudes to the Patriarch and about the workings of Church blessings during war'.

During wars, peasants would pray fervently, begging God 'to grant victory to Russian arms'. When describing the general devastation and despondency during the Russian retreat at the beginning of the Patriotic War of 1812, Glinka noted 'only churches remained open day and night; they were full of people praying, weeping, and arming themselves'.

According to correspondents of the Ethnographic Office, during the Russo-Turkish War of 1877–8, the people 'attended church more regularly'; peasants did not miss a single service 'in their eagerness for news from the front'; and they joyfully rendered thanks for victory. In the Khvalynsk *uezd* of Saratov province, they attended divine service 'when our arms prevailed; but when rumours percolated that the Turks "were beating our side", they wept and implored God to help overcome the foul enemy'. Peasants attended requiem services for the dead, prayed for victory and collected donations 'for the wounded'. There was a belief that 'the Turks have begun to beat and torture Christian peasants in order to force the Muslim faith on them'. In some localities, aged literates explained to fellow villagers that the Slavs were 'our brothers' because 'they are descended, like ourselves, from the same son of Noah Japheth. ...'

The popular sympathy for their oppressed brother co-religionists was reflected in the volunteer movement to the Balkans. With the outbreak of hostilities between Serbia and Turkey, several thousand volunteers, including peasants, set out 'for the relief' of the Slavs. In one of the village communities of Orlov *uezd* of Orlov province 'some peasants decided to abandon their families and go to war ... and the community rewarded them appropriately'. The people felt that 'were they to be killed in action for the Christian faith, God would forgive them their sins'.

To the peasant, the war always had the Christian purpose of defending the humiliated and downtrodden. Alexander II, according to them, was 'compassionate and good, and he intervened on the behalf of Christians', and 'he took pity on his brother Christians'. Peasants were convinced that 'if our sovereign lord declared war, it meant a fight for the truth, for the Orthodox faith, for those who had been hurt'.

In the Russian consciousness this was an awesome trial for Orthodoxy and for the entire fabric of Russian life. Interestingly, peasant sympathies during the Greco-Turkish War of 1894 were for the Greeks, although they knew of it only from newspapers. Many expected Russian troops to be despatched to their aid and 'some announced their resolve to volunteer for service in Greece'.

One of the most complex questions about popular consciousness is the relation between the social and the national. Even during national wars of liberation which witnessed expressions of Russian national unity, social interests continued to be formulated. This was especially the case in 1812. The concept of the freedom of the Motherland and of the individual were conflated in the patriotic movements of the Russians.

As research has shown, the notion of 'the estates rallying round the throne', as in official pre-revolutionary historiography, is not tenable.

Before the war and in its early phases, peasant attitudes could vary. Some claimed: 'When Napoleon comes, he will free us.' The beginnings of the war saw instances of Russian peasants and French soldiers combining against Russian landlords: 'In Polotsk *uezd* of Vitebsk province, in the El'ninsk, Sychevsk, Porechsk, and Iukhnovsk *uezd*s of the Smolensk country, and in a number of villages around Moscow, ... the local peasants sacked seigneurial estates with French help or did it on their own, beat up their landlords and delivered them for trial and punishment to the French, as happened in the Porechsk and Velizhsk *uezd*s of Smolensk province.'[9] However, as Napoleon penetrated deeper into Russia, 'the illusions of a few quickly dissipated, and the hopes of striving for individual freedom now merged with the liberation of Russia'.

A historical understanding, as a component of national consciousness, conserved chiefly the memory of events and persons of national history. The correspondent of the Ethnographic Office reported about Vladimir *uezd* of Vladimir province thus: 'Our people love, above all, to talk about power, wealth, and the might of our Mother Russia. They take pleasure in listening to stories about it.'

Nonetheless, national consciousness absorbed information and representations about other people with whom Russians came into contact during their ethnic history, in military campaigns and during the conquest and settlement of new lands, and so on. Peasant historical folklore extensively employed, for example, the ethnonym 'Tatars'. During the nineteenth century it denoted in most cases many eastern peoples indiscriminately. The usage had local variations also. Tatar raids were remembered chiefly in the south Russian region. On the other hand in Siberia, owing to prolonged peaceful contact between Russians and Tatars, the word 'Tatar' ceased to connote enmity. Such a metamorphosis in ethnic representations even led to revisions in the history of the incorporation of Siberia: the colonization of the territory was regarded as peaceful in popular opinion. According to N. A. Minenko, 'the very suggestion that their legendary Ermak "conquered" the Tatars' appeared 'ludicrous'.[10]

The ethnonyms 'Lithuanian' and 'pan' were likewise relative. Traditionally they had no clear-cut ethnic basis and generally denoted all newcomers from the west. During P. Iakushkin's travels in Pskov country, his guide recounted stories of 'how the Lithuanians came and wished to take Opskov'. Old inhabitants informed him that 'the Lithuanians approached and took up position on the hill of Mitinsk. ... They bombarded Izborsk, destroyed the gates and slaughtered large numbers', and that 'Stephen Bathory approached our monastery'. (This referred to the Pechersk monastery and the siege of Pskov, and other events of the Livonian War.) Songs and legends contain ethnonyms of not only enemies but also of allies in wars and campaigns. For example, the Volga folklore about Ivan IV preserved memories about the participation of the Mordva in the Kazan campaign. In this matter the notes assembled by P. I. Mel'nikov, the writer and ethnographer, in Nizhnii-Novgorod, Kazan and Simbirsk provinces in the 1840s are especially interesting.

Growing knowledge about the wider world began to erase traditional concepts about social structure. The experience of Russian soldiers in the liberation campaigns of 1813–14 had a profound impact on the peasant world-view. Soldiers had the opportunity to observe countries and peoples freed from serfdom as a result of the bourgeois revolutions. As A. A. Bestuzhev recalled,

> armies, from general down to the common soldier, on returning home, talked only about how wonderful it was abroad. Comparisons led to the question of why it could not be the same at home. ... Impoverished peasants began to record police harassment, and they felt the oppression by the nobility all the more because they began to understand peoples' rights.

In the growing wave of peasant movements after the wars, the majority of leaders were veterans of these wars.

In the second half of the nineteenth century, and especially during its last quarter, liberal and revolutionary democratic ideals penetrated the peasantry ever more. This was to a significant degree under the influence of the Narodnik ideology. The report of the Kirsanov *uezd* police chief to the Tambov governor (17 September 1878) speaks of how in the village assembly the peasant Mikhail Fedorov Shirshov of Viaz'minsk *volost*

> began denouncing the current system in Russia: 'Why is it not like France here; we must have a republic. There, that is in France, they have an elected ruler, but we have whoever comes by royal descent. And since the tsar's family is vast, it consumes huge amounts and they take the skin off the peasant's back.

Further, one of Shirshov's distant relatives, A. Gavrilovskii, called on him in 1875 to 'instil liberal ideas into him such that from that moment Shirshov altered his way of thinking'.[11]

The following conclusions may be suggested. During all of the nine-teenth century and especially after the reform of the 1860s, more impinged upon the national consciousness than in earlier times. With the growth of literacy, the oral tradition was significantly comple-mented by textual knowledge. The growing tempo of the Russian peasant struggle left its imprint.

Historical knowledge was assembled around persons. The lives and achievements of tsars, military leaders and other political figures were appraised for their national significance. The most important measure of a historical personage among the people was his contribution to the consolidation of the might of the Russian state.

The reciprocal relation between the image of the motherland and of Orthodox ideas led to the most highly regarded historical figures being seen as expressing 'the will of God'. This was especially the case with monarchs and the most powerful military leaders. The attributes which attracted peasants to such individuals, whether worker-tsar or common soldier-commander, were democratic comportment and simplicity. Many major figures of the past, contrary to fact, were represented by peasants as defenders of their social aspirations and needs, and were set against the traditional 'internal' enemy, the 'bad' boyar and landlord. It was a firmly held belief throughout the nineteenth century that the peasants of different parts of the country enjoyed a common under-standing of national interests.

Notes

1. Translated from the Russian by Hari Vasudevan.
2. For more on peasant reading habits, see M. M. Gromyko, 'Krug chteniia russkikh krest'ian v kontse XIX veka', in *V nachale bylo slovo* (Leningrad, 1990); B. Eklof, *Russian Peasant Schools: Officialdom, Village Culture and Popular Pedagogy, 1861–1914* (California University Press, 1986); A. V. Buganov, 'Chto chitali russkie krest'iane', in *Rossiiskaia provintsiia*, no. 1 (1994).
3. Arkhiv Gosudarstvennogo Muzeia Etnografii [hereafter GME]. Otdel pis'mennykh istochnikov, *fond* [*f.*] 7, *opis'* [*op.*] 1, *delo* [*d.*] 1397, *list* [*l.*] 15.
4. *Revoliutsionnaia situatsiia v Rossii v seredine XIX v.* (Moscow, 1978) p. 54.
5. Otdel rukopisei Gosudarstvennoi publichnoi biblioteki imeni M. E. Saltykova-Shchedrina [hereafter ORGPB], *f.* 478, *op.* 1, no. 34, *l.* 1, *oborot* [*ob.*].
6. D. N. Sadovnikov, *Skazki i predaniia Samarskogo kraia*, in *Zapiski Imperatorskogo Russkogo Geograficheskogo Obshchestva po otdeleniiu ethnografii*, *t.* 12 (St Petersburg, 1884) pp. 371, 372.

7. M. M. Gromyko, *Dukhovnaia kul'tura russkogo kres'ianstva*, in *Ocherki russkoi kul'tury XVIII v.*, ch IV (Moscow, 1988) p. 323.
8. *Materialy dlia istorii goroda Borovska i ego uezda*, t. 1 (Borovsk, 1913) p. 77.
9. N. A. Troitskii, *1812 velikii god Rossii* (Moscow, 1988) p. 219.
10. N. A. Minenko, *Istoriia kul'tury russkogo kres'ianstva Sibiri v period feodalizma* (Novosibirsk, 1986) pp. 29–30.
11. Gosudarstvenny Arkhiv Tambovskoi Oblasti, *f.* 4, *op.* 1, *d.* 2792, *l.* 42.

5

Regulating Conflict through the Petition

Madhavan K. Palat

The petition considered here was the collective representation by peasants and workers during the second third of the nineteenth century. It was a form of action that atrophied with the Great Reform. The petition was addressed to autocracy, it invoked its might and mercy, it affirmed its law and it denoted craven submission. It accused a mendacious bureaucracy of disfiguring the sublime majesty of autocracy, and it proposed instead another autocracy, in direct relation with the peasantry. It legitimized autocracy rather than challenged it; as such it was one of the latter's instruments of social regulation. The petition was composed, not by the peasants themselves, but by others who knew or claimed to know the mind of autocracy and the manner of pleasing it. It reveals an ideal relation as seen by the autocracy, a negotiating instrument used by the peasantry, and a reciprocal mobilization by either. It was not the peasant's voice, it did not describe his condition, and it does not suggest naive faith in the tsar. It was a routine re-statement of a relation, routinely stated in order to ensure that the relation held, and therewith pointing to a possible mutation.

The structure of the typical petition may be summed up as follows. In formal terms it consisted of a salutation, a narrative of grievances, the claim and a concluding prostration. Being addressed to high authority, whether tsar, senators, ministers or governor, the salutation and conclusion were suitably humble and self-abasing. The narrative of grievances had its own design. It was intended to rouse the tsar to anger by demonstrating that his law had been infringed upon; and it was meant to move him to pity through heart-rending accounts of privation. Its legitimation was restorative, through the contrast between an ideal past when the law was upheld and social relations were just, and the present when both had degenerated. The structure of the claim was invariable as advocacy, citing both law and custom in justification. The content of the claim was nearly invariable; it concerned status in the social hierarchy, as sanctified by law, to rise within it, to pre-empt a derogation, or to restore a lost position.

This standard format of the petition was a looser version of the traditional *chelobitnaia* established in the sixteenth century. This was a general term for every type of address to high authority, be it the tsar, the princes of the blood, the patriarch, feudal magnates or high officials. It was an official document as part of the record; it followed a rigidly prescribed pattern; it was the basis for official action, judicial or otherwise; and the collections constitute archives on major events like flights, deaths, threats, treason, the exercise of the prerogative of mercy and the like.[1]

This structure in four parts was *de rigueur* until the middle of the nineteenth century. Its standardized form betrayed its official character as it prepared the recipient for the contents. The rhetorical devices were directed at the emotions of the addressee and were distinguished from the laconic style of other official acts like laws. The narrative section was vivid and 'genetically' related to folklore.[2] The modern petition and the *chelobitnaia* were comparable for threatening consequences, in case of frustration, to the petitioners themselves, not to the addressee.[3] They warned that they would perish from hunger, flee, become destitutes or orphans, or be ruined in some fashion. They affirmed the freedom of the will and of action of the recipient and the impotence of the author. This is the single most important difference from the demand, which negotiated by threatening sanctions against the audience and circumscribing its discretion.

Restoration

The narrative of grievances contained its own justification. It purported to present an ideal or better condition, which was to be restored. The state so described could have been truth or fiction insofar as such statements can at all be valid; but it necessarily aimed to be plausible. It was a form of defending a right or making an improvement on it.

In the case of the landlord serfs, the ideal occasion arose with a succession to the estate. Law and practice were intermeshed; practice, with time, became custom, and therewith acquired the sanctity of law. A succession usually brought a new serfowner with novel ideas about administering the estate. He could be ignorant of the previous owner's practice, or he might choose to repudiate them. He did so either through a strict interpretation of the law or in flagrant violation of it. In addition, he brought with him a new team of bailiffs, clerks and overseers, whose personal dealings with the peasants were of consequence.

Thus the 2,700 peasants of the late Countess Varvara Petrovna Razumovskaia in the villages of Bolshie and Malye Poliany of Lukoianovskii *uezd* in Nizhnii Novgorod *guberniia*, complained in 1826 about the excesses of the new steward, Fedor Ivanovich Zeiman fon Izerskii. They painted a picture of a lost golden age under the late countess when they were never taxed in excess or otherwise troubled.[4] In September 1841 500 souls belonging to Nikolai and Vasilii Chulkov in Gribanovo village in the Volokolamsk and Klinsk *uezd*s of Moscow *guberniia* fixed the year of the fall in 1814 when their previous owner, Major-General Aleksei Evgrafovich Tatishchev passed on the administration of the estate to his serf, Chulkov, the father of the present two owners. According to them, it had been unending misery ever since.[5] Such was the standard pattern.

A succession usually entailed a will which could be disputed by the heirs or peasants or defended against presumed violations. In such cases the peasants demanded restitution of rights that had been promised even if not yet exercised, or sometimes rights that had been permitted informally by the late owner who had then entered them in his will. More often than not, this concerned freedom to the serfs.

In July 1829, peasants of Artemii Ivanovich Kharlamov, of Lugsk *uezd* of St Petersburg *guberniia*, complained for the second time to the tsar that they had been granted their freedom in the will of their late owner, Olimpii Anisimovich Kharlamov, but had been illegally enserfed again by his cousin's illegitimate son, Artemii Ivanovich.[6] In summer 1830 the peasants of the Gradobit' estate in Valdai *uezd* of Novgorod *guberniia* claimed that their previous and late owner, Nikolai Bazarov, had freed them by his will of 1818 but that his brother Aleksei now refused to honour the pledge.[7] In August 1853, the peasants of I. P. Petrovskii of Samarino village (Bolshie Rzhavtsy) of Ranenburg and Riazhsk *uezd*s in Riazan *guberniia* discovered their owner to be illegitimate as their previous owner, Natalia Ivanova Samarina, had died without issue and had granted them freedom in her will; but Petrovskii was none other than her former serf and steward Polit Varlamov Poluekhtov, since freed and with this new name. The case rested on legalities of course, but also on restoring a supposed freedom.[8]

The situation among the state and appanage peasantry was comparable, save that before the reform of 1861 they were obsessed with the innovations by Perovskii and Kiselev, that is, the new land surveys, tax assessments and potato sowing.

In April 1836 the state peasants of the Triputin estate or *starostvo* in Mstislav *uezd* of Mogilev *guberniia* protested against the regime of their new lessee, Major-General Gerngross, by contrasting with the ideal past thus: 'In past times when the peasants of the aforesaid villages lived in tranquillity and possessed good horses', they used to labour six *sokha* a day, but had now reduced it to just four.[9] In August 1846, the state peasants of the Orlov office (*okruzhnaia palata*) of State Domains complained about atrocities committed by troops quartered on them for wanting to be subject to the jurisdiction of the *zemskii sud* as before and not under the *palata* which the Kiselev reforms had introduced for more rational tax assessments.[10] In 1851–2, the appanage peasants of the villages Truevskaia Maza and Iulovskaia Maza in Vol'skii *uezd* of Saratov *guberniia* protested against the new method of tax assessments[11] which led to great losses of allotment and increases of *obrok* compared with what they had enjoyed by the seventh, eighth and ninth revisions.[12]

A vast number of protests concerned status that had been lost or might soon be; such petitions invariably combined the legal argument about status with an ideal past.

In August 1829, 175 male souls, formerly of Aleksandra Nesterova of Kasimov *uezd* in Riazan *guberniia*, petitioned the tsar that they used to belong to the murzas. Following the prohibition on murzas owning serfs, they were to be translated to state peasantry, instead of which they had been enserfed and would soon pass to the Don Cossacks. They based their argument chiefly on their violated status as presumed state peasantry.[13] In April 1830, 5,000 appanage peasants of Urenskii *volost'* in Varnavin *uezd* of Kostroma *guberniia* petitioned against the levy of *obrok* from 1829 on their *kulizhnye* or allotment lands which had been exempted until then. The opening justification presented the idyll in which they had 'lived peacefully, discharged all state obligations accurately, and submitted humbly to our superiors, that is, to the Urenskii *volost'*, which protected us graciously and justly until today.'[14] In April 1837, the appanage peasants of Syzran and Sengileev *uezds* of Simbirsk *guberniia* protested against the new obligation of 'social cultivation' or *obshchestvennye zapashki*. But their argument was vintage traditionalism, thus:

> From ancient times our ancestors, known by ancient usage as ploughing soldiers, and after them we ... peasants of our commu-

nity, living in the town of Syzran in our houses, have taken to commercial and artisanal occupations. We do not and formerly never did carry on peasant agricultural activity, and many of us do not even do any stockbreeding.[15]

After this came the new obligations, which reduced them to ruin.

The argumentation by workers, or those who were now called workers but were in fact industrial serfs, was symmetrical. The occasion and the cause, however, differed. Their idealized past was their life as peasants in agriculture from which they had been rudely plucked to work in factories and mines; they recalled their time in another factory from which they had been shifted; or more prosaically, the higher wages they had once enjoyed. Unlike their posterity, in their own understanding they were not aiming at a better future so much as at the gentler past.

One of the famous examples of the nineteenth century is that of the Osokin workers. They ceaselessly complained, from 1803 until their eventual emancipation in 1847, that their ancestors had come to the Kazan cloth factory as free persons in the first half of the eighteenth century, but had since been enserfed.[16] In February 1805, the assigned, purchased and landlord peasants of the Iakovlevs' Greater Iaroslav Manufactory commenced their petition with a history of their arrival there as free workers from the times of Peter and Anna, when they were paid adequately, unlike now when prices have become exorbitant.[17] On 7 June 1809, the state workers of the St Petersburg Foundry complained of extremely low wages, but explained it by their self-sufficient agriculture at the Lipetskie ironworks on the Lipovka river in Tambov *guberniia*, from where they had been transferred to the Olonetskie plants in 1796, and then on to the St Petersburg Foundry where they were now entirely dependent on their meagre wages.[18] If it was not a deliberate image of a better past, it was a tale of prolonged privation and unheeded complaints such that happier days were to be inferred or were communicated inter-subjectively.

Among workers, the question of rations, wages and work norms was central. Wage claims were always made in the form of compensation for inflation since the original order, usually of the eighteenth century, and never of a demand for better conditions in principle. These should not therefore be confused with modern wage demands, as too much of Soviet historiography has done. Such indexation of values or legal briefs were presented in appropriate detail in many of the petitions already noted above, especially those of the St Petersburg Foundry workers in 1809, of the Iakovlevs' Greater Iaroslav Manufactory in 1805, and as usual of the Osokin workers in 1813 and 1826.

Advocacy

The argumentation on an idealized past was logically related to advocacy. Such a past was legitimate at law, and enforcing the law merely entailed a restoration. The law was a given, it did not need to be enacted. It had been issued by the tsar or under his authority; and the customary law they asserted was presumed to enjoy such imperial sanction because it had not been repudiated during the years of its practice. Custom, the tsar's law and the golden past were a series of propositions whose relations were meant to be internal and logical, not contingent. The detail of legal claims therefore are wholly consistent with the other attributes of the petition.

The telling legal argument regarded status, as would be evident from the examples of demands for restoration. Among landlord peasants it concerned freedom granted or abrogated, or conversion to state peasantry; among the state peasantry, it was to retain their status as such for fear of derogation to landlord serfdom; and among workers, it was to deny their landlord serf status in favour of factory serf (*na zavodskom prave*), possessional, state, or free status. In each case the claim was supported by the equivalent of a lawyer's brief, often in excruciating detail.

But the first explicit or implicit assertion in such petitions was their innocence at law. The petition arose from an infraction of the law; they were at pains to proclaim that they were not the guilty party. This was usually placed at the beginning; but it could also be scattered liberally through the body of the document.

In early 1826, 757 peasants belonging to A. I. Griazev and his daughter, E. A. Filosofova, of Varnavinskii *uezd* in Kostroma *guberniia*, petitioned for reduction of *obrok*; but they began by proclaiming innocence of wrongdoing at law, that they had been paying their taxes properly, and by promising to continue doing so. It was not even a claim to restitution of rights.[19]

The Osokin cloth workers of Kazan, in their long litany of complaints against the lessee, Osokin, in 1803, began by protesting their innocence at law, and even cited the very laws by which they would have been liable. 'We have been properly obedient to the lessee and his agents, and diligent and industrious in our work, lest the provisions of article 5 of the *ukaz* of 7 January 1736 be applied.'[20] In 1817, the workers of the Greater Iaroslav Manufactory had to open by repudiating charges of insubordination, 'we can never be insubordinate; we have been commanded to work at night; we work without insubordination'.[21]

If there were no specific legal points to make, protestations of innocence sufficed. They admitted in principle the legal grounds on which they could be punished, as the Osokin workers did in 1803 or the Princess Belosel'skaia-Belozerskaia's workers of the Iurezan'-Ivanovskie ironworks in Orenburg *guberniia* did in 1,828 about 'Tarakanov, our attorney and protector of innocently perishing 2,500 and more souls'. The management was incorrigibly vicious, 'yet each and every honest one among us strove as always without compulsion to discharge our duties, never were insubordinate to our superiors, and were always submissive'.[22] Batashev's ironworkers in Tambov *guberniia* could even strike at a sensitive point; after cataloguing the atrocities of lower officialdom, they noted that 'by the laws of your imperial majesty, it has been ordered that it were better to forgive ten of the guilty than to punish one innocent'.[23]

If their claims to innocence at law were not always explicit, it was only because the claim was implied throughout, especially in their tearful wails at their extreme misery. They felt obliged to demonstrate that they were not taking unilateral action, still less threatening sanctions against their superiors, unlike what workers later were to do with strike demands. These assertions therefore were equally protestations of loyalty or acts of self-mobilization on behalf of autocracy through its implied commands.

Anger and pity

The petition could not end with an ideal past framed by the positive law of the sovereign or a customary law sanctioned by autocracy: it had to create sympathy. This was to be achieved through a dramatic narrative of wrongdoing and rhetorical appeals to the might and mercy of their sovereign. They were designed to move their superiors to outrage at the injustice and illegality perpetrated in the imperial name, and to dismay at the enormity of the misery and distress endured. They could adduce vast quantities of evidence and of course embroider the facts. The historian today is in no position to establish whether these atrocities had in fact been committed; nor do we need a *Roshomon* to remind us of the futility of the exercise. Our concern is the image the peasants proffered of themselves. Whether these appeals produced that effect is another matter; but they were couched with that apparent intent. The design and the manifest hope of success, not necessarily the eventual result, legitimized the appeal. They were aimed at mobilizing the tsar's affections against his officials and nobles in their own favour, not to challenging him in any respect.

The agony of Countess Razumovskaia's peasants is typical of hundreds of such accounts. When they complained of the steward's excess levies, 300 soldiers descended on the hapless villagers, committed every atrocity that invading soldiers must, and seized all the grain. The peasants were whipped and beaten every day, everyone between the ages of fifteen and seventy was forced to drill, the elderly were left broken in health, and the rest faced starvation.[24] When the appanage peasants of Piskovskaia *volost'* of Sychevka *uezd* in Smolensk *guberniia* dared to present a petition to Nicholas during his progress through Sychevka in 1828, the Kostroma infantry regiment was let loose on them with the usual horrors to follow. In one lot thirty-nine men were shaven and shorn, then another twenty-seven, finally, as a bonus (in the logic of the petition), even the governor arrived to beat them up with his own hand; and now 'so that nobody goes out to petition, they do not issue passes, so that our earnings have dried up and we suffer the most appalling poverty and intolerable burdens and are deprived of even a crust of bread'.[25] In 1837, the Glazenap peasants of Mar'inskoe village of Bogodukhov *uezd* in Khar'kov *guberniia* heaped abuse on their landlord, that 'insatiable serpent' who had tormented them every day of the previous 20–25 years, had not once addressed anyone by name, and had refused to lift a finger when the harvest failed, and so on.[26]

The best points in such cases were made with respect to the physically helpless – the aged, women and children. Thus, in the description of the tyranny of Aleksei Bazarov of the Gradobit' estate in Valdai *uezd* when forty-eight men were thrown into Valdai gaol, others confined to their huts on a bread-and-water regimen for three weeks, and the hayricks confiscated, the cattle, women and children were left to starve.[27] In the summer of 1836, the peasants of the Triputin *starostvo* in Mogilev *guberniia* described how the lessee, Major-General Gerngross, had permitted them to eat only once a day and had driven nursing mothers to work in the fields.[28] In the tale of woe of the 5,000 appanage peasants of Urenskii *volost'*, leading members of their community perished of hunger after arrest by Frolov, the director of the Appanage Office (*udel'naia kontora*); others were beaten up, driven away from harvesting or ridden down by horses; pregnant women, old men and children were assaulted, children were tied up all night, cattle and money were seized, and sixty deputies were thrown into prison; and when they fell on their knees to Turnov, the appanage administration official, he shot at them.[29]

Tearful descriptions of misery substituted for legal claims which were inadequate or impossible. The flow of petitions against excesses fluctuated according to rumours of an impending freedom or even a general emancipation of serfs, which naturally could not be demanded outright.

There were strong rumours in early 1826 that serfs were to be freed; on 12 May therefore an imperial manifesto issued a severe warning against such rumours. It was to be read on Sundays and holidays in all churches, markets and fairs for six months.[30] Between March and May 1826, P. V. Golenishchev-Kutuzov, governor-general of St Petersburg, had to deal with a series of petitions for the freedom supposedly decreed by the tsar. The Gdovsk and Lugsk *uezds* were particularly affected. But, as he noted, a large number of petitions preferred to dissemble by complaining against the excesses of officials and serfowners or about high taxation.[31]

Their case was to be made foolproof by the extreme nature of self-abasement. Petitions began and ended customarily with prostrations appropriate for approaching divinity. They reassured their sovereign, explicitly or otherwise, that they dutifully and patiently waited upon imperial discretion. At this point they did not presume even to press their legal right. In this matter they were constitutionally correct: the tsar's judgement, like that of god, was inscrutable; he was the source of law; and if it were his decision to contradict his own previous law, it was valid as such, and amounted to a new law.

They debased themselves therefore by presenting themselves as singularly unheroic, even cowardly, necessarily passive, incapable as it were of resistance. The petition revelled in the image of fainthearted peasants scampering away like mice. This is how the Urenskii *volost'* peasants portrayed themselves in encounter:

> Driven by such unbearable cruelty and menace, up to 1,000 of us fell on our knees [to request] Turnov to forgive us. But he worked himself up into a frenzy at this and began firing at us from his double-barrelled pistol. He dashed up and down waving a naked sword and ordered the gendarme with the convoy to beat us all up into pulp. This atrocity now compelled us to flee and hide several

days in the woods, leaving our farms untended, our children helpless and all our property at the mercy of the troops and their
leader.[32]

While all this may have done the peasant self-image no good, they certainly inflated that of the tsar. These were clearly no rebels.

This self-image contrasts well with official depictions of them as
violent, uncouth, hysterical and fully mobilized, with even the women
and children in arms against officials performing their duty. Witness
now the official account of these same Urenskii *volost'* peasants:

> At this, the coachmen were ordered to harness the horses. As soon
> as this was done and the officials had taken their places, they were
> informed that the peasants were streaming in to Karpovo village,
> mounted and on foot, armed with stakes. At once the departure was
> halted and the troops were told to dispose themselves around the
> official's residence for the latter's security. No sooner had this been
> done than suddenly at 7 o'clock they spotted the peasants
> approaching the house from all sides, with stakes, cudgels, hooks,
> pikes, rifles (which were fired eventually from near the tavern),
> enormous spades, stakes with stones attached, and staves with balls
> (of iron five pounds or more weights on cords). By this time there
> were more than 500 peasants. They surrounded the house and
> blocked all exits; they howled dreadfully at the coachmen all set for
> departure, 'Don't move, detach the horses.' They screamed at the
> elder, Komarov, who happened to be on the street with them, 'How
> dare you turn up; you were told not to go. We will beat up every-
> one!' And in fact, the most insolent of the lot, Larion Fedotov from
> Karpov village, also called Kobelev, struck him with the staff and
> ball on the chest and spine, which is why he retreated to the house.
> But the rest surrounded Komarov and grabbed him by the collar,
> and abused him in the foulest language, declaring unanimously 'If
> the officials get out we shall deal with them properly, break their
> bones, and shatter the panes.'[33]

The contrast is of black and white, and it is invariable. That the same
events were always painted in opposed colours thus suggests deliberate
image-making on either side to establish guilt and innocence.

One of their favourite arguments concerned women and children
abandoned to fate; but from official accounts it would appear that they
were the dangerous, not the endangered, species. Here is a typical

version, arising from Nikonov's Insar workers in Penza *guberniia* resisting recruitment in 1809:

> Hearing which, the other workers of the factory, without leaving the premises, collected in crowds; and not just the men but even the women, with cudgels and staves, began a riot in great passion.[34]

In 1828, the official account of P. M. Volkonskii's peasants resisting their leaders' arrest in Arkhangel'skii village of Balashov *uezd* ran thus:

> but immediately after the departure of the village constable and his assistants, the bells sounded the tocsin. At once peasants, women, and even children dashed out of their houses, the streets, and the barns, wielding rods, chains, and staves and, yelling wildly, hurled themselves at the ...[35]

In 1828 again, the womenfolk of Turchaninov's workers in Perm *guberniia* were reverted to *barshchina* (the servile labour obligation) for three days a week on the Kuiashskaia estates of the landlord. The women refused on the ground that their men were already discharging equivalent duty. In the official description of the argument, the women,

> running out of the houses into the streets, shouted out to women from many villages gathered there: 'women, do not give up', and all of them, taking leave of their senses, ran down the streets in a demented frenzy, some beating on doors with cudgels and threatening.[6]

The contrasting versions reveal the polemical technique. Either side had to show itself injured, helpless and passive until the final moment, but always as reactive, not active. By their own presentation, they were the objects of social processes, not the subjects or agents of history. Mironov has suggested that this feeling might have rendered their unhappy fate more tolerable.[37] But this is to treat their projections of themselves as 'true' feelings about themselves. It is more illuminating to see it as a deliberate instrument. It is significant that even officials so showed themselves. The self-abasement, the humility, the tales of woe, all belong to the single tactic of rousing the tsar to passion.

The peasants' autocrat

An obvious question is why peasants should have petitioned their class enemy with such futile perseverance. Soviet historiography has routinely explained it as ideology, as 'naive monarchism', as lack of consciousness in Leninist terms, or, with more liberal prejudice, as typical of peasant primitivism. Others, like Daniel Field, have rejected the Soviet version in favour of the objective circumstance of the plenitude of autocratic powers generating the humble petition.[38] But there exists the more obvious objective circumstance of the real success of petitions in sufficient quantity to have warranted faith and hope. Litvak has suggested as much, which Field has rejected for statistical reasons, wrongly in my opinion, both on the ground of statistics and of judgement.[39]

The autocracy undoubtedly rested on the nobility and serfdom, but it was not wooden and unreflecting in the exercise of its powers. It sought to manipulate social groups, as it needs must. The tsar embodied autocracy beyond the mere class interest of landholding and nobility. The autocracy made claims to impartiality, just administration and, most of all, to a direct relation with all its subjects. The tsar was no liege lord in a feudal hierarchy, and the serfs were not bound by homage to their serfowners, still less to the bureaucracy. Officials were servants, and nobles were slaves of the autocracy, as Speranskii famously observed. Power lies in its exercise; and nobles, like bureaucrats, were regularly punished for that purpose. Redress of peasant grievances was one form of it. It yielded the obvious dividend of peasant loyalty also. But more than such simple rationality, the irrational exercise of power, its unpredictable whimsicality which so exasperated generations of liberal intelligentsia, stimulated a deliberately irrational hope in and tortuous intrigue around the throne. It multiplied the rate of manoeuvre by different social interests, among them the peasantry, and it expanded the field of manoeuvre for the autocracy. But it was legitimized by the formal irrationality, in Weberian terms, of imperial jurisprudence, that is, of the tsar's monopoly of power, executive, legislative and judicial, answerable to none on earth and not guided by any predictable principle.

The petition, establishing a direct relation between autocracy and peasant, was useful to autocracy both as an instrument of social regulation and as an expression of Uvarov's novel nationalist ideology. Peasants, however, were not seizing such nationalist initiatives; they were living by an older tradition of outflanking the bureaucracy and nobility to link up with the autocracy. It was a tradition that the autocracy had also constituted and even formalized as a means of social regulation.[40] The results of petitions gave peasants ample ground for hope. Between 1810 and 1884, the Petitions Office received 600,000 petitions from all classes of the population. Twenty-six per cent of these were successful and 6.3 per cent were reviewed by the emperor himself. The flow of petitions provided high authority with insights into realities on the ground and served as additional channels of vertical communication.[41] Such action also cohered well with the new doctrines of official nationality propagated by Uvarov; and the direct relation between tsar and *muzhik* (peasant) corresponded to the vision of the ideal autocracy in communion with the *narod* (people) as seen by Konstantin Aksakov in his dream. Peasant and bureaucrat were speaking different languages and pursuing distinct strategies; but the format of the petition induced an apparent congruence and eased the transition to the modern for the autocracy.

The success of the petition should come as no surprise to the historian, just as it was the hope that sustained these peasants. The heroic contests of the eighteenth century have been investigated in detail and presented in Semevskii's authoritative pages. Thus Catherine II ordered the resumption of Count Repnin's workers to the state in 1769, the *nepomniashchie* workers at Khlebnikov's Krasnosel'skaia cotton factory in 1796, and of the Kopninskaia cotton factory workers in 1794.[42] Semevskii has provided similar graphic accounts of movements at Evgenii Demidov's Avziano-Petrovsk, Sievers's Voznesenskii, Nikita Demidov's Kyshtymsk and Kaslinsk, Shuvalov's Kamskie, Gur'ev's Alapaevskie, and the Vorontsov, Chernyshev and Osokin plants in the middle of the eighteenth century, and the extensive Viazemskii and Bibikov commissions of inquiry, leading to severe strictures on factory owners and penalties for innumerable lower staff.[43]

Unfortunately, petitions have always been treated only as a form of protest, even of class struggle by other means, not as a means of regulation also by autocracy. Therefore, both the tsarist intelligentsia and Soviet scholarship have investigated the grievances at the expense of the results in order to expose the odious despotism that was autocracy. Positive consequences could not possibly have issued from such a source. But occasionally other researches have scrutinized the consequences and meaning of petitions rather than the mere statements within them. These reveal a manipulative autocracy that was flexible in its repression.

In 1923 Iurovskii examined the archives of the Nobles' Deputies Assembly for Saratov after the imperial rescripts of 19 June and

6 September 1826 demanding surveillance on landords' treatment of their peasants. A petition was treated as a serious matter since it was not easy to complain against the nobility, especially as it required absence, which amounted to flight. Generally the police were ready to investigate, the nobility were anxious to maintain standards, and both grew keener with the approach of the abolition of serfdom. It was a difficult squaring of the circle. Landlords were often made to sign promises of good conduct, for which there was no warrant at law, for example:

> I hereby furnish a signed undertaking to the Saratov provincial marshal of the nobility that I shall not harrass my servants [*dvorovye*] or peasants and I shall not permit any domestic harrassment of them. Failing which, I submit myself to investigation as by law prescribed. Saratov, 11 January 1860. Provincial Secretary, Sergei Alekseev, son of Fofanov.[44]

Out of the 198 investigations in the Assembly archives for the period 1826–61, the decisions in favour of peasants were seventy-six, against them only forty-four, while seventy-eight were unclear. Official endorsement of the complaint did not save the peasant from condign punishment; but it is significant that the peasants won their case in more than one-third of the plaints in an entirely provincial situation where the nobility had to judge their fellows. These were not even addresses to the tsar.[45] Nor is the author remotely prejudiced in favour of the nobility as an *émigré* might well have been; this is a Soviet scholar in the first flush of revolution seeking to demonstrate the *ineffectiveness* of imperial reform attempts.

Later research has revealed the frequency with which the autocracy acted. Circulars were issued in 1832 against the harshness of landlords; in 1841 marshals were reproached for poor surveillance of *pomeshchiki*; in June 1842, May 1845 and September 1846 further instructions were sent out to keep a watch on them; and in 1846 for the first time two marshals were removed from office for slackness in this regard. The reports of the Third Section and of the Corps of Gendarmes are replete with accounts of excesses by landlords and penalties imposed on them.[46] Similarly, Varadinov, the chronicler of the Ministry of the Interior, has recorded the frequency with which serfs shifted status to state peasantry at the instance of their owners, and the numerous cases of action against landlords for misdemeanours.[47] The Druzhinin series has published records of many such complaints and of punitive action against landlords. Between the years 1834 and 1845 as many as 2,838 landlords were tried for excesses in twenty Great Russian provinces alone; of these 630 or 22.2 per cent were convicted. Rakhmatullin reproduces Varadinov's figures: for the three years 1836, 1851 and 1853, 848 estates in all of Russia passed under guardianship. Not all action resulted from serf complaints, but these are significant nonetheless.[48] Regional and case studies reveal many more details.

In the late Soviet epoch, Litvak now questioned whether petitions had ever been prohibited. Several laws forbade direct appeals to the tsar and severely punished wrong procedures, but not the actual submission. The Druzhinin series on the archives on peasant movements has noted 876 direct addresses to the tsar for the years 1796–1861. Laws were not enforced, they were highly contradictory, and they were variably interpreted. When the Petitions Commission was set up in 1810 and the Committee of Ministers proposed that direct appeals to the tsar be forbidden, Alexander I minuted that lower instances could not be trusted to redress grievances, which was of course the peasants' most ancient charge.[49] Subsequent enactments made the provisions clearer and easier. A resolution of the Committee of Ministers in 1821 explicitly permitted petitions; in 1835 the tsar assumed direct control of the Petitions Commission; further instructions followed on the formula for the petition. The law could not logically prohibit petitions altogether since they could be patriotic acts of denunciation of treason; the *Ulozhenie o nakazaniiakh* of 15 August 1845, or the Penal Code, prohibited them by article 1909 and allowed them by article 311. Consequently, there are innumerable instances of action against landlords after a petition.[50]

Rational functioning yields rational results sometimes; but irrational operation also is founded on rational calculations. The right hand of bureaucracy may not always know what the left is up to, but they may knowingly differ also. The confusion in Russian legislation suggests such a strategy. A series of laws prohibited direct appeals to the tsar, but petitions were nonetheless accepted in large numbers. Numerous other laws gave detailed instructions on how the petition was to be composed; the *ukaz* of 1767 was interpreted in many ways; the *ulozhenie* of 1845 contained directly contradictory articles; and the law of 21 January 1846 encouraged denunciations of treason. Such confusion provided for the arbitrary exercise of power, not as corruption, but in order to ensure greater subservience and freedom of action through its unpredictability. It is a technique that all leaders understand well: it keeps hope alive among the people, be they noble or peasant.

Beyond rational justice and deliberate whimsicality, the tsar could also appear as the source of inscrutable mercy, which is the supreme and perhaps most ancient form of irrationality in such contexts. Nicholas I resorted to this device thus. During the rumour of 1826 that freedom was imminent, courts martial were ordered on 9 August 1826 to try cases arising out of this dangerous trend. Military units set about their repression, and courts martial discharged their duties with terrifying ferocity. In November 1826, Nicholas permitted governors to reduce the sentences of these courts, and the Senate and governors-general to reprieve altogether. It created an entire cycle of offence, sentence, petition, anxiety and hope, and exhilarating pardon, reprieve, commutation of sentences, and other forms of mitigation from on high. The viciousness of the courts, the gentleness of the governor, and the clemency of the tsar, were lucidly structured. To the peasant, however, it appeared utterly arbitrary at all levels, attributable to the instinct of cruelty and the quality of mercy, with the petition playing a crucial role in remission of sentences. The same cycle went on in many other ways, but not perhaps with the same deliberate clarity.[51]

Peasants hoped, and with justification. Calamities were visited upon them like the scourge of God, and forgiveness dropped like manna from the heavens; serfdom was of the former, and freedom of the latter. The irrationality of their existence made the hope of freedom utterly rational. Freedom meant different things at different times. Soviet scholars have examined the possible meanings and have suggested that until the 1850s it meant change of status, usually the shift to state peasantry, but that towards 1861, especially after the Nazimov Rescript, it meant full freedom. Similarly, they have disputed what peasants meant by demanding land, whether it was that under their own cultivation or also that of the nobility.[52]

But we are concerned here with the rationality of the culmination of all hopes, in freedom to be granted by the tsar, whatever it meant at different times. Those who had been but recently enserfed in the late eighteenth or early nineteenth centuries, expected to get out of it also. This was especially applicable in the ecclesiastical estates of the west, the so-called 'economic' peasants, state peasants in the Ukraine, and workers enserfed to factories.[53] The year 1812 bred many such hopes. In a cruel irony, the Decembrist movement appeared to the peasants as a succession crisis triggered by Grand Duke Konstantin's attempt to free the serfs and the Decembrist officers' conspiracy to foil it.[54] Therefore 1826 was full of expectation. The *ukaz* of 2 April 1842 now permitted landlords to free the *obiazannye* peasants; peasants at once interpreted it as a decree on freedom. Similarly, the law of 8 November 1847 permitted the peasants of an indebted estate the first right to purchase it at auction; again it was treated as a fresh right to gain freedom. There were major movements during the Crimean War on the ground that military service in this war would bring freedom. The law of 31 December 1856, on the procedures to be followed for converting to state peasant status, was at once interpreted as a general invitation to convert to such freedom, and copies of the law sold at high prices on the black market.[55] As late as during the Revolution of 1905, peasants interpreted revolutionary calls for rising as summons from above; courts rejected accusations of instigation on the ground that peasants had assumed imperial sanction; and priests and officials strove hard to block news of the October Manifesto, evidence that traditional peasant suspicion about their mendacity had been well grounded.[56]

Finally, all their naïvety and fortitude seemed justified. For no apparent reason other than his angelic character and the persistence of peasant appeals for justice, the good tsar allowed their most ancient dream to materialize: he emancipated them in 1861. This singular event seemed as incomprehensible to the class enemies, nobility and peasantry alike, as the destruction of both communism and the Soviet Union by the General Secretary himself in our own times has been to the *nomenklatura* and their enemies in the cold war. Only the most tortuous mathematical exercises by latter-day scholars on the profitability or otherwise of serfdom can invest its abolition with such rationality. Certainly none of the interested parties in 1861 could do so. It was divine dispensation. Faith in the tsar did seem amply vindicated; this was the climax of innumerable lesser acts of kindness. Peasants were not making a simple 'mistake', as too often asserted in interpretations of 'naive monarchism'; nor were they in any sense 'correct' in their judgement; but their faith in the tsar was meaningful to them and is intelligible to us without its being right or wrong.

The petition as authored by autocracy

Who wrote the petition? The simplest answer is that it was some petty clerk from a provincial town hired by the peasantry and writing at their dictation. Towns always had dismissed, retired or even serving clerks, soldiers, accountants, school teachers and others who found this a source of added income; otherwise any literate person of humble origin would do so, like the priest or especially the *raznochinets*; there would be the occasional scribbler, autodidact or village philosopher among the peasants, like the *volnodumtsy*, by whom Soviet historiography has been much exercised in the hope of discovering a peasant intelligentsia; and there are many instances of even a landlord or factory owner resorting to this intrigue as a means of ruining his neighbour, rival or foe. The usual model is of the clerk painfully indicting what illiterate peasants laboriously dictated, and putting it into something resembling Russian prose; the end product was then sent up to authority and bequeathed to posterity as the authentic voice of the peasantry and a reliable record of class tension.

The novelist Reshetnikov, in his memoirs composed as fiction, has left us a typical example of the process. The peasants would approach this literate adolescent, a nephew of the impecunious local postmaster, with requests to compose their correspondence. He did so willingly, as a proper *raznochinets*, and they were delighted with him, not only because he charged them only 15 kopecks against the more than double that amount demanded by the other regular document writer, but also that he 'improved' the document considerably. He enforced such improvements as the name of the addressee in proper intelligentsia and bureaucratic sequence of Christian name, patronymic and surname, whereas peasants would 'wrongly' dictate it as Christian name, surname and then 'son of so-and-so', which was in effect the patronymic. The patronymic would appear thus in the last of the series whereas it should have gone into the middle. Such letters always went astray; from his redaction they did not. In sum, he told them what the state demanded and they gladly acquiesced instead of attempting to impose their subaltern culture. As for the contents, they were in the habit of inserting 'useless' greetings to all and sundry. He excised such verbiage. The news they wanted to convey was hopelessly jumbled, both logically and chronologically. He cleared it all up and made it readable and intelligible as a straight narrative. He wrote what they wanted; but his advice on what they wanted and how it should be presented prevailed over their preferences.[57]

Reshetnikov was being ordinarily helpful; he was ensuring the best effect, both for passage through the post and on the recipient; and the peasants were grateful for guidance. In the event, the document had been restructured to suit its audiences, postmasters and peasant relations. Unbeknownst to both the peasant and Reshetnikov, an abstract social and political presence had intervened. The cultural and bureaucratic dictates of the intelligentsia and state, through style and form, had been imposed on the letter and moulded it entirely.

The petition partook of this procedure. The extreme case was of the peasant signing a document placed before him. The typical instance is the deposition in the court martial. Here the prisoner explained his conduct to authority in order to exculpate himself; but he followed a form rigidly prescribed; and it corresponded to the structure of the questionnaire or application form in which the signatory merely fills in the details. Such persons are not authors in any sense of the term; they are at best informants, whether about themselves or about others. The author's freedom of composition and self-expression is expressly denied to the signatory, and no matter considered extraneous by the court martial, or for that matter, the sociologist wielding the questionnaire, is admitted. In effect, it revealed more of the world-view of the court (ultimately, the tsar), than of the deponent.

Faced with such a court during the Karmaliuk affair of 1826 in Podolsk *guberniia*, the peasant Vasil'ev, son of Grits, explained why he had not been energetic enough in assisting his landlord, Ianchevskii, in arresting Karmaliuk. The response began astonishingly, like so many petitions, that he was a good Christian who observed the rituals and had never been tried for any crime, that is, he was innocent of any wrongdoing in general. His reactions had been tardy, he said, only because he was obeying orders, that is, holding the horse outside, while Ianchevskii plunged into the hut where Karmaliuk and his gang were holed up. The next argument also came out of the petition, that he had served his landlord faithfully by dashing in a moment later with another peasant and seizing another of the gang, Dobrovol'skii. In short, he had always lived correctly and had obeyed his serfowner during this encounter. Thus, although a response to an accusation, the defence, in the abstract, stated the ideology of the regime, that of submission to God and the landlord. The deposition of Gariton Romaniuk was almost identical, with names, ages, family details and action different, but otherwise utterly loyal to God and to his landlord.[58]

In February 1829, sixty of the *odnodvortsy* of the Shebelinka settlement of Zmievskii *uezd* of Slobodsko-Ukrainsakaia *guberniia* were mown down for refusing to line up as military colonists. The deposition by one of the main leaders, the twenty-two-year-old Stepan Demin, approximates to the official report by Senator Lt.-Gen. Gorgoli in language and style. It describes the peasant action as a 'riot' (*bunt, vozmushchenie*); that 'all of us began to shout out, by previous agreement ...'; that the priest Petr came to cajole them, the *miatezhniki* or mutineers, into submission or *poslushanie*. The style was as fluent and effortless as that of a *sanovnik*. It condemned the peasants in the manner of an official, not even that of a mutineer betraying his comrades. It was terse, lucid and focused, presenting just the necessary evidence of responsibility. It listed the guilty persons, then singled out those more guilty than others. There was not a trace of the peasant's hand in it, nor even of the *pisar'* or village clerk who officially took it down on account of the deponent's illiteracy.[59] The deposition by the twenty-four-year-old Polikarp Nepochatyi was identical in structure and style. It incriminated the others to the extent of it reading like an official police account; it freely used words like *miatezh* or mutiny and *usmirenie* or pacification: 'They agreed among themselves not to go into the Uhlans. I agreed also and was in the crowd of mutineers [*miatezhniki*] until the pacification [*usmirenie*].' It was equally free with other official terms like *povinovenie* meaning submission and *krichali* or yelled; it was quite as comfortable with pejorative accounts: 'Then ... we hurled ourselves at the Uhlans with spears and began to beat them.'[60]

The deposition at a court martial is perhaps the extreme case of the official account passing for subaltern expression; the identity between the peasant statement and bureaucratic report should now be noted. The diametrically opposed images of peasant action in the petition and report on the Urenskii *prikaz* appanage peasants in 1830 have already been shown. It is now worth re-examining them to discern the remarkable identity of style. They read as if they could have been composed by the same author for the same audience to describe the same events. The differences lay in the salutation, recommendations, requests and endings. The petitioners made prayerful submissions with tearful requests; they threw themselves at the foot of the throne and alter. The report merely used prescribed ritual bureaucratic submissions and conclusions. Each employed a set of code words for the persons, places and events, as shown in the table below.

Petition	Official report
Peasants (*krest'iane*)	Mutineers or rioters (*miatezhniki*)
Meeting (*sobranie*)	Disorder (*besporiadki*) or violence (*buistvo*)
Declaration (*ob'iavlenie*)	Yelling (*kriki*)
Threats (*ugrozy*)	Gentle urging (*krotkie vnusheniia*)
Submissive (*pokornyi*)	Insolent (*derzkii*)
Fled to the woods	Went into hiding in the woods

Similarly, the petition would present the peasants as defending themselves and officials as attacking: attackers would be diabolic tormentors and defenders would be helpless babes in the wood, sometimes literally, and otherwise more like Christians thrown to the lions. In the report, the reverse would be the case: peasants would be attacking hordes of drunken, violent louts, armed with fearful weapons that seem to have emerged from antique myth; and officials would be helplessly rational, conscientiously defending imperial majesty, desperately and as a last resort firing to restore his, the tsar's, order.

Within these coded differences, both described the same range of action in comparably racy narrative styles, especially since both were drafted by virtually the same level of official, and both were addressed to the same superior, but on behalf of two different constituencies. Both have the same structure of rousing anger in the tsar for order violated, laws flouted, a perfect past corrupted, with the supremacy of the imperial will as legitimation. It appears like asking the tsar to mediate between two fractious contestants; and it was not so very obvious who were inferior and superior, with both seeming to want independent hierarchies to the tsar.[61]

In 1844, when the state peasants of Kozlovka village in Borisoglebsk *uezd* of Tambov *guberniia* rioted because the remission of dues announced by the manifesto of 16 April 1841 had not been implemented, the reports by the acting governor, Petr Bulgakov, and the petition by the peasant deputy, V. M. Popov, read entirely alike, in favour of the bureaucratic specimen, of course. Most of Popov's complaints were directed against the *pisar'*, Mikhail Bolovin, who later became the village head or *golova*. Popov's description of atrocities and iniquities was composed in the same colourful style as that of the governor; today it would read like an enjoyable piece of journalism. But more than that, it employed all the code words of officialese, but now against the meanest of officialdom, the *pisar'* or the village clerk. Thus Bolovin's group were called 'conspirators' (*soumyshlenniki*); they 'burst' (*vtorgnulis'*) into his homestead; this provoked a 'noise' or (*shum*); Bolovin then threw himself at Popov 'in a passion' (*v azartnosti*) intending to 'beat' (*bit'*) him, but he was restrained by his neighbours in this 'violent' (*buistvennyi*) conduct; Bolovin harboured 'evil intent' or (*zloumyshlennost'*) towards Popov; he and his gang descended on the village of Kozlovka 'in a thoroughly intoxicated condition' (*sovershenno v p'ianom vide*). It went on in this official style; and only a close look at the document would reveal that this was a peasant account of official attacks on them, not the official version of a peasant riot. The identity with official reportage is uncanny.[62]

The petition followed the prescriptions of the audience in the manner that application forms and lawyers' submissions must. The scribe advised them on the precise case to be made out, the laws to cite in their defence, the extent of hyperbole to be employed, the degree of fiction or exaggeration that would be plausible, and so on until it assumed shape. The most important advice was the issue to be focused. This had to be negotiable or tenable as a case. If peasants wanted freedom, they could not demand it since it was not in the canon; instead they looked for a point at law, and, if nothing could be found, the tyranny of the steward was always a safe bet, since he was not even a *dvorianin*. For these reasons it demanded considerable expertise at drafting; and monographs are full of examples of how so many *raznochintsy* lived by them.[63] There is occasional evidence of bureaucrats doing so in the discharge of their official duties. Thus the Kaluga provincial gazetteer, in its section on the duties performed by sundry officials, records how the *striapchii* in the Department of State Properties 'helped 300 petitioners from among the State peasantry with advice, composing petitions, and by providing information'.[64] In certain cases it could rise to higher levels of authorship, as with priests at the Alexander Nevskii monastery in the first half of the eighteenth century officially composing or certifying them with their own signature.[65]

Those who have had to supplicate understand this process well; and Laurence Sterne has captured the predicament of Russian peasants perfectly. He had to petition the duc de Choiseul at Versailles that he be excused for not having a passport. The problem was not the subject matter so much as the form of the petition, so that it caught the duke's mood of the moment:

Then nothing would serve me, when I got within sight of Versailles, but putting words and sentences together, and conceiving attitudes and tones to wreath myself into Monsieur le Duc de C____'s good graces. This will do, said I. Just as well, retorted I again, as a coat carried up to him by an adventurous taylor, without taking his measure. Fool! continued I; see Monsieur le Duc's face first. Observe what character is written in it; take notice in what posture he stands to hear you; mark the turns and expressions of his body and limbs; and for the tone, the first sound which comes from his lips will give it to you; and from all these together you'll compound an address at once upon the spot, which cannot disgust the Duke – the ingredients are his own, and most likely to go down.[66]

Sterne and Russian *muzhik* were possessed of the same vital insight, that 'the ingredients are his [duke's or tsar's] own, and most likely to go down'. The petitioner was obliged to perform like the courtier; the style was the substance; the courtesy of the aristocrat and the self-abasement of the peasant belonged to the same genre of representing the monarch, not themselves. Only in the rational discourse of bourgeois public opinion did the rationality of the argument, or its substance, assume its autonomy from style and assert its privilege over form.[67]

Not for nothing then did the autocracy legislate upon and prescribe the form and nature of the petition. From the seventeenth century onwards instructions ceaselessly flowed. Only relevant matter was to be stated; it was to be set down in manuscript pages, not in columns; in the early eighteenth century came the order that the day, month and year be shown. The name itself went through numerous changes. The Petrine *Generalnyi Reglament* altered it from *chelobitnaia* to *proshenie chelobitchikovy*, which narrowed the meaning from any form of address to what we now understand by petition. Each emperor or empress issued further instructions on the forms of address and the appropriate contents. Peter III named it simply *proshenie*; Catherine II restored the old term *chelobitnaia*, and then turned to *donoshenie*, so that all three came to be synonymous. For the sake of respectability in Europe, she then ordered the terms *zhalobnitsa* or *proshenie* and that the conclusion should give up the demeaning 'most humble slave' (*vsepoddanneishii rab*) in favour of just *vsepoddanneishii*. The *zhalobnitsa* then became the simpler *zhaloba*. The nineteenth century witnessed the final atrophy of *chelobitnaia* and currency of *zhaloba* and *proshenie* for all types of address to Court, even if it were not a complaint. There were specific instructions on how it should be set out in points sequentially, how all lower instances were to be exhausted before approaching the emperor, yet how denunciations for treason were permitted direct. These contained their usual contradictions also, which have been noted. In 1810 a Petitions Commission was set up to deal with them; and in 1835, the tsar took it under his direct supervision, evidently because he found it sufficiently informative and otherwise useful.[68] There were as many clauses prohibiting petitions as permitting them.[69]

Clearly the autocracy had a purpose in legislating so regularly on this matter. It acted as a summons to faithful subjects to report on the state of the empire, and at least one Soviet scholar in the palmy days of the 1950s has suggested as much, rather baldly:

> The peasantry considered themselves the economic foundations of the state; so they sought to expose, through petitions, the relation

to the peasantry, of landlords, monasteries, local officials, and also the higher instances of government, the Senate and Synod, with the result they resorted directly to the supreme power, – the empress.[70]

This, along with Pushkarenko, argues that it was an imperial instrument of regulation, against the usual Soviet view that it was the only means available of class struggle.[71] An approach to the problem that incorporates the class struggle without being limited by it would suggest how the petition established communication between autocracy and peasantry so that the latter could 'represent' the autocracy, assume it, rather than be merely absorbed or otherwise suppressed by it. The petition was more than just peasant resistance; it was the peasant's attempt to be the subject of history and the autocracy's harnessing of that energy. If the petition was a blank application form distributed by autocracy, it was the peasantry that filled it up, and thereby determined autocracy also.

Notes

1. S. S. Volkov, *Leksika russkikh chelobitnykh XVII veka. Formuliar, traditsionnye etiketnye i stilevye sredstva* (iz-vo Leningradskogo Universiteta, 1974) pp. 11–13.
2. Ibid., pp. 22–30, 71, 92.
3. Ibid., pp. 102–6.
4. Petition to Nicholas I, 21 March 1826, in N. M. Druzhinin (ed.), *Krest'ianskoe Dvizhenie v Rossii v XIX-nachale XX veka* (Moscow, 1961 onward). Each volume deals with a specific period. They will be referred to by the abbreviation *KD*, followed by the period, and the documents by their number in the volume and pages. Here *KD 1826–49*, no. 7, pp. 57–8.
5. Petition to A. Kh. Benkendorf, Chief of the Corps of Gendarmes, 27 September 1841, *KD 1826–49*, no. 140, pp. 406–7; I. G. Seniavin to A. G. Stroganov, director in the Ministry of the Interior, 10 September 1841, *KD 1826–49*, no. 139, pp. 404–6.
6. Petition to Nicholas I, 29 July 1829, *KD 1826–49*, no. 35, p. 137.
7. Petition to Nicholas I, earliest May 1830, *KD 1826–49*, no. 51, pp. 182–4.
8. Petition to Nicholas I, latest 6 August 1853, *KD 1850–56*, no. 49, pp. 152–3.
9. Petition to Nicholas I, 13 August 1846, *KD 1826–49*, no. 99, pp. 310–12.
10. Petition to Nicholas I, 13 August 1846, *KD 1826–49*, no. 181, pp. 541–3.
11. *KD 1850–56*, p. 628, n. 158.
12. M. L. Kozhevnikov, governor of Saratov, report to D. G. Bibikov, Minister of the Interior, *KD 1850–56*, no. 52, pp. 164–5; petition to P. M. Volkonskii, Minister of the Imperial Court, ibid., no. 53, pp. 166–7; Groshev's petition to Perovskii, ibid., no. 56, pp. 182–7.

13. Petition to Nicholas I, before 12 August 1829, *KD 1826–49*, no. 36, pp. 140–2.

14. Petition to *chastnyi pristav*, P. Popov, 30 April 1830, *KD 1826–49*, no. 45, p. 161.

15. Syzran town peasants' petition to assistant director, Syzran *udel'naia kontora*, N. V. Mil'kovich, before 19 April 1837, *KD 1826–49*, no. 112, pp. 335–7.

16. Petitions to V. P. Kochubei, Minister of the Interior, November 1803, 25 June 1807; to Alexander I, 20 January 1813; and to Nicholas I, 20 August 1836, in A. M. Pankratova (ed.), *Rabochee dvizhenie v Rossii v XIX veke. Sbornik dokumentov i materialov* (Gos. iz-vo pol. literatury: 1950 onward). Volumes are by periods, hence references will be to *RD* and the years covered, followed by document number and pages. Here *RD 1800–1860*, no. 3, pp. 123–4; no. 4, p. 126; no. 5, p. 127; no. 162, pp. 556–62.

17. Petition to Alexander I, February 1805, *RD 1800–1860*, no. 18, pp. 164–5.

18. Petition to Alexander I, 7 June 1809, *RD 1800–1860*, no. 37, p. 208.

19. Petition to Nicholas I, before 22 January 1826, *KD 1826–49*, no. 3, pp. 48–9.

20. Petition to V. P. Kochubei, November 1803, *RD 1800–1860*, no. 3, p. 119.

21. Petition to G. G. Politkovskii, the governor, September 1817, *RD 1800–1860*, no. 24, p. 117.

22. Petition to A. A. Boguslavskii, 27 December 1828, *KD 1826–49*, pp. 471, 473.

23. Petition from Unzhensk factory, September 1830, *RD 1800–1860*, no. 149, pp. 506–7.

24. Petition to Nicholas I, 21 March 1826, *KD 1826–49*, no. 7, pp. 57–8.

25. Petition to Nicholas I, 23 November 1828, *KD 1826–49*, no. 33, p. 132.

26. Petition to Nicholas I, 18 June 1826, *KD 1826–49*, no. 114, p. 341.

27. Petition to Nicholas I, earliest May 1830, *KD 1826–49*, no. 51, pp. 182–4.

28. Petition to Nicholas I, 1 April 1836, *KD 1826–49*, no. 99, pp. 310–12.

29. Petition to P. Popov, the *chastnyi pristav*, 30 April 1830, *KD 1826–49*, no. 45, pp. 161–4.

30. *KD 1826–49*, p. 646 n. 21; *Polnoe Sobranie Zakonov Rossiiskoi Imperii*, 2nd series (St Petersburg, 1830–84).

31. P. V. Golenishchev-Kutuzov to Lanskoi, director in the Ministry of the Interior, 5 July 1826, *KD 1826–49*, no. 9, pp. 62–6.

32. Petition to P. Popov, 30 April 1830, *KD 1826–49*, no. 45, p. 163.

33. P. Popov's report, 4 May 1830, *KD 1826–49*, no. 46, p. 166.

34. Moscow Mines Board to Golubtsov, 17 May 1809, *RD 1800–1860*, no. 43, p. 225.

35. A. V. Golitsyn, civil governor of Saratov, to A. N. Bakhmet'ev, governor-general of Nizhnii-Novgorod, Kazan, Simbirsk, Saratov and Penza, 6 March 1828, *KD 1826–49*, no. 31, p. 126.

36. Ekaterinburg lower *zemskii* court to K. Ia. Tiufaev, governor of Ekaterinburg, 12 September 1828, *KD 1826–49*, no. 30, pp. 119–23.

37. B. N. Mironov, *Istoriia i sotsiologiia* (Leningrad, Nauka, 1984) p. 146.

38. Daniel Field, *Rebels in the Name of the Tsar* (Boston, Mass.: Unwin Hyman, 1989) pp. 9–14.

39. Ibid., pp. 16–18.

40. For one of the few Soviet scholars to suggest the autocracy's purpose in encouraging petitions, see A. A. Pushkarenko, 'Krest'ianskie chelobitnye kak istochnik dlia izucheniia klassovoi bor'by rossiisskogo krest'ianstva v feodal'nuiu epokhu', in V. L. Ianin et al. (eds), *Sovetskaia istoriografiia agrarnoi istorii SSSR (do 1917 g.)*, (Moscow, 1968) pp. 168–78

41. B. N. Mironov, *Sotsial'ndia istorria Rossii perioda imperii (XVIII–nachalo XXV.)*, vol. 2 (St Petersburg, 1999) pp. 249–50).

42. V. I. Semevskii, *Krest'iane v tsarstvovanie Imperatritsy Ekateriny II*, vol. 1, 2nd edn (St Petersburg: M. M. Stasiulevich, 1903) pp. 487–508.

43. V. I. Semevskii, *Krest'iane v tsarstvovanie Imperatritsy Ekateriny II*, vol. 1, 1st edn (St Petersburg: M. M. Stasiulevich, 1901), chs 2–6.

44. L. N. Iurovskii, *Saratovskie votchiny: Statistiko-ekonomicheskie ocherki i materialy iz istorii krupnogo zemlevladeniia i krepostnogo khoziaistva v kontse XVIII i v nachale XIX stoletiia* (Saratov: izdanie Saratovskogo Universiteta Narodnogo Khoziaistva, 1923) pp. 150–4, citation pp. 153–4; see also, for rescripts of 19 June and 6 September 1826, M. A. Rakhmatullin, *Krest'ianskoe dvizhenie v velikorusskikh guberniiakh v 1826–1857 gg.* (Moscow: Nauka, 1990) pp. 169–71.

45. Iurovskii, *Saratovskie votchiny*, pp. 159–61.

46. E. A. Morokhovets, *Kreest'ianskoe dvizhenie 1827–1869*, vol. 1 (Moscow, 1931), see *passim* under sections '*zhestokoe obrashchenie*' and its equivalents for each year.

47. N. Varadinov, *Istoriia Ministerstva Vnutrennykh Del*, 8 vols (St Petersburg, 1858–63). These are recorded under an appropriate heading for each year, starting with 1810.

48. Rakhmatullin, *Krest'ianskoe dvizhenie v velikorusskikh guberniiakh*, pp. 33, 168–9.

49. B. G. Litvak, *Ocherki istochnikovedeniia massovoi dokumentatsii XIX-nachala XX v.* (Moscow: Nauka, 1979) p. 273, also pp. 270–2.

50. Ibid., pp. 273–5.

51. Rakhmatullin, *Krest'ianskoe dvizhenie v velikorusskikh guberniiakh*, pp. 168–9.

52. B. G. Litvak, *Krest'ianskoe dvizhenie v Rossii v 1775–1904 gg. Istoriia i metodika izucheniia istochnikov* (Moscow: Nauka, 1989) pp. 179–81; Rakhmatullin, *Krest'ianskoe dvizhenie v velikorusskikh guberniiakh*, pp. 226–38; for the argument that peasants had developed a programme, shifting from mere demands for improvement to a general one for the end of the noble presence, especially of all noble landholding, see V. A. Fedorov, *Krest'ianskoe dvizhenie v tsentral'noi Rossii 1800–1860 (po materialam tsentral'no-promyshlennykh gubernii)* (iz-vo Moskovskogo universiteta, 1980) pp. 148–61; V. I. Krutikov, 'Nekotorye voprosy istorii krest'ianskogo dvizheniia v Rossii v period razlozheniia i krizisa krepostnichestva', in V. N. Ashkurov et al. (eds), *Iz istorii Tul'skogo kraia* (Tula, 1972) pp. 159–69.

53. Litvak, *Krest'ianskoe dvizhenie v Rossii v 1775–1904 gg.*, pp. 150–52; Fedorov, *Krest'ianskoe dvizhenie v tsentral'noi Rossii*, pp. 76–80.

54. I. I. Ignatovich, *Bor'ba krest'ian za osvobozhdenie* (Leningrad and Moscow: iz-vo 'Petrograd', 1924) pp. 39–44.

55. V. A. Fedorov, 'O krest'ianskikh nastroeniiakh', pp. 4–5; Fedorov, *Krest'ianskoe dvizhenie v tsentral'noi Rossii*, pp. 95–100.

56. P. P. Maslov, 'Krest'ianskoe dvizhenie 1905–7 gg', in L. M. Martov et al. (eds), *Obshchestvennoe dvizhenie v Rossii v nachale XX-go veka, tom 2, ch. 2* (St Petersburg, 1910) pp. 212–16, 240.

57. F. M. Reshetnikov, *Mezhdu liud'mi (zapiski kantseliarista)* [orig. edn 1864–5], reprinted in *Mezhdu liud'mi. Povesti, rasskazy i ocherki* (Moscow: Sovremennik, 1985) pp. 184–6.

58. Their respective depositions, 25 June 1827, *KD 1826–49*, nos 14 and 15, pp. 77–9.

59. Demin's deposition, 13 June 1929, *KD 1826–49*, no. 40, pp. 150–2.

60. Nepochatyi's deposition, 13 June 1829, *KD 1826–49*, no. 41, pp. 152–3.

61. *Chastnyi pristav* P. Popov's testimony, 4 May 1830, *KD 1826–49*, no. 46, pp. 165–73; peasants' petition to Popov, 30 Apr. 1830, ibid., no. 45, pp. 161–4.

62. P. A. Bulgakov, governor of Tambov, to L. A. Perovskii, 22 February 1844, *KD 1826–49*, no. 170, pp. 517–18; Bulgakov to Nicholas I, 8 February 1844, ibid., no. 171, pp. 518–20; petition to Nicholas I, 29 March 1844, ibid., no. 172, pp. 520–4.

63. S. V. Dichkovskii, 'K voprosu ob uchastii raznochinnykh elementov goroda v krest'ianskom dvizhenii vo vtoroi chetverti XIX veka', in Ashkurov et al. (eds), *Iz istorii Tul'skogo kraia*, pp. 211–16.

64. M. Poprotskii, *Materialy dlia geografii i statistiki Rossii, sobrannye ofitserami general'nago shtaba. Kaluzhskaia guberniia* (St Petersburg: Tipografiia E. Veimar, 1864) ch. 2, p. 282.

65. D. I. Raskin, 'Krest'ianskie chelobitnye v krupnoi monastyrskoi votchine v pervoi chetverti XVIII veka', in A. L. Shapiro et al. (eds), *Problemy istorii feodal'noi Rossii. Sbornik statei k 60-letiiu prof. V. V. Mavrodina* (Leningrad: iz-vo Leningradskogo universiteta, 1971) pp. 187–8.

66. Laurence Sterne, *A Sentimental Journey* (London: Dent, Everyman's Library, 1962 edn) pp. 80–1.

67. Jürgen Habermas, *The Structural Transformation of the Public Sphere: An Inquiry into a Category of Bourgeois Society* (Cambridge: Polity Press, 1989) trans. Thomas Berger, orig. German edn 1962, *passim*.

68. Litvak, *Ocherki istochnikovedeniia*, pp. 267–75.

69. L. B. Genkin, 'Krest'ianskie zhaloby pervoi poloviny XIX v. kak istoricheskii istochnik (po materialam Gos. Arkhiva Iaroslavskoi oblasti)', in L. M. Ivanov et al. (eds), *Voprosy istorii sel'skogo khoziaistva i revoliutsionnogo dvizheniia v Rossii. Sbornik statei k 75-letiiu Akademika Nikolaia Mikhailovicha Druzhinina* (Moscow: iz-vo AN SSSR, 1961) pp. 164–6 for a list of publications.

70. P. K. Alfirenko, *Krest'ianskoe dvizhenie i krest'ianskii vopros v Rossii v 30–50-x godakh XVIII veka* (Moscow: iz-vo AN SSSR, 1958) p. 293.

71. Pushkarenko, 'Krest'ianskie chelobitnye', p. 174.

6
The Stolypin Land Reform as 'Administrative Utopia': Images of Peasantry in Nineteenth-Century Russia

Judith Pallot

The call in recent years for historians of Russia to show sensitivity to language and semiotics in their research is especially relevant to studying the history of the Russian peasant. Peasants were quintessential 'others' in Russian society; they were an objectified class which was 'spoken for, debated over, represented and categorised, central to any vision of future polity, but excluded from the process of envisioning it'.[1] The historiography of the Russian peasant in the nineteenth and early twentieth century shows that at that time there was no universal understanding of 'peasantry'; rather, it was a category that was ambiguous and contested. In addition to the legal definition of a peasant as a person born into a particular social estate, there were numerous competing understandings of the category that projected a range of personal qualities, and social and political attributes, onto peasants. Educated Russians might be touched by the idea of the peasant as a primordial human being or, alternatively, impatient with peasant 'backwardness', but their imaginings always dramatized the distance between themselves and the peasants. The Stolypin Land Reform was an important moment in this process of 'othering' the Russian peasant.

The competing images of the peasant in the nineteenth century have been explored by Cathy Frierson in her pioneering book, *Peasant Icons: Representations of Rural People in Late Nineteenth-Century Russia*, and more recently by authors in the collection, *Transforming Peasants*.[2] Frierson showed how the search for the peasant's soul gave way under the pressure of enlightenment thought in the last two decades of the nineteenth century to new ways of essentializing the peasant as backward and helpless in the face of overwhelming forces confronting him. These images found their expression in the literary works of Maxim Gorky, Ivan Bunin, Anton Chekhov and in the analyses of the zemstvo statisticians. The picture could not have contrasted more sharply with the comforting images of the peasant as 'man of the land', judge or teacher in the works of Leo Tolstoy and Fedor Dostoevsky. Whereas in these representations peasants had remained spiritually pure despite the victimization they suffered, the late nineteenth-century representations revealed the peasants as degraded by it. Subjugation to the corrosive influence firstly of the feudal landlords and, latterly, of the market had left their mark on the peasants, reducing them to their current state of helplessness and dividing the village into winners and losers – the kulaks and the vast majority of poor peasants upon whom they preyed. It was an extremely pessimistic view, one that did not apparently hold out much hope for the future.

However, there were those in late nineteenth-century Russia who, while accepting unreservedly the backwardness and helplessness of the peasants, were convinced that there was an exit from this state. These were Russia's social reformers, who argued that the peasants could rise above their current problems and take their place as citizens alongside others in tsarist Russia. The precondition for their doing so was the intervention in the village of people with the education and specialized knowledge, as well as the practical means, to show the way forward. In the latter decades of the nineteenth century discussions about rural reform among sections of Russia's educated classes had turned to the need to modernize peasant farming along 'Western' lines.[3] A 'perceptual revolution' had taken place in favour of radical reform, and against the status quo, which formed the basis for the various social and agrarian reforms imposed on the Russian countryside in the twentieth century. These all began from a common standpoint which defined peasants *a priori* as backward and which discounted their initiative and agency. As Dan Field has commented: 'the peasant might be conceived as impulsive, bestial or as vulnerable and innocent. In either event, he required authoritative guidance'.[4] Thus whether it was in the field of education, health care, scientific agronomy or land reform, the agents of change in rural Russia were outsiders. The image of peasant backwardness justified an interventionist approach to the affairs of the village that was to characterize state–peasant relations long into the twentieth century.

Reform programmes, such as the Stolypin Reform, created the context within which new visions of the peasant could be realized. On the one hand, the Reform made the usual assumptions about peasant backwardness and the inability of peasants to progress using their own intellectual resources; but, on the other, it was optimistic about their longer-term capacity for change. This optimism derived in large measure from the Reform's teleology which supposed that all peasants were bound, sooner or later, to follow the path of farm individualization; the state's role was merely to help this 'natural' transformation along in a sort of 'wager on history'.[5] It was thus inevitable that the Reform would challenge the pessimistic understanding of the peasant's capacity for change, substituting in its place a vision of a peasant who was capable of enlightenment and who, under appropriate conditions, could develop into a modern agriculturalist. For the Stolypin Reform's authors, the appropriate conditions were disengagement from the land commune (*obshchina*), land privatization, and enclosure.

The well-ordered landscape

Although it aimed at creating a new type of peasant farmer, the Stolypin Land Reform was not really about people at all. The Reform consisted of a number of rather narrowly drawn technical and legal measures which were necessary in order to effect a change in the manner in which peasants held the land. Laws, passed between 1906 and 1914, gave peasant heads of household in villages throughout Russia the right to take the land to which they were entitled in the commune into personal/private ownership and to seek technical and financial help to reorganize it into fully integrated, or enclosed, farms. Initially, the change was conceived of as a two-stage process; first, the peasants would take their strips in the open fields into personal ownership (*ukreplenie v lichnoi sobstvennost'*) and then, later, they would gather these into an integral unit (*uchastkovoe zemleustroistvo*).[6] Together tenure change and physical consolidation would provide Russia's peasants with the independence and security it was thought they needed to become productive farmers. But the importance attached to these changes was understood by the Reform's supporters to go beyond providing a framework for agrarian improvement; individualization was supposed to have a transformative effect on peasant psyche and behaviour. The Stolypin peasant would be more hardworking and sober than the ordinary village peasant and more inclined to want to innovate.

The farm landscape the Reform set out to implant in Russia would stand in sharp contrast to the 'chaotic' strip fields and common pastures of the land commune. It would consist of a chequer-board of individual farms in which all of a peasant's needs in arable, pasture and meadow would be satisfied within the boundaries of each new farm unit and there would be no call on common lands. The Stolypin landscape was, above all else, a well-ordered landscape. A preoccupation with order was not new for Russia's rulers but the order the Stolypin Reform sought to impose was more concerned with the extension of 'disciplinary' authority over the peasants than with old-style *opeka* (or tutelage). In this respect the Reform was true to the changes taking place more generally in how power was exercised in Russia; through its educational reforms, the collection of socio-economic statistics on the peasants, and the development of social agronomy, the state had been seeking to make peasants more comprehensible and controllable. This was the precondition for their incorporation into 'civilized' society.[7] The land reform project, involving as it did enclosure and separation, recalls Michel Foucault's ideas about the relationship between 'space' and power in the transition to disciplinary authority. 'Disciplinary space', Foucault maintained, avoids collective dispositions and analyses confusion:

> Each individual has his own place; and each place its individual. ... Disciplinary space tends to be divided into as many sections as there are bodies or elements to be distributed. ... Its aim was to establish presences and absences, to know where and how to locate individuals, to set up useful communications, to interrupt others, to be able at a moment to supervise the conduct of each individual, to assess it, judge it, to calculate its qualities or merits.[8]

The repositioning of peasants in space and the reorganization of their land was a means of removing the Russian peasant from the 'confusion and collectivity' of the village with its mass of 'untidy' strip fields and common use resources, communal assemblies and traditions of mutual aid. It was to be replaced by a landscape of physical partition and enclosure in which peasants were physically and symbolically isolated. The iconographic form of these arrangements was the *khutor* landscape of enclosed farms, each a perfect square, distributed evenly over the landscape and connected by a grid iron network of roads. In this schema villages as units of settlement would disappear from rural Russia, their sites becoming little more than distant folk memories.

Farmers in this imaginary landscape would have little horizontal vision, but would themselves be subject to maximum vertical visibility – they would become easily identifiable targets for investigation, enumeration and improvement. This was an arrangement that, following Foucault, was a guarantor of order.

For earlier periods in Russian history, Richard Stites has referred to state-directed attempts to impose order on society through extreme rationalism as the pursuit of 'administrative utopia' by those in power. The utopian dream he describes consisted of:

> a desired order, an extreme rationalism, an outlet for the constructive imagination of organisers who wished to build environments and move or control people like men on a chess board.[9]

He cites as his examples the tsarist police state, the 'parodomania' of Gatchina and Arakcheev's military colonies, and Catherine the Great's utopian town planning, which used 'Western reason, geometric shapes and lines to contain and control people' in the name of production or combat. In its obsession with order and geometrical shape the Stolypin Land Reform was heir to these crude projects of control, but it was more sophisticated than them in its attempt to obtain popular consent to the transformations. Compared with the constant drilling of peasant soldiers on Arakcheev's estates, the Stolypin Reform's methods of achieving peasant compliance with its vision were subtle and varied, employing 'persuasive pressure' and the old art of 'divide and rule'.[10] It was the Reform's 'voluntary' nature, together with various ambiguities in the law, that created a space for the peasants to resist and modify the Stolypin utopia.

The purpose of breaking the power of the peasant land commune over its constituent members was obvious in the land reform project; the change in property rights removed the control the community at large had previously exercised over the distribution of peasant land, while physical separation removed many of the excuses for collective interference in individual peasants' lives. In their turn, these changes would end the need for peasant assembly at the *skhod*. From 1911, under the provisions of the Law on Land Settlement, physical consolidation automatically conferred a change of property rights on household heads withdrawing from the commune, without the need for a separate application for tenure change. This change concentrated responsibility for the reform process into the hands of the new, and new-style, bureaucracy set up to administer the Reform, which consisted of the Chief

Administration for Land Settlement and Agriculture and its 'army of land reform specialists'.[11] It also signalled the partial withdrawal from the reform of the Ministry of Internal Affairs and the land captains, representatives *par excellence* of the old-style *opeka*.

The Stolypin Reform was not merely a reaction against the commune, however. As has been observed above, it was informed by a very clear idea of the new agrarian landscape that was to replace the old. Among the 'texts' that can be read for the utopian character of the Stolypin Land Reform are the circulars and memoranda that passed from the reform centre to local agents (the permanent members of land settlement commissions, land captains and land surveyors) charged with the task of familiarizing the peasants with enclosure and providing them with the technical and legal means to adopt it. Local land reform agents were left in no doubt that the physical separation of peasant from peasant was a priority of the Reform. In a very detailed and precise way they were instructed by the centre in the sorts of changes they were supposed to introduce into the village and what they had to avoid, and how their efforts were to be prioritized. These priorities were codified in an addendum to the Law on Land Settlement of May 1911. This addendum contained a list of enclosed farm types ranked in order of priority, and recommendations about how local agents should deal with a range of problems to do with the partition of land that might arise in specific enclosure projects. Principal among these latter was the fate of common-use resources such as permanent pastures and the untangling of complex patterns of existing land use which made full farm integration difficult to achieve.

Whether the project at hand was the consolidation of individual peasant land involving whole communities (*razverstanie*), or groups of individual peasants (*vydelenie*), the priority schedule for the formation of enclosed farms was as follows:

> Type A *khutor*. This was a farm that approximated as nearly as possible to a square and consisted of a single parcel of land incorporating the house and garden plot with no residual land, such as pastures and meadows, left outside its boundaries;
>
> Type B *khutor*. This was similar to type A in all respects except that it was oblong in shape, with the length of its sides not exceeding the width by more than five times;
>
> Type C *khutor*. This was a farm that consisted of more than one parcel of land in which the house and garden plot were united with

the arable, but some other types of land, such as wood and meadow, were enclosed in separate parcels;

Type D *otrub*. This was a farm that consisted of a single parcel of land, the length of which did not exceed the width by more than five times, that was physically detached from the house and garden plot but located as near as possible to it;

Type E *otrub*. This was similar to type D but consisted of several land parcels detached from the house and garden plot.[12]

The meticulous detail with which these farms were distinguished one from another is indicative of the land reform organization's obsession with classificatory order. Each of these farms was vested with certain attributes which, however minute these might have been when viewed from the perspective of agrarian improvement, nevertheless were important to the land reform project's ultimate aims. The ranking of enclosed farms, for example, reveals the importance the reform organization placed on physical arrangements of land which involved the dispersal of peasants from their native villages. Thus, priority was given to *khutora* which failed to unite into a single parcel all types of farm land – meadow, pasture and arable – over an *otrub* that did achieve such full integration. Arguably, 'scientific agronomy' could be better served by the latter than the former, but what made it less desirable from the point of view of the land reform utopia was its failure to disperse peasants' dwellings. *Otruba*, according to the instructions, were a last resort to which permanent members should consent only when physical conditions made the formation of *khutora* difficult and, then, they should preferably be implanted in new settlements (*otrubnye poselki*) hived off from a parent village, rather than fashioned around the existing settled area.[13] In an early draft of the instructions, the formation of *otruba* other than in conjunction with the founding of a new settlement had, in fact, been excluded from the list of acceptable enclosed farms – a significant omission considering that this was precisely the sort of land reorganization that had dominated the work of local commissions in the proceeding years. The draft read:

If it is impossible to form the first category (of *khutor*), then the second must be formed; but if the second is impossible then the third, and only when none of the enumerated categories of *khutor* can be adopted is it appropriate to resort to the *otrub* settlement system (*posel'kaia sistema*). With this latter system it is better to have as few households as possible in the settlement.[14]

The priority accorded to *khutora* was affirmed by the fact that among all types of enclosed farms, it was only *khutora* that were fully protected in law against further reorganization of their lands in future land settlement projects.

The instructions sent to land reform agents in the localities did not stop at distinguishing between different general types of farm. Local agents were also apprised of the desirable shape and configuration of land on the new farms; no angle on a farm boundary, for example, should be less than forty-five degrees, and the length-to-width ratio of each farm was not to exceed 5:1. The preferred position of the peasant's hut was even a matter for recommendation; it was to be in the centre of the *khutor*, 'so that the farmer's wife can call her husband for lunch'.[15] This was social engineering on a grand scale – no longer were peasants to take lunch together in the fields, they were to return home to their wives. The method of dividing commons by substituting one type of land use for another was also a matter for central direction. Where such substitutions proved impossible, local land reform agents were instructed that dividing the commons into discrete parcels, one for each household, was preferable to leaving them in collective use. In 1915 P. P. Zubovskii, recently promoted to head the Reform, was arguing that it was better to postpone a land settlement project than allow peasants to keep any land in common use.[16] Zubovskii's predecessor, A. A. Rittikh, was more inclined to compromise with peasant wishes if they resisted the division of pasturelands, but even so he urged his local agents to divide the commons whenever circumstances dictated that this was possible.[17] The retention of land in common use was believed by some in the reform organization to provide a 'breeding ground for ideas about communal use'.[18] The language of this objection provides an interesting example of the way in which communal landusership, like communal living in the village, was conceptually linked to the spread of disease.

The elaboration of the details of the *khutor* landscape was in large part the brainchild of A. A. Kofod, a naturalized Dane who became head of the Reform's inspectorate. It was he who drafted the instructions about land settlement 'technique' for local commissions. Kofod's influence on the Reform organization must not be exaggerated but his appointment as the chief inspector for the Reform was an important moment in cementing the administration's commitment to its utopian vision of a *khutor* landscape. Kofod's authority on the 'technical' side of land consolidation was deferred to by everyone, even though occasionally he was ridiculed for his 'liking for squares'.[19] Kofod was the author of official texts on the Reform designed for a variety of audiences ranging from peasants, to educated society, to foreign dignatories. One of his influential texts was *Khutorskoe razselenie*, which was commissioned by the Chief Administration for Land Settlement and Agriculture in 1907.[20] The pamphlet was produced in half a million copies in Russian, Lithuanian and Tatar and was distributed to all provincial and district land settlement commissions to be made available to peasants. References to the pamphlet in local and national newspapers and other official publications confirmed it as the main source for the public and members of the reform organization on the landscape changes the Reform was seeking to achieve. *Khutorskoe razselenie* contained a clear statement of the Land Reform's priorities. In it Kofod produced a carefully argued case against what he referred to as 'defective' and 'inferior' land consolidations. These included the star-shaped arrangements and longitudinal *khutora* that he had observed in his earlier investigations of the western provinces, where peasants had enclosed their land without uprooting themselves from their villages.[21] Significantly, these 'defective' consolidations were the product of the peasants' own, 'spontaneous', attempts to enclose their land. To Kofod and his peers they spoke of the necessity for specialized land surveyors to be involved in enclosure. Kofod retained the reputation as the authority on all matters to do with the technical side of land consolidation through his publications and public appearances. Furthermore, his vocabulary was internalized by the reform administration – even with those who were doubtful about the possibility of implanting the *khutor* landscape – employing terms such as 'perfect', 'correct' and 'defective', and 'inferior' and 'incorrect' to refer to configurations of farm land.

The *khutor* landscape was unrealizable. In the event, the majority of farms that came into being under the terms of the land settlement legislation corresponded to the lower priority types of farm: *otruba* with incomplete integration of land uses and with their peasant proprietors remaining in their native villages. This departure from the model has suggested to some historians that the Reform administration was not really serious about breaking up the commune and implanting *khutora*; once it was understood at the centre that peasants would not move on to *khutora*, the administration jettisoned the idea and let itself be guided instead by peasant preferences for a more limited land reform.[22] There is some force to the argument that the limited restructuring of peasant farms that resulted from the Reform's operation in rural Russia was the product of some sort of compromise between peasants and the state, but this does not constitute evidence of the centre's abandonment of its utopian vision, or its acceptance that the peasant knew better than the experts what constituted a rational farm structure. The compromises that were made in the localities were often wrung out of the local commissions by peasant resistance, or they were concealed from the centre. The most the Chief Administration for Land Settlement and Agriculture was prepared to concede publicly was that the sequencing of changes on the ground was different from planned. It acknowledged that *otruba* were being formed rather than *khutora*, but this had to be set against the fact that overall numbers responding to the Reform far exceeded expectations. The conclusion the Reform administration drew from this was that the mass of the peasantry had been successfully converted to the idea of enclosure but that their understanding was not yet sufficiently advanced to see the need to disengage from the village – hence their preference for partially enclosed units. In time, and with experience of more independent farming, they would come to realize the benefits of rejecting the vestiges of communal practice. Accordingly, *otruba* were re-theorized as an intermediary stage in the formation of *khutora*. Boris Iurevskii, one of the publicists for the Reform, claimed to have found proof of a progression from *otrub* to *khutor* among farmers in Khar'kov province who, a few years after the initial enclosure of their land, began moving their houses and farm buildings onto it. This constituted,

> the best indication of the point I have made several times: that, so long as there is sufficient water, *otrub razverstanie* is only a transitional step towards full *khutor* dispersal.[23]

Kofod, similarly, presented 'proof' of the transitional nature of partial enclosures in examples of post-enclosure divisions of common pastures and in other examples of the spontaneous transformations of *otruba* into *khutora*.[24] By 1916 the representation of *otruba*, and other departures from the model *khutor*, as intermediary forms of enclosed farms was firmly entrenched in official discourse.

Reform advocates, despite the theoretical adjustments made to the sequencing of enclosure, were never wholly comfortable with *otruba* and felt bound to explain and excuse them. Thus, *otruba* invariably appeared in reform literature accompanied by an explanation for why, in the circumstances of the particular enclosure project, it had not been possible to form *khutora*. In the southern arid provinces, for example, *otruba* were explained away by the unsuitability of hydrological conditions for settlement dispersal. Elsewhere in European Russia, other explanations had to be found.[25] For example, in Smolensk province the domination of *otruba* among enclosed farms was attributed to the peasants' involvement in subsidiary employments which had resulted in their lack of interest in farming.[26] Had the peasants been more committed to farming, the implication was, they would have chosen *khutora*. There was a host of other reasons given for the failure to form *khutora* including the catch-all 'cultural backwardness' and 'unfounded' fears of isolation. Peasant backwardness was thus put to the service of explaining problems that arose during the course of the Reform's implementation; this was obviously preferable to the alternative of having to concede that there might be flaws in the original model. Whether the centre believed its theory or whether it was merely employed to keep critics of the Reform at bay, *khutora* remained the symbol of the Reform and of its agenda of division, separation and partition.

Exhibiting the reform

To counter opposition claims that the Reform was failing and to try to convince sceptics in government, the Chief Administration for Land Settlement and Agriculture engaged in a considerable effort to publicize its achievements. It produced popular publications, staged lectures and public exhibitions, in addition to encouraging regular coverage in pro-Reform newspapers. This public record of the Reform was a celebration of science, measurement and bureaucratic efficiency. The messages it sought to convey were usually clear-cut and unambiguous and, in this respect, it differed from some other contemporary representations of the peasantry. Lewis Siegelbaum, for example, has found that exhibitions of peasant handicraft industries which took place at the turn of the century were imbued with a sentimental nostalgia and contained 'mixed and even conflicting messages' about Russia's encounters with modernity.[27] Not so the exhibitions and other representations of the Stolypin Land Reform. They were uncompromising in their rejection of the past and enthusiastic in their acceptance of modernity. The visitor to land settlement exhibitions and readers of popular literature on the Reform were left in no doubt that the agrarian future of Russia lay with a Western-style, individualized system of farming and not with the archaic communal forms that still dominated the Russian countryside. They were also left in little doubt about the pivotal role of professionals and specialists in the rural transformation.

These emphases in representations of the Reform were particularly obvious in the enclosure exhibits which, from 1909, were regularly included in regional and national agricultural shows. In August 1910 the Reform administration was presented with an especially prestigious venue in which to exhibit its work when it was invited to participate in the exhibition celebrating the bicentenary of the founding of the Tsar's summer palace at Tsarskoe Selo. The Chief Administration for Land Settlement and Agriculture's exhibit was contained in a pavilion and on an adjacent open-air lot. Exhibited in the pavilion were diagrams and charts of enclosed farms, scale models of *khutora* (not *otruba*), plans of villages before and after consolidation, photographs illustrating how peasant huts could be moved without having to be dismantled, land surveyors' equipment and a library, which exhibited, among others, the Tatar translation of Kofod's *Khutorskoe razselenie*.[28] The lot next to the pavilion was given over to a life-size replica of an 'authentic' *khutor* and officials of the St Petersburg province land settlement commission were on hand to answer the public's questions. A *Novoe Vremia* reporter at the exhibition noted with satisfaction the 'quality' of these men; they were, 'young, fresh, strong with the sun-tanned faces of people who spend their working life in the open air', people who 'have the contented air of the pioneers of a great era'.[29] Visitors to the exhibit were able to see that it was these people, together with their scientific instrumentation, who were the agents of land consolidation, rather than the peasants.

However, one peasant did intrude and spoil what would otherwise have been one of the administration's finest hours, when a reporter from the opposition newspaper *Rech'* revealed the 'truth' behind the pictures on display. The reporter wrote of a visit he had made to one of the *khutora* exhibited in plans and a scale model on which, according to the exhibition publicity, a four-field rotation had been established. A visit to the site had revealed a different reality. Peasant Rokko's house had no roof, he was carrying out no rotation on his land and had abandoned attempts to dig a well because he ran into rocks. Thus alerted, the *Rech'* reporter took his investigations further and alleged that he had found similar discrepancies in the case of six other exhibits.[30] The story of Rokko's *khutor* ran for some time in the national press. The Tsarskoe Selo land settlement commission was forced to issue a public defence; the exhibit, it claimed, was only of its *projected* work with Rokko's farm, a case that was difficult to sustain as the caption at the exhibition had read 'completed'.[31] A more ingenious defence came in *Rossiia*, which argued that it was the land settlement commission's modesty that was at fault:

> if the Tsarskoe Selo commission should be criticised for something it is for its excessive modesty. Usually at exhibitions the very best examples of things are shown off, but the local commission decided against just showing the best *khutor* knowing that, compared with it, others in the exhibition would have no chance of winning the Emperor's prize.[32]

An important aim in the representation of the Reform was to show how enclosure in Russia was part of a Europe-wide process of agrarian change. At Tsarskoe Selo, one of the exhibits compared the area of enclosed farms in Russia with that in other countries, while histories of enclosure pointed to its diffusion into Russia through the western borderlands or from the Baltic states. Western audiences could be linked to the Reform in Russia through bilingual publications or by being invited to view progress on the ground. On one notable occasion in 1911 the Chief Administration for Land Settlement and Agriculture organized a tour of enclosed farms for a large party of visiting Germans. The party consisted of 104 people and included, on the Russian side, a provincial governor, twenty-four judges, three directors from the Ministry of Land Settlement and Agriculture, nine professors and thirteen district marshals. The party first visited Khar'kov province where, setting out in seventy-five carriages, it had a five-hour excursion to see *khutora*, the whole party decanting from their carriages at various points to take refreshments and ask questions. The party was also taken to Moscow and Tver provinces and treated to a lecture by Kofod with slides of *khutora*. Boris Iurevskii wrote up the trip in the most positive terms; the visitors, 'were beside themselves with wonder', at the 'amazing results that had been achieved in three to four years'.[33]

The year 1911 was also the year in which the Chief Administration for Land Settlement and Agriculture produced the first anniversary volume of its work.[34] It contained statistical tables which, as in the administration's annual reports, were a record of the Reform administration's efficiency in processing applications for enclosure and other land settlement works. It did not include any socio-economic data on the households involved in the Reform, an omission which, together with its failure to include a breakdown of types of enclosed farms, was to excite opposition criticism. As in the Tsarskoe Selo exhibition, plans showing the disposition of land in a sample of villages before and after land settlement work were included in the anniversary volume. These plans were to become a familiar feature in representations of the Reform. Their purpose was to give the reader the opportunity to 'see' for him- or herself the radical changes being effected in the village by the juxtaposition of plans of unreformed and reformed villages. The comparisons were dramatic. 'Before' plans showed the multiplicity of strips dividing the open fields, with the land of one peasant farmer shaded to enable the reader to count for him- or herself the number of parcels in which the peasant's land was held. The *khutor* landscape of the 'after' plans was altogether more tidy. They showed the orderly partition of land into near square farms, including the one belonging to the peasant whose strips were shown on the 'before' plan. In addition to these plans, the 1911 volume included some photographs which confirmed the 'authenticity' of the plans. One pair of photographs of adjacent fields, simply labelled as belonging to a *khutorianin* and an ordinary peasant farmer, was designed to convey a clear message about the efficacy of the Reform. In the first photograph, the land has been recently cleared of stones (these are piled at the edge ready for carting away) and is grazed by healthy-looking cattle; but in the second, the land is strewn with stones and has a thin grass cover and there are no grazing cattle. Since the caption to the photographs did explain the reasons for the difference, it must be assumed that the authors thought that this would be readily understood by the reader to be a consequence of adoption of the Reform; what precisely enclosure did to bring about these changes, evidently, did not need spelling out. Interestingly, and perhaps inadvertently, the family groupings shown in the photographic representations of enclosed farms, contained a message of the continuing relevance of the household unit to *khutor* farming, even though enclosure involved the transfer of sole ownership to the head of household. This was one of the few examples of ambiguity in the messages contained in representations of the Reform.

The Stolypin Reform's critics were scathing of the 1911 publication. *Russkoe Bogatstvo* accused the Chief Administration for Land Settlement and Agriculture of using it simply to show pictures of 'perfect *khutora*' and it likened the village plans to pictures in a child's story book, with the comment:

> But these are not pictures in a child's story-book – they are, as a matter of fact, produced by a ministry in charge of one of the most important branches of the national economy which purports to be

giving an account of the results of four years' hard work undertaken in order to effect a full-scale revolution in this branch of the economy. ... But this publication looks as though it has been produced exclusively for government juveniles.[35]

The substance of the criticism was sound. The plans, in all probability, were of idealized distributions, with even the 'before' plans looking suspiciously symmetrical. Paradoxically, the pattern of strip use, as distinct from theoretical entitlement, was often even more 'chaotic' in the unreformed village than shown in these representations.

The criticisms of how the Reform was reported did not abate and they clearly rankled the authorities. Omissions in reporting of the Reform fuelled the suspicion that the Chief Administration for Land Settlement and Agriculture was withholding something. This suspicion was given force by the results of surveys of enclosed farms carried out by the *zemstva* and other independent authorities which began to appear from 1908–09, some of which called into question the Reform's benefits to the mass of the peasantry. In response, the Chief Administration for Land Settlement and Agriculture decided to make its own survey of enclosed farms and to include in this comparisons of their performance before and after enclosure. Twelve *uezdy* were chosen for the survey, which was intended as the most comprehensive of enclosed farms to date. The results were published in 1915 in a volume designed for popular consumption. It consisted of statistical tables, colourful graphs and diagrams, comparative plans, and locational maps of enclosed farms and agricultural extension services.[36] The volume was notable for its repeated affirmation of two of the Reform's central tenets; that the configuration of the land, not the amount of land or size of labour force a farm possessed, was the principal determinant of a household's well-being, and that among all the possible ways of holding land, the *khutor* was the best. General economic data about the sample of households was displayed not, in the zemstvo convention, by size of sowings, total land area or livestock numbers, but by the degree of consolidation and separation that had been achieved on the sample farms. In other words, a similar classification was used as in the technical instructions with farms divided into different types of *khutor*: those that had involved peasant households moving out from their villages and those formed by land being gathered in around an existing dwelling site – *otruba* and *otrubnie poselki*. The tables showed *khutora* to be consistently out-performing *otruba* and ordinary peasant farms; here was 'proof' of the relationship between enclosure and agrarian advance. The survey thus could be presented as contradicting the opposition argument that it was their superior command over resources compared with other farms that explained the *khutora*'s success. In reality, it was difficult, even using its classificatory scheme, for the authors of the survey to disguise the fact that *khutora* were, on average, larger and better resourced than other types of farm.

Stolypin's farmers

It has already been observed that the peasant was absent from much of the discourse surrounding the Stolypin Reform. When peasants appeared in Land Reform narratives, it was generally as the grateful recipients of progress and enlightenment. Typically, the permanent member of the land settlement commission arrives in a village and gives the assembled peasants the good news that they can leave their commune and set up individual farms and he explains how, with modern surveying equipment, a precise, and equal, division of land can be achieved. At first the peasants are sceptical, but among their number there are those who recognize the importance of the specialist's words and determine to follow the path of agrarian improvement. Other peasants are eventually won over to the idea, sometimes by argument and sometimes by the example of the first 'separators', and the idea of enclosure spreads to embrace the whole community and, then, on to its neighbours. A metaphor frequently used to describe the peasants' reception of the Reform was of their awakening from a deep slumber. One popular publication on the Reform directed at the St Petersburg audience, *New Agrarian Russia – Essays on Land Settlement*, opened with a cameo sketch of enclosure in one village which was entitled *The Awakening Village*.[37] The title, of course, was a play on A. I. Shingarev's well-known 1902 publication, *The Dying Village*, which had painted such an affecting and dismal portrait of the Russian village.[38] In *The Awakening Village* we encounter one of the few peasant agents of change in the popular representations of the Reform. The narrator describes how in one village in Zhitomir province a single progressive peasant won his neighbours over to the idea of enclosure by lecture and example: 'one peasant, a clever and energetic *muzhik*, gets up at sunrise and, having led out his cattle to the fields, sits beside his hut and delivers whole lectures about land settlement'.

The peasant in Zhitomir province was one of the 'sober' and 'strong' upon whom Stolypin had placed his 'wager'. Although Soviet historians interpreted Stolypin's words as a 'wager on the *kulak*', it is accepted now that this was not the intended meaning. Stolypin's strong and sober peasants were precisely that; they were peasants who had energy sufficient to carry through the transformation of agriculture, an important precondition for which was that they did not participate in village drinking bouts. According to the Reform mythology, these peasants could be drawn from any social class in the village, so that whenever they were described it was invariably in terms of their personal attributes, such as energy, sobriety, vigour and independence of mind, and not in terms of their class position. To have located the peasants coming forward to take up the Reform in a particular socio-economic group would have contradicted the myth of the Reform's universal appeal and relevance. The link between the Stolypin Reform and temperance has been recently explored by Stephen Frank.[39] It was not simply that the sober peasants were those most likely to respond to the Reform, but that the life on an enclosed farm was supposed to engender a new, sober lifestyle. According to some contemporary observers, the changes in peasant character could be accomplished remarkably quickly. Boris Iurevskii in *Rossiia* assured his readers that an immediate effect of transferring on to *khutora* was that the peasants were more inclined to religious reflection and less inclined to drink.[40] However, it was more consistent with society's view of peasant backwardness that the realization of the peasant as citizen, modern agriculturalist or upstanding individual, would follow some time after enclosure. Just as the mid-nineteenth century portrayal of the peasant as a 'rational man of the land', in the works of G. I. Uspenskii and A. N. Engelgardt, had argued that the peasant was the product of the natural environment, the Stolypin farmer was the product of a refashioned, human-made landscape.[41] The peasants' transformation into modern agriculturalists would, in most cases, have to await the physical recasting of the landscape.

By far the most celebrated of the strong and sober peasants was Sergei Semenov.[42] Author of numerous writings on the agrarian question, Semenov wrote a personal account of his attempt to set up an enclosed farm.[43] Semenov was the embodiment of enterprise and progress in the peasantry. He was determined to try to rise above the 'darkness' of the village and to embrace the opportunities offered for improvement by the Stolypin Land Reform. He tried to persuade his co-villagers to consolidate their land but when their ignorance and 'fear of learning' defeated him in this task, he determined unilaterally to withdraw his land from the commune. He and his family suffered various privations as a consequence – his children were debarred from school, his livestock were denied access to the communal woodland and pasture, and his wife was beaten. It took two years for Semenov to set up his new farm, which was located on poor scrub land on the periphery of the village. Nevertheless, Semenov soon turned the tables on his former neighbours; his became a model farm with yields double those in the village. Semenov's account of his experiences is an example of the heroic genre in Reform narratives. Peasant Solovev's story, recounted in a Tver agricultural journal, is another example:

> When I applied to secede, the *muzhiki* shouted and made a din but all the same I would not back down. I agreed to take any land whatever it was like only it had to be in one place ... in the end I received it, stuck out of the way in a corner, of worthless quality; much had been cropped year in, year out with flax and had finally been completely abandoned, and needless to say it had never seen an ounce of manure. This was the best part of my holding, the rest, more than half, was covered with stones and every type of weed imaginable ... the commune would not give me any meadow land and it refused to take my livestock into its herd on the commons, and pasturing them on my *otrub* was very difficult.[44]

Despite these privations, Solovev persevered and within a few years had established a multiple-field rotation on his farm and was doing well.

The description of the people who opposed progressive peasants such as Semenov and Solovev is significant for its denial of systematic opposition to the Reform. The failure of enclosure to catch on in most provinces was publicly attributed to the work of a varied but predictable cast of saboteurs, even though in internal memoranda, officials often admitted that the peasant 'backwardness, ignorance and complete lack of understanding about a more rational way of doing things' was preventing the Reform spreading.[45] The cast list of the Reform's villains was predictable and included students, clerics, left revolutionaries, teachers, doctors, veterinary doctors, black shirts, Jews and the right nobility from outside the village, and women, the elderly, children, *zakhvatchiki*, *kulaks*, 'steppe wolves', lower ranks of the police, commune officers and the landless, from within. While there was some mileage to be gained by showing how a determined sober peasant could overcome the dark forces symbolized by these opponents of enclosure, the Reform administration was generally at pains to present adoption of the Reform as unproblematic. It was, precisely, an absence of drama that characterized most official representations of the Reform.

The Stolypin Reform did not succeed in transforming the physical landscape of rural Russia and, probably, made even less headway in transforming the peasant psyche. But the assumptions upon which it was based about the state's guiding role in agrarian change and the pursuit of order through the intervention of specialists, survived. Under pressure from the Ministry of Finance, which had always opposed expenditure on land reform, the initiative for agrarian modernization passed from the Chief Administration for Land Settlement and Agriculture to the *zemstva* and their programmes of agricultural aid and peasant cooperatives.[46] However, this was more a shift in emphasis than a paradigmatic change because, just like the Stolypin Land Reform, social agronomy sought to achieve the transformation of the peasantry through the introduction of agrarian progress 'from above'. It was a paradigm that, in obvious ways, appealed as much to Russia's revolutionaries as it did to the members of the tsarist government.

Notes

1. Yanni Kotsonis, 'How Peasants became Backward: Agrarian Policy and Co-operation in Russia, 1905–1914', in J. Pallot (ed.), *Transforming Peasants: Selected Papers from the Fifth World Congress of Central and East European Studies* (Basingstoke, 1997) p. 16.
2. Cathy A. Frierson, *Peasant Icons: Representations of Rural People in Late Nineteenth-Century Russia* (Oxford, 1993); Pallot (ed.), *Transforming Peasants*.
3. D. A. Macey gives a comprehensive account of the early theorization of the land reform in the last decades of the nineteenth century in D. A. Macey, *Government and Peasant in Russia, 1861–1906: The Pre-History of the Stolypin Reforms* (Illinois, 1987).
4. Daniel Field, *Rebels in the Name of the Tsar* (Boston, Mass., 1976) p. 213.
5. David A. J. Macey, 'A Wager on History? The Stolypin Agrarian Reforms as Process', in Pallot (ed.), *Transforming Peasants*, pp. 149–73.
6. There was another procedure possible under the reform, *gruppovoe zemleustroistvo*, which involved the reorganization of village lands without the holdings of individual peasants being enclosed or title to them changing. Group land settlement was understood in the reform theory as constituting an intermediary step in the progression towards individual farms in parts of the country where village lands were intermingled with each other or with private land. It was not understood as an end in itself.

7. See M. R. Echlin, 'The Statistics of the Russian Peasant in the Nineteenth Century: A History', unpublished D.Phil thesis (University of Oxford, 1990); B. Ekloff, *Russian Peasant Schools: Officialdom, Village Culture, and Popular Pedagogy, 1861–1914* (Berkeley, Cal.: University of California Press, 1986); Y. Kotsonis, 'The Agrarian Question in Russia: Agricultural Cooperatives and Social Integration, 1861–1914', unpublished Ph.D. thesis (New York: New York University Press 1995).

8. Michel Foucault, *Discipline and Punishment: The Birth of the Prison* (London, 1987) p. 143.

9. R. Stites, *Revolutionary Dreams: Utopian Vision and Experimental Life in the Russian Revolution* (Oxford, 1989) p. 19.

10. J. Pallot, 'Did the Stolypin Land Reform Destroy the Peasant Commune?', in Robert B. McKean (ed.), *New Perspectives in Modern Russian History: Selected Papers of the Fourth World Congress of Slavonic and East European Studies* (Basingstoke, 1992); P. N. Zyrianov, *Krest'ianskaia obshchina Evropeiskoi Rossii, 1907–1914 gg.* (Moscow, 1992).

11. For a discussion of the administrative organization of the Reform, see G. Yaney, *The Urge to Mobilize: Agrarian Reform in Russia, 1861–1930* (Urbana, 1982) pp. 367–79.

12. J. Pallot, '*Khutora* and *otruba* in Stolypin's Program of Farm Re-organisation', *Slavic Review*, vol. 42, no. 2 (1984) pp. 242–5.

13. Rossiiskii Gosudarstvennyi Istoricheskii Arkhiv [hereafter RGIA], *fond* [*f.*] 408, 1909, *opis'*[*op.*] 1, *no.* 116, *list*[*l.*] 441.

14. RGIA, *f.* 408, 1909, *op.* 1, *no.* 116, *l.* 214.

15. RGIA, *f.* 408, *op.* 1, *no.* 272, *l.* 61.

16. RGIA, *f.408*, 1914, *op.* 1, *no.* 518, *l.* 14.

17. RGIA, *f.* 408, 1911, *op.* 1, *no.* 161, *l.* 12.

18. RGIA, *f.* 408, 1909–10, *op.* 120, *no.* 19.

19. This remark originated with B. D. Brutkus in a seminar at the Imperial Free Economic Society, when Kofod addressed academics on the land reform. *Trudy vol'nogo ekonomicheskogo obshchestva*, 1–2 (St Petersburg, 1900) p. 50.

20. A. A. Kofod, *Khutorskoe razselenie* (St Petersburg, 1907).

21. A. A. Kofod, *Krestianskie khutora na nadel'noi zemle*, 2 vols (St Petersburg, 1905).

22. Yaney, *The Urge to Mobilize*, is the strongest advocate of this position.

23. Boris Iurevskii, *Chto dostignuto zemleustroistvom* (St Petersburg, 1912) p. 20.

24. A. A. Kofod, *Russkoe Zemleustroistvo* (St Petersburg, 1914).

25. See, for example, the long list given in *Zemleustroistvo, 1907–1910* (St Petersburg, GUZiZ, 1911) p. 42.

26. Iurevskii, *Chto dostignuto zemleustroistrom*, p. 20.

27. Lewis Siegelbaum, 'Exhibiting *Kustar* industry in late imperial Russia/Exhibiting late imperial Russia in *Kustar* industry', in Pallot (ed.), *Transforming Peasants*, pp. 37–63.

28. *Katalog sostoiashchei pod vysochaishim ego imperatorskogo velichestva pokrovitel'stvom tsarskosel'skoi 1710 iubileinoe 1910 vystavki* (St Petersburg, 1911).

29. *Novoe vremia* (14 August 1911) p. 3. The author of the article also claimed that the *khutor* movement had assumed 'gigantic proportions' and was expanding 'in geometrical sequence'.

30. *Rech'* (21 September 1911) p. 2. In his report of the last day of the exhibition the reporter, S. Liubosh', wrote that he had revisited Rokko's *khutor*

and that it was still in a sorry state. He reported other 'incorrect' exhibits. One whole village consolidation he claimed to be fictitious – the peasants from the village in question had written to him saying there were no *khutora* there. See *Rech'* (8 October, 1911) p. 5.

31. *Rech'* (9 October 1911) p. 5.
32. *Rossiia* (9 October 1911) p. 1. The prize referred to were the livestock and equipment that had been used to stock the exhibition 'Khutor' and were to be awarded to the best 'real' *Khutor* portrayed in the exhibition.
33. Iurevskii, *Chto dostignuto zemleustroistvom*, p. 13.
34. *Glavnoe upravlenie zemleustroistva i zemeldeliia, Zemleustroistvo, 1907–1910* (St Petersburg, 1911).
35. *Russkoe Bogatstvo*, no. 11 (1911) p. 188.
36. Glavnoe upravlenie zemleustroistva i zemledeliia, *Zemleustroennye khoziaistvo. Svodnye dannye sploshnogo po 12 uezdam podvornogo obsledovaniia khoziaistvennykh izmenenii v pervye gody posle zemleustroistva* (St Petersburg, 1915).
37. S. Bel'kii, 'Probudaiushchaia derevnia', *Novaia zemledel'cheskaia Rossiia – ocherki zemleustroistva* (St Petersburg, 1910).
38. A. I. Shingarev, *Vymiriaiushchaia derevnia: Opyt sanitarno-ekonomicheskogo izsledovaniia dvukh selenii voronezhskogo uezda*, 2nd edn (St Petersburg, 1902, 1907).
39. Stephen P. Frank, 'Confronting the Domestic Other: Rural Popular Culture and its Enemies in Fin-de-Siècle Russia', in Stephen P. Frank and Mark D. Steinberg (eds), *Lower Class Values, Practices and Resistance in Late Imperial Russia* (Princeton, NJ, 1994).
40. Iurevskii, *Chto dostignuto zemleustroistvom*.
41. For a discussion of the peasant as 'rational man of the land' see Frierson, *Peasant Icons*, ch. 4.
42. For a description of Semenov's life see Orlando Figes, *A People's Tragedy: The Russian Revolution, 1891–1924* (London, 1996) pp. 232–9.
43. S. T. Semenov, 'Legko li u nas vydeliastsia iz obshchiny?' *Sovremmenik*, nos 5–6 (1911); 'Novye Khoziastva', *Sovremennik*, no. 10 (1913); *Dvadtsat'-piat let v derevne* (Petrograd, 1915).
44. A. Solovev, 'Kak ia vydelilsia iz obshchiny i pervye moi shaga na otrube', *Sel'skokhoziaistvennyi listok* (Tver, May 1914).
45. RGIA, *f. 408, op. 1, no.* 161.
46. Kotsonis, 'How Peasants became Backward'.

7
Broken Identities: The Intelligentsia in Revolutionary Russia[1]

Dietrich Beyrau

The nomadic identities of the intelligentsia

There are as many definitions of the term 'intelligentsia' as there are authors writing about it.[2] Consensus is to be found only in the statement of the equivocal nature of the term as well as the realities it connotes. Alexander Blok had once characterized it as the 'nomadic and winged faculty' (*imushchestvo kochevoe i krylatoe*),[3] a definition that we find again eighty years later in the wake of intellectual opposition in Eastern Europe, that of the intelligentsia as

> a separate category of people assigned the role of manipulation and interpretation of elusive but crucial factors of social integration called values, meanings and symbols. On the other hand, we might be looking for a distinct 'intellectual mode', 'idiom', or 'pattern' articulated, codified and practised by such manipulators and interpreters simultaneously as a tool of self-definition and as part of a bid for social power.[4]

In the context of Russia of the nineteenth and twentieth centuries, the concept of intelligentsia acquired additional emphasis on account of the politically repressive conditions of the tsarist regime and the Soviet Union. Various metaphors that were in use – the intelligentsia as a 'critical thinking being' (*kriticheski mysliashchaia lichnost'*),[5] who had only the welfare of the general public in mind, or the 'knight of the living word'[6] – describe normative models, which could be activated in phases of social and political mobilization. Identity, on the other hand, is primarily used today with reference to two social dimensions: since class and class-consciousness as determining factors of social processes are now perceived as old-fashioned, they are often replaced by the more sublime concept of identity.[7] Its role becomes increasingly important where consciousness and the mobilization of ethno-nationalism is concerned. Members of ethnic minorities, or peoples, are straitjacketed into national identities.[8] To what extent do collective identities determine the bleak reality? Common sense tells us that identities and normative models enforced through propaganda compete with a number of other identities and roles. This is also valid for members of the intelligentsia. Identities can be based on regional, corporate, religious or social origins, on family status, on profession, on extra-professional activities, on wealth, poverty, lifestyle or prestige, as well as on political and ideological convictions. Depending on the question and object of study, different characteristics are highlighted. The problem of establishing the identity of the intelligentsia arises out of the ubiquity of the intelligentsia, out of its manifold functions in society and out of the changes in the wake of industrialization, commercialization and political upheavals since the end of the nineteenth century.[9] For the period before 1914, Soviet historians as a rule chose criteria of political conviction (ideology) in order to arrive at conclusions regarding class affiliations.[10] Other authors proceeded from origins, from social status, or from professional standing. For the period after 1917, official Soviet rhetoric linked the ethics of political conviction with functional and social aspects while talking about bourgeois specialists, about the Red and later the Soviet intelligentsia. This intermediate stratum (*prosloika*) was divided into creative (*tvorcheskaia*) and scientific and technical groups (*inzhenerno-tekhnicheskie rabotniki*).[11] Where criteria of ideological ethics in the populist tradition are emphasized,[12] the pre-history of the Russian Revolution is written even today as the drama of the moral revolt of the intelligentsia.[13] Its social history, however, has come to be concentrated on certain professional groups and their process of professionalization,[14] or, as of late, on cultural milieux.[15]

The diffuse nature of the term intelligentsia suggests that it might be necessary to give it up in scholarly discourse – a process that has already begun. On the other hand, we see its continued use in everyday language. What cannot be defined unequivocally for academic purposes does not necessarily disappear from social reality, a classical dilemma of all theories dealing with human beings. This paper seeks to grasp this dilemma by outlining the scope of action of professional intellectual groups on the one hand, and on the other by describing historically conditioned attributes and models as well as patterns of behaviour resulting from them.

Social profiles of the intelligentsia

The term 'intelligentsia' became popular in Russia in the 1860s. It was used for those intellectual groups that arose in the niches of the crumbling estates structure and that belonged neither to the tax-paying population nor to the privileged estates. At best their members moved in the lower rungs of the Table of Ranks (*tabel' o rangakh*). The secular system of education established under Peter I and extended from Catherine II's day, was entirely orientated to the civil service. Civil and military educational institutions contained mainly the children of the nobility, the bureaucracy and the clergy. Along with the concept of intelligentsia there emerged that of the *raznochinets* from the 1860s. This term referred to a group which had no definite position in the hierarchy of the estates or which had outgrown its traditional place in this order.[16] This was an indication of a reorganization of the social milieu which could no longer be classified by the criteria of the estates order, even though the legal system still upheld the old categories, hereditary and service nobility, honoured citizens and so on.

Although the nobility and the clergy continued to function as an important reservoir for the recruitment of the educated classes, the majority of high school and university students before the First World War came from the 'taxable' strata, mainly the peasants and the so-called petty bourgeoisie (*meshchane*). From the 1890s, technical institutes became almost as important as the universities. Whereas in 1912–13 over 35,000 students were enrolled at universities, technical institutes already had over 25,000 students.[17] In relation to the population, university graduates still remained a tiny minority, comprising just about 1 per cent of the population. They were also concentrated in the big cities: 46 per cent of all scholars and writers, 30 per cent of all engineers and technicians, as well as about 15 per cent of all doctors and lawyers worked in St Petersburg and Moscow.[18] The socio-cultural gap with regard to the mass of the population remained very large, although a massive literacy campaign had been initiated since the turn of the century. It is claimed that before the First World War about 40 per cent of the rural and about 60 per cent of the urban population had been made literate. The concept of literacy used here, however, covered a wide range – from the laborious deciphering and writing of a few words to the active ability to read and write.[19]

With the growing success of institutionalized education from the middle of the nineteenth century, we may observe professionalization among bureaucrats and the military on the one hand, and the development of professionals on the margins of and outside the civil service on the other. They worked partly in an independent capacity and partly within the framework of the civil service or the local administration, here mainly the zemstvo. Thus new social categories penetrated the fast disintegrating dualistic structure of taxable and privileged orders. In keeping with the concepts of those times, they were termed 'Society' (*obshchestvo*), by which was meant the educated, including the rich insofar as they were educated. They were to be found among the nobility and the upper levels of bureaucracy as well as among strata which did not belong to the privileged. This 'Society' was given a place outside of and in antithesis to the masses.

With the spread of education, the arena of the public also expanded. In the wake of reforms under Alexander II an anonymous public sphere arose in the place of the salons, the assemblies of the nobility, and military headquarters in the provinces. Its points of crystallization were the daily newspapers and more particularly the 'thick journals' (*tolstye zhurnaly*). Whereas the circulation figures of journals and newspapers for the educated public hovered around some 10,000 in the 1860s and the 1870s, the market for these expanded greatly from the 1890s, by which time it was already serving the urban masses. The market for books also boomed. The number of published books multiplied almost threefold between 1887 and 1913, from about 3,000 to 8,000 titles, and the editions quadrupled from 13 to 54 million.[20] The publishing market collapsed during the civil war, and these figures could be restored only towards the end of the 1920s.[21] Before 1905, daily newspapers and the more intellectual journals played the role of a substitute parliament. Sundry secondary forums flourished for the general public: the societies and associations of the different professional groups; the universities with their rituals of public lectures and scholarly disputes, especially the highly regarded defence of doctoral theses; but also the law courts with their spectacular trials of criminals and revolutionaries; and, last but not least, the subculture of the revolutionary circles (*kruzhki*) and conspiratory groups comprising mainly students. It was only in the 1890s that the revolutionary underground parties developed out of this – the General Jewish Workers' Union (or the Bund for short), the Socialist Revolutionaries (SRs) and the various Social Democratic parties. Although they touched the fringes of that part of society to which artisans and workers belonged, they remained at first parties of the intelligentsia in the sense that their leadership consisted almost exclusively of members of the intelligentsia.[22] In contrast to the agile and for the most part youthful revolutionary intelligentsia, the associations of the professionally established intelligentsia at first led a relatively unremarkable existence. It was only the Volga famine of 1891–2 that pushed the associations into politics. At the beginning of the Revolution of 1905 they came together in the Union of Unions in order to provide the slogans and an organizational framework in the first phase of the Revolution. This umbrella organization brought together mainly the professional associations and interest groups of the tertiary sector, from the professors to the 'third element', the employees of the zemstvo, railway personnel, the Womens' Union, or short-lived associations like the Union for the Complete Equality for Jews (*Soiuz polnogo ravnoupravneniia evreev*).[23] The precarious situation of these professional and interest groups of the intelligentsia was to become apparent during the Revolution of 1905–6. Bloody Sunday in St Petersburg triggered off rebellious risings in the national borderlands before the Revolution again seized the Russian centre. With the strikes, the setting up of soviets, the peasant unrest and the subsequent civil war conditions in the countryside as well as in the industrial centres, the professional associations soon lost control of the Revolution. Their goals of differing forms of constitutional and democratic politics and society were overtaken by national and social revolutionary movements which expressed at best only a secondary interest in a constitutional state. Both the political right and left articulated and organized their anti-bourgeois and anti-liberal tendencies. Their roots lay in the relatively traditionalist agrarian structure on the one hand, and on the other in an initially undefined but potentially socialist radicalization mainly of factory hands. As studies of the liberal judiciary after 1864 and of the functioning of the parties after 1905 suggest, constitutional and participatory models of the liberal sort had little response, even in times of peace, outside 'Society'.[24]

The commercialization and modernization of society in the wake of Alexander II's reforms opened up many opportunities for the professional groups among the intelligentsia and stimulated their social and political demands; but it also exposed them, according to their field of activity, to political hazards and economic vicissitudes. The expansion and professionalization of the bureaucracy gave rise to a class of experts[25] whose demands could only be met by a reform of the political system. It was this socio-political constellation which led to the success of the Union of Unions at the beginning of the Revolution of 1905. Its political goals, as we have seen, could only be partly achieved. This was due as much to the revolutionary process not being subject to regulation as to the tenacity of the old authorities, but most of all to the transformation of the traditional socio-cultural dualism. In the process of the transformation, the old ruling powers – the nobility and the autocracy – were divested of their legitimacy; yet the majority of the population did not invest the newly formed 'Society' with a corresponding dose of power.[26] Despite this, and given all the post-revolutionary repression, a return to the status quo ante was no longer possible. The growth of the tertiary sector opened up options for the professional intelligentsia that had not been available to them before 1880, until which date multiple forms of censorship were in place. Censorship lost much of its bite owing to the quantitative growth of the book market alone. After 1905 it had to confine itself to a few radical journals.[27] When the reactionary Minister of Culture (*prosveshcheniia*), L. A. Casso, dismissed professors because of student unrest and the struggle for university autonomy, or when these professors gave up their jobs, most of them found employment elsewhere, partly again as professors and scholars in the private Siniavskii University or in private laboratories.[28] In the face of political repression, members of other groups such as doctors, engineers or writers of all kinds could look for and find jobs free of state control. The prevailing attitude of opposition among the intellectual professions afforded a certain amount of protection, which also penetrated the professional administration. Although members of other intellectual professions comprised all ethnic groups and social classes, including the nobility, there are remarkable differences to be observed from an ethnic point of view with regard to the old upper classes of the nobility and the bureaucracy right until the end of the regime. The higher posts in civil and military service were still almost exclusively occupied by members of the hereditary and service nobility. In ethnic terms these consisted mainly of the Russian nobility, the Baltic German barons, and the formerly Polish but now russianized *szlachta* or nobility of the western region (*zapadnyi krai*).[29] The ethnic profile of the professional and the better researched revolutionary intelligentsia shows that they contained even those ethnic groups that were systematically discriminated against, such as, in different degrees, Jews and Poles; otherwise it revealed those from traditionally subaltern positions like the peasants or the scattered and diasporic peoples such as the Tatars or the Armenians. Jews, Poles, Letts, Armenians, Georgians and even Muslims, whose political activists were accommodated among the Constitutional Democrats after 1905, were comparatively well represented in the professional and revolutionary intelligentsia.[30] These spheres of activity on the margins of, or outside, the civil service opened up career possibilities for the mobilized ethnic groups, especially the Jews, although the civil service and particularly higher posts were denied to them. This change from the 'aristocratic' to the former plebeian or discriminated ethnic groups was to be reflected in the post-revolutionary political elite. A new 'coalition' was formed with a Russian majority as before, but with prominent representation especially of Jews, Letts and Caucasians.[31]

The formation of a new socio-ethnic profile of intellectuals was accompanied by a counter-culture which set itself against that of the nobility. Important writers and opinion makers reacted strongly to the official politics of anti-semitism which obtained after the pogroms of 1881. In contrast to the latent or openly anti-semitic literature of the decades before 1880, there now appeared a literature of guilty conscience. It was positively disposed towards Jews, didactic in nature and of mediocre quality, like N. G. Chernyshevsky's novel *Shto delat'?*, the cult novel of the nihilistic intelligentsia.[32] Jews found it relatively unproblematic to gain entry into the counter-culture. They already played an important role in the various, even established, professional groups of the intellectuals, like lawyers, doctors and revolutionaries. Among their 'enlightened' contemporaries, anti-semitism was seen almost exclusively as a mark of the reactionary nobility and the police. The counter-culture of the intelligentsia was, on the contrary, indifferent to the question of nation: it was internationalist, sometimes even philo-semitic. Another distinguishing characterstic *vis-à-vis* the ruling elite was the support extended by the (male) members of the intelligentsia to the question of the emancipation and employment of women. The struggle in this case revolved around their access to universities and other institutions of higher education.[33] Until the turn of the century the counter-culture was characterized by secular values, by the demand for freedom of public life from religious domination, by their distance from religion in general and the official Church in particular. Materialism and positivism dominated the sciences.[34]

The intelligentsia between the state and the people

The growing professional class soon became a rival of the bureaucracy, which had proved its incompetence in the eyes of the public in the famine of 1891–92, in the disaster of the Russian–Japanese War, and in the First World War. Given the inadequacy of infrastructure, be it in transport, education or health facilities, and the 'backwardness' of the rural and the proletarianized population, the associations and opposi-

tional parties drew up distinctly protectionist and paternalistic programmes. After 1905, two tendencies, called *kul'turniki* and 'politicals',
appeared among the many professional groups. They differed on
whether 'progress' was to be achieved through professional work or by
political struggle. The paternalism and *kul'turtregerstvo* of the professional groups reappeared in their programmes as the politics of
'enlightenment' (*prosveshchenie*) and of political education; among the
radicals they emerged as agitation and propaganda or, in an extreme
form, with Lenin and the Bolsheviks, as the concept of the Party as the
vanguard of the proletariat. This implied that workers, their spontane-
ity notwithstanding, needed the leadership of the Party in order not to
fall prey to trade-unionist limitations. The programmes of intelligentsia
groups reflected their opposition to the regime but revealed that they
did not represent the 'people', whatever their claims to the contrary. In
their lifestyle, their professional work, and especially in their forms of
discourse, they were as ever far removed from the scarcely literate
masses and seemed to have more in common with the elite than with
the 'working people' (*trudiashchiisia narod*). The latter also no longer
lived within the structures of the seventeenth century as at the time of
the peasant emancipation, but were also subject to processes of modernization. These included the rise of an urban mass culture, ever
deeper contacts with the outside world through seasonal labour
(*otkhodnichestvo*), and handicraft and factory labour outside the home
villages. These were accompanied by the commercialization of agriculture, often over generations, and an expanding book and information
culture, which touched the villages too. We could talk of a plebeian
modernization which altered the divide between ruler and ruled,
without overcoming it. In this context the excesses against the intelligentsia during the Revolutions were symbolic of the cultural rift they
embodied. The indiscriminate violence in villages, in factories and
among troops was equally traumatic. The elite could be targeted and
the intelligentsia could be included. As such the intelligentsia's claims
to leadership and participation was questioned not only by the establishment, but by the 'people' as well. Since the working class and especially the peasant movements could not be institutionalized after 1905,
the gulf between them and the professional groups only widened.

The intellectual professions drew a number of conclusions from the
Revolution of 1905. There was a tendency towards depoliticization and
a growing distance between the professional groups and the increasingly marginalized revolutionaries. Their response to the growing militancy, especially among workers in St Petersburg, was limited; and it

would be said in 1917 that they had betrayed the revolution.[35] While the figures on political repression before 1915 reveal a considerable proportion from the intelligentsia still, the number of workers, crafts-men and petty officials in the revolutionary movement had increased.[36] In 1920, the university-educated among the Bolsheviks were about 1 per cent, which was roughly their share of the popula-tion.[37] It was clear, however, in the intellectual debates, especially among the metropolitan intelligentsia, that the hegemony of the nihilist-materialistic tradition was receding. Symbolism and 'deca-dence' in art and literature, the pull of 'idealism' and the philosophy of religion, or the rise of the Dostoevsky cult, all suggest a paradigm shift which would not leave even the debates of the revolutionaries untouched.[38] This change was provocatively announed in the *Vekhi* anthology (1909). It forsook the materialist-revolutionary tradition and mocked the revolutionay group culture as an infantile stage of the intelligentsia.[39] It is not clear how far these debates indicate the embourgeoisement of the intelligentsia and their reconciliation with the semi-constitutional regime in the manner of the German *Bildungsbürgertum*. A more detailed analysis would have to distinguish between separate professional and status groups, since the post-revolu-tionary period was a time of ambivalence for the intelligentsia. They wanted constitutional politics, but the nobility and higher bureaucracy retained the political initiative. Many intelligentsia circles were perse-cuted. The universities, which were important as revolutionary terrain in 1905, were again put under strict control. As against the pre-1905 situation, student and professors' protests which culminated in expul-sions and dismissals were due more to specific university concerns than to general political demands. The teaching community in particular suffered from repression after 1907. However, the race for literacy between the state and the Church on the one hand, and the zemstvo and the local bodies on the other, opened up new areas of activity for the 'lesser' intelligentsia. The same holds true for the public health service. The zemstvo doctors who carried out populist programmes of preventive medicine faced the new challenge of the developing science of bacteriology. The Stolypin Reforms, although condemned politically, provided agronomists with new tasks and opportunities through their measures for the clearing and improvement of farm land. Agronomy as a whole received a fresh impetus, which would continue after the Civil War.[40] Similarly, engineers, technicians, architects and artists profited from urban growth and the opening up of new territories for agriculture and mining. The expansion of the book market and of the free professions offered career opportunities, especially for discriminated and underprivileged groups (Jews and women). (A third of the literary professions, in a broad sense, was staffed by women.)[41] Political quiescence and career through intellectual work made for greater ambivalence, in which radical political programmes like those of the Social Revolutionary Maximalists or the Bolsheviks lost their lustre.

In the course of the First World War, however, it was to become apparent how weak the support for the regime among the educated classes actually was. As against Germany or France, where the educated classes, with few exceptions, indulged in an uninhibited enthusiasm for the war, as expressed in the *Burgfrieden* or the *union sacré*, patriotic fervour remained muted in Russia[42] despite a long anti-German tradition among those with property and education. Identification with the war developed only after the February Revolution, when the professional intelligentsia assumed specialized administrative functions and were given a chance for the first time to carry out their reform programmes. The defeats on the war front and the growing instability within the country demonstrated, however, the impotence of the old, but now democratically legitimized institutions, as well as of the new ones. The focal points of liberal-democratic aspirations like municipal government and the zemstvo, the legal system or the newly formed committees in the towns, the rural areas and the front, functioned from the summer of 1917 like mills without water. Authority did not grow in these institutions, but in the 'grass-roots' soviets – the factory and village committees, and their executive bodies. It is here that we find the pre-1914 marginalized intelligentsia, who emerged from the underground or out of obscurity, and those who returned from emigration. As spokesmen and organizers of the activist core among workers, soldiers and sailors, they stepped into the important positions of power after October 1917, which had earlier been occupied by the nobility and the higher bureaucracy. With this, a section of society came to power, which before 1917 had been marked by its precarious existence and its marginality, by exile, emigration or a dangerous life in the underground or on the fringes of legality. It had only known the repressive side of the old regime. Only ceaseless political activism and commitment could make their privations tolerable (*ubi doctrina, ibi patria*). These circles had preserved the tradition of a community of thought, established during the Nihilist movement of the 1860s and flourishing under changing labels.

Several inputs of early Bolshevik politics may be explained by this tradition of marginalized existence and firm commitment. It accounts for the singular combination of ideological intransigence and political flexibility; unrealistic political programmes and an implacable will to power; adapting to the moods of the 'masses', which were exploited when required, but firmly suppressed if need be, by invoking the vision of socialism; and last but not least, always imagining itself in the 'last battle' in a Manichaean world divided into friend and foe.

Changes of role: winners and losers of the 1917 revolution

The Bolshevik Revolution led to a dramatic change of roles within the intelligentsia. The new people in power enjoyed material resources and political power thanks to their agitation and propaganda adapted to the psychology of the masses.[43] The hegemony of agitational rhetoric, which had asserted itself then, was in a few years to monopolize discourse. In place of the plurality of public speech, which had surmounted all obstacles since the middle of the nineteenth century, what Peter Kenez has termed the 'propaganda state' had come into being.[44] To the professional groups the Revolution was like a 'bear stepping on their ear' (*tochno medved' na ukho nastupil*).[45] Whereas the revolutionary and professional intelligentsia appeared to have fought on the same front in 1905, they confronted each other almost as enemies in 1917–18. While the Bolsheviks and many Social Revolutionaries celebrated the Revolution as the dawn of a new age, the years after 1917 were a civilizational catastrophe for the other side. Intellectuals located in the tradition of symbolism and idealism freely resorted to the metaphor of the apocalypse to explain the events. The Revolution was a troika running away, a popular explosion, the 'fusion of the darkest forces of barbarism and civilization' (*soedinenie samykh temnykh sil varvarstva i tsivilizatsii*), the triumph of the *smerdiakovshchina*, the 'evil animal' (*zloi zver'*), and finally the 'absolute evil'.[46] More sober observers and the victims spoke of the educated as the shipwrecked in an ocean of barbarism.[47]

Many revolutionaries looked upon the professional intelligentsia as mere 'lackeys of capitalism' (*lakei kapitala*),[48] and for that reason highly suspect. Given their dependence on the 'monopolists of knowledge' (A. V. Lunacharsky), however, greater pragmatism prevailed. By Petrine standards this meant using the experts, but imposing Party control and political abstinence on them. The concept of the 'bourgeois specialist' thus came into being. As the revolutionaries mutated into rulers and bureaucrats of the Russian type, they assumed authority in political, social and ideological matters, formerly the classical terrain of the intelligentsia; the bourgeois specialists, on the other hand, were to place their expertise at the disposal of the new regime without commenting on issues of general concern. Given Bolshevik enthusiasm for science and technology, natural scientists and the technical intelligentsia were relatively quickly accommodated. The agreement with the otherwise anti-Bolshevik Academy of Sciences was more than symbolic. In the spirit of the 'materialism' of the nineteenth century, science and technology were promoted despite limited resources. The Plan for the Electrification of Russia in 1920 (GOELRO) then advertised their importance with a flourish. This Plan may have been more propaganda than plan, and it may have served more to 'feed' semi-starved technical and scientific experts that any scientific leap forward; but it certainly revealed what this new Socialism believed it had to offer to technical and scientific progress.[49] The relationship between specialists and Party was structured in model form in the army and factories. The officers who enlisted in the Workers' and Peasants' Army, whether freely or under compulsion, had political commissars attached to them. Similarly 'Red' Directors, often those who had risen from the ranks of the workers, kept an eye on engineers in the factories, in part to protect them from the wrath of the workers. This division of roles could not be imposed everywhere. In the field of education, and especially in higher education, other methods had to be employed. Teachers were organized in communist-led trade unions, and universities lost the autonomy they had just gained.[50] Each professional group, according to its worth, worked out and attempted to assert its professional interests. Scientists, engineers and technical experts, but also doctors, were probably the best placed. These groups survived the turbulence of the Revolution and Civil War relatively well. The problem of their political views was secondary to their usefulness to the process of reconstruction. The attacks on bourgeois specialists by sundry left Bolshevik and anarchist groups were short-lived. The political leadership could claim credit for having tamed the egalitarian fury of workers and for having prevented another Bartholomew's Night for the specialists. Indeed, orders were issued not to shoot them or take them hostage on account of their political past.[51]

These professional groups being assigned their functions and the relatively privileged conditions they enjoyed did not convert them into soulless automatons, the public reproach that Lenin had to suffer.[52] The outstanding work of Vladimir Ipatiev (the chemist and later émigré) under the Bolsheviks was justified on the ground that before 1914 service under the autocracy did not necessarily entail being a supporter of the monarchy; the same would hold true for the majority of specialists. In like fashion, one could work under the Bolsheviks without being a communist.[53] Similarly, the question of professional opportunities in Soviet Russia (or in the West) guided the geologist and biochemist, Vladimir Vernadskii, a former Kadet and briefly deputy minister in the Provisional Government, on the issue of emancipation. He discerned destructive tendencies at work, which he ascribed to the religious fervour of the Bolsheviks and their anti-elitist politics; but he respected their efforts in the fields of science and technology. Science, he felt, must in any case insulate itself from the excessive demands of democracies as well as dictatorships.[54]

It was clear soon enough that the Bolsheviks would not grant to either the Academy of Sciences or academic institutions a formal and legal autonomy of the kind enjoyed by the Kaiser-Wilhelm Society in Germany or the Royal Society in England despite their public funding. In effect, however, even in Soviet Russia, it was the scientists in the Academy as well as in other academic bodies who determined research policies more or less autonomously, although these were subordinated to the Supreme Council of the National Economy (VSNKH) or the Peoples' Commissariats.

Often troubled by a bad conscience and many reservations, the scientific and technical intelligentsia found legitimizing arguments in *Smena Vekh*, a collection of articles published in Prague in 1921 and circulated in Soviet Russia.[55] The remarkable response to the volume was due to its interpretation of the Revolution and its consequences as unfortunate, its acknowledgement that the Bolsheviks had both inherited the Russian state and Russian universalism and had subdued the latent anarchy of the masses. It appealed to the intelligentsia emphatically to forego political ambition and maximalism and instead to reflect more on this function as representatives of culture in a barbarized land. The metaphor of China after the Mongol invasion and the role of the mandarins in containing Mongol barbarism was commonly employed to describe and justify their own conduct under the Bolsheviks.[56] Although many different intellectual trends flourished under the aegis of the *Smena Vekh* movement, the Bolshevik leadership tolerated the expansion of this 'transitional ideology' as long as it was grist to their mill, as Stalin formulated it.[57]

The expulsion of more than a hundred intellectuals chiefly from the disciplines of the humanities and social sciences in the autumn of 1922 exposed the limits of action. Given the powerful anti-Bolshevik sentiment in the country, the catacomb existence of these 'notorious corrupters of the youth' (*zavedomye rastliteli ... dlia mladshego vozrasta*) with their 'old bourgeois rubbish' (*staromu burzhuaznomu khlamu*) was to be snuffed out.[58]

As in the case of scientists, Bolsheviks enjoyed little support even among writers and artists. Among these were mainly the heterogeneous movement of the 'Proletkult',[59] the futurists, and a few bourgeois authors like the symbolist Valery Briusov, who was attracted mainly by the prospect of power. The collapse of the market for publications in the wake of the Revolution and Civil War, combined with its gradual nationalization, created suitable conditions for expanding the net of censorship. The State Publishing House (*Gosizdat*), which was established in 1919, soon accounted for two-thirds of all publications in the Russian Soviet Federated Socialist Republics (*RSFSR*). The Gosizdat licensed private publishers, organized paper distribution and price fixation, monopolized the editing of text books, music and literature, and administered the newly nationalized copyrights of Russian classical authors. A Political Department (*Politotdel*) was attached to the State Publishing House, which carried out a pre-censorship until 1930. This was especially strict with respect to private or cooperative publishers. The State Publishing House functioned therefore as a monopoly and as a political authority, which asserted its economic privileges and its political power rigorously against its competitors. From 1927 to 1928 this power was used to eliminate competition.[60]

In June 1922 the Main Committee on Literature and Publishing (Glavlit) was set up. Until 1931 it was run by P. I. Lebedev-Polianskii, a long-standing party activist who was to become a member of the Academy (Academician) and to continue to exert considerable influence in matters of literature. At first Glavlit coexisted with the Political Department of the State Publishing House, the Glavlitprosvet, which controlled the public libraries. These suffered several purges.[61] The literature of the Comintern, the Party, as well as of the Academy and the military was at first subject to its own censorship bodies.

These bodies shifted fairly early on from pure prohibition, inherited from the tsarist regime, to prescription. It was meant to be pedagogical, made much easier by coordinating the appointment of editorial bodies and publishers' readers with the Glavlit (after 1924). Pre-censorship therefore shifted to the editorial offices, a practice which was to be retained and perfected upto the end of the Soviet Union. The scattered information available for the 1920s shows that 1–10 per cent of the manuscripts were affected by pre-censorship. Already in 1924 authors were complaining about pathologically suspicious and often incompetent controlling bodies. Their censorship was felt to be 'worse than the sword of Damocles' (*khuzhe nozha bulatnogo*) resulting in a 'terrible self-censorship by writers' (*i v samom pisatele eshche zhivet surovaia tsenzura*).[62] The pedagogic impulse was contained in the instructions to editors and publishers' readers to ensure that the 'objective' view of the Party was duly expressed in the fictional work of the so-called fellow-travellers.[63] By the mid-1920s pre- and post-censorship was severe. The latter was organized through campaigns and, in individual cases, through police action against authors and their manuscripts. Even relative liberals in the domain of politics like A. V. Lunacharsky, Commissar for Education, were afflicted by the power of the censorship bodies. Despite the storm raised by communist critics, the famous Central Committee resolution of 18 June 1925 confirmed the politics of a supposedly cooperative re-education of fellow travellers; but it insisted on retaining the Communist monopoly over the criticism and control of the institution of literature, which had already been achieved. A desperate Kornei Chukovsky noted in December 1925 what this meant for non-confirmist writers:

> I am silenced as a critic, since RAPP [The Russian Association of Proletarian Writers] has assumed the functions of literary criticism. The Party card, not talent, informs judgement. I am reduced to being a writer of children's literature. But I have been driven out of this field ... by the disgraceful events concerning my children's literature. I found the last refuge, the comic novel, in the newspaper under a pseudonym. Who compels me to be novelist rather than a critic or a poet? I, Kornei Chukovsky, am no novelist but a former critic, a former human-being.[64]

Kornei Chukovsky's desperation reveals how censorship promoted by Lebedev-Polianskii and his bureaucracy had long become the norm. Re-education now meant 'that even those who are beaten up, smile' (*shtoby ulybalis' dazhe te, kotorykh derut*).[65] The case of Boris Pilnaik was a perfect example of how this was to be achieved. He was induced to engage in 'auto-polemics' (*avtopolemika*) and to make changes voluntarily even in foreign editions of his works. Eventually he prayed for official guidance. However it was not possible to re-educate all fellow-travellers and some put up strong resistance.

The workshops of change

Among the followers of Proletkult, futurists and artists of revolutionary inclination, the Bolsheviks encountered groups that used the Revolution as a stage from which to reveal their visions of an entirely new culture, of the new human being, and of a 'bright future'. To conventional politicians such revolutionary fervour was alien, even if initially tolerated. The extent to which such visions anticipated totalitarian ambitions is a controversial question in academic literature.[66] In the long run however, the party leadership looked upon these artists and writers as being too undisciplined. While some were persecuted, others allowed their work to be used for Party purposes. Mayakovsky's mutation from a poet of revolution into a poet of resolutions was typical in this context.[67]

The party leadership was politically concerned with the systematic training of a new generation of intellectuals who would combine specialized knowledge in a discipline with Marxist preparation and the 'correct' social background. This generation would free the Party from its dependence on bourgeois specialists and the exalted left. With the founding of the Communist Academy (1918–36), the Institute of Red Professors (1921–8) and other academic institutions under the control of the Party, educational and scientific institutions were created for the purpose of generating a 'red' intelligentsia. The example of the Institute of Red Professors permits a detailed reconstruction of the contradictory results of the ambitious politics of the 1920s. The political recruitment of students and faculty was combined with grass-roots democracy in the organization of teaching and research. The latter included student representation in matters related to teaching and often considerable internal checks on research, performance and ideology among students and faculty. These prepared the ground for the later ritualized forms of criticism and self-criticism, of ideological snooping and denunciation, and even 'academic' and political purges. After the first generation of students had exhibited Trotskyite susceptibilities, the Party leadership insisted upon wider recruitment from the working class and peasantry. With this it hoped to recruit material that could be more easily moulded. In addition, the use of students for political campaigns of all kinds combined learning with praxis, whatever its nature. The purpose of education in a narrower sense was thus often not achieved. Instead, the students mastered the rules of political argument, as was publicly demonstrated by the Party leadership. In short, the communist educational institutions became the playing ground for political rituals of struggle and ideological self-indoctrination. Here the new generation learned those codes of conduct that were necessary in order to succeed and rise in the system. From the middle of the 1920s these rules of the game were applied to the Workers' and Peasants' Faculties, to the other universities, and from the Communist party cells to other research institutions. The 'teachers' soon found themselves subjected to vehement criticism based on an ever-narrowing understanding of Marxist doctrine. The catechization of Marxism–Leninism, which had already begun in the 1920s, was rooted not only in the relatively low standard of education of the new generation, but also in power hunger. The sundry debates were concerned, not so much with academic differences of opinion on history, economics or philosophy, but rather with consolidating opinion through reprisals by the Party leadership, through control of editors' offices, through university chairs, and positions in the Party administration. The warring factions increasingly appealed to the Party leadership, which was inexorably sucked into the disputes. It was, however, interested in arming and mobilizing student groups to its purposes. The activity concerning communist historians provides a clear picture of these procedures. Finally even the supreme arbiters of official education and science policy like D. B. Riazanov, A. V. Lunacharsky, M. N. Pokrovsky or Emel'ian Iaroslavskii were immersed in these debates and power struggles.[68] Similar trends may be observed in literature. Communist writers and critics took charge of editorial offices and functioned even as official censors. The first generation of cultural bureaucrats like A. K. Voronskii or V. P. Polonskii tended to benevolent re-education in the spirit of cooperation; but they were subjected to increasingly vehement criticism by communist circles, which always argued politically. In the 'will to victory' these circles demanded, ostensibly in the interest of readers, a relevant class literature, its unambiguous standardization, and finally curbs on publishing troublesome works.[69]

The new 'red' generation deployed and radicalized a concept inherent at least in the rhetoric of the generation of revolutionary intelligentsia. This saw the word as a weapon that could not be entrusted to all and sundry; they looked upon the literature of fellow-travellers as 'poison' for the masses (Lunacharsky); it could at best be tolerated as 'fertilizer for a new culture' (Trotsky);[70] and a bourgeois science could after all exist. All these notions were further reduced by the new generation in their fight for recognition and influence. The main concern now was to establish a canon of 'correct' opinions and methods and to enforce them administratively.

Stalin's 'answer' to the journal *Proletarskaia Revoliutsiia* proved to be decisive for the humanities and social sciences – and in certain respects also for literature – insofar as it set the standard for a Party science. It was not to allow any 'worthless liberalism' in historiography, which might permit Trotskyist and bourgeois penetration. The historians' task was to 'systematically tear off the masks from the faces of ... deceivers'.[71] Stalin's intervention led to an orgy of self-flagellation among communist historians. Stalin's sanction to Party history being made into a catechism now affected other fields in the humanities and the social sciences. A new generation of Party intelligentsia, with more of the Party than intelligentsia about them, was called upon to determine the public discourse with their uninhibited militancy.[72]

The First Five-Year Plan period saw these campaigns culminate in attacks on bourgeois professionals. The accompanying 'cultural campaign' (*kul'tpokhod*), like the Five-Year Plan itself, was marked by a utopian fervour. Education, science, culture and production were to be directly related to each other through a reorganization of all fields of activity. Art was called upon to mobilize producers. Artists and writers would work collectively.[73] Universities and scientific establishments would be part of the production process and would organize themselves according to the requirements of collective production. Through greater recruitment from workers and peasants and with the help of 'brigade methods', the new proletarian generation was led as quickly as possible to education and science. The education of others and self re-education according to 'proletarian' standards formed, to a certain degree, a dialectical scenario of 're-forging' (*perkovka*). In this context bourgeois science and art appeared to be superfluous and were consigned to oblivion.

The manner and the intensity with which the heights of science and culture were captured, was different in each field. In literature, the (V)RAPP, the Russian Association of Proletarian Writers, played a dominant role from the end of the 1920s. The new generation that had captured the official channels of censorship, the editorial offices and the posts of sub-editors, had to a great extent pushed the old revolutionary intelligentsia into the background. The fellow-travellers had either adapted themselves or were quiet. Open resistance was no longer possible. At best one could appeal to Stalin and the OGPU. There was a change only when Maxim Gorky, who had been wooed by Stalin, became the target of attacks. The existing literary organizations were disbanded and the formation of a new Soviet Writers' Organization was announced (1932), to which even the re-educated fellow-travellers were to belong.

The process of dealing with bourgeois historians was a different one. Here a long-simmering debate between the Academy and M. N. Pokrovsky was used by Party authorities to remove bourgeois historians from the Academy and other institutions. The OGPU therefore invented the story of a conspiracy against the Soviet system. Professional and political rivalries, along with the administrative clutches of the OGPU, formed an opaque net in which more than a hundred historians were trapped, including many prominent ones like E. V. Tarle, Iu. V. Got'e, S. V. Bakhrushin and, as the leader of the conspiracy, S. F. Platonov.

The persecution of historians and other social scientists – including those from the humanities – was part of a campaign for the sovietization of the Academy of Sciences. The attack on this remnant of bourgeois science was carried out variously, whether through arrests or through dismissals, especially in the departments of humanities and in the administrative branches of the Academy. With this, the remaining natural scientists were pressured into accepting reforms. It was known, for example, that Party circles were considering the dissolution of the Academy. Since the formation of the VARNITSO in 1927, the Association of Technical and Scientific Workers in Support of Socialist Reconstruction (*Vsesoiuznaia assotsiatsiia rabotnikov nauki i tekhniki dlia sodeistviia sotsialisticheskomu stroitel'stvu*), the Party began to organize natural scientists, technicians and engineers in the Academy as well as outside it. In an emergency, therefore, an entire reserve could be mobilized to take over the work of the Academy. After intense discussion the majority therefore voted in favour of a restructuring of the institution. The Party sought to gain influence by doubling the membership of the Academy to over eighty persons. While the Academy formally retained the right of co-opting members, the Party leadership began a careful and well-planned campaign in the late summer of 1928 to induce universities and scientific organizations to name the right candidates for election to Academy membership. In this manner, 'social pressure' was simulated. The Party leadership had lists drawn up, which clearly showed which candidates were to be supported as sympathizers, which were to be opposed as enemies, and which were to be ignored as neutrals. Hitches could have arisen between the intention and its execution, since the campaign expected too much competence of local Party authorities. Therefore the Academy could still enjoy a certain latitude, since its members were concerned with preserving the Academy's right of co-option.[74]

The campaigns and the measures of criminal prosecution associated with them had different goals. First, it was obvious that scapegoats for all the problems of forced industrialization had to be found. The Shakhty engineers, who found themselves in the dock again after May 1928, had to bear the brunt of this. Second, bourgeois experts in the management of the economy were pilloried. These had in different ways advocated a more balanced politics of development and had spoken out against unrealistic plan targets, against forced collectivization, and against a pure distribution economy.[75] These issues had been under discussion at official instances and in professional journals from the mid-1920s. With the beginning of the campaigns of denunciation, critics of official policies were accused of being saboteurs and spies. In the show trials against the so-called Industry Party (1930) and against the equally fictitious Central Bureau of Mensheviks (1931), or in the secret trial against the Working Peasants' Party (1932), critics faced the most absurd charges. Stalin and his associates apparently believed in these conspiracies that had been invented in the ofices of the OGPU and at the same time used them to discredit the Party right-wing.[76] The denunciations and the spy hysteria in the political leadership as well as among activists demand explanation. They seem to have been a product of communist militancy which by then had lasted over a decade. Capable of thinking only in categories of friend and foe, they saw themselves in a world ringed by enemies, at first open, later 'masked'.

Although Stalin's speech of 23 June 1931 marked the official end of the witch-hunt on bourgeois professionals (many of whom resumed their positions after 1933),[77] it by no means meant the end of group persecution of the professional intelligentsia. A prominent example is the so-called Slavist affair, an alleged conspiracy of a 'Russian National Party' in 1933–4. Prominent linguists such as V. V. Perets, V. V. Vinogradov and scientists from other disciplines were dragged into it. V. I. Vernadsky and N. S. Kurnakov also figured in the prisoners' statements, along with the Ukrainian historian M. S. Hrushevskii as leader of the party. They were, however, not arrested.[78] Despite further arrests, bourgeois professionals, as ones who had been denounced, were no longer a collective focal point of public campaigns. Isolated records of hearings and statements made in prisons, which have now become accessible, show that the prisoners were victims of ludicrous accusations and insinuations as well as all kinds of blackmail. At the same time, however, they were made to cooperate with the OGPU in order to produce the desired results. In a manner of speaking, the accused mastered the rituals of self-examination, confession, self-accusation and the expression of regret. At the same time, the officials conducting the hearings took on the role of father confessors. They initiated and guided the composition of the statements, confessions and accusations. From the mid-1930s, physical torture began to be used along with psychological terror.[79] The traumatic consequences of these procedures for the survivors, for their social behaviour after their release, can perhaps only be analysed by analogy with the relationship between the hostage and the abductor. The gratitude expressed by former accused for the trust reposed in them by the Party or for their successful 're-education'[80] – a fact often quoted by Soviet historians – has to be understood in this context. Boris Pasternak was to capture this state of affairs in the metaphor of a horse wanting to narrate how it had ridden itself around the circus ring (*Eto kak by loshad' rasskazyvala, kak ona sama ob'ezzhala sebia v manezhe*).[81]

Summary

The reference to broken identities in the title of this article means above all the changed role of the revolutionary and professional intelligentsia as a result of the Revolution of 1917. Under the authoritarian, but liberally 'infected' old regime, many members of intellectual groups found themselves subjected to all kinds of persecution. However, as is evident from their activities and their own testimonies, a network of social protection and solidarity existed within different groups, which as a rule insulated them from total isolation and demoralization. Between revolutionary antagonism and variants of oppositional attitudes, there were many options that allowed full scope for the most diverse individual and collective dispositions.

Revolution and Civil War destroyed this liberal atmosphere. The revolutionary intelligentsia triumphed and found itself catapulted into positions of leadership. It not only assumed all the attributes of an absolute power, but also the form of a secular religion, which not only demanded obedience, but – in the long run – also 'conversion'. It was a matter of establishing their visions of socialism against a society – by no means against the professional intelligentsia alone – which wanted change, but not necessarily in the direction of Communism. Kronstadt and the peasant revolts in the Civil War, as well at the violent measures during collectivization, made this abundantly clear. The incremental realization of their visions after 1921 may be described up to a point as a 'colonization' of society. The professional intelligentsia, which had envisaged its future in a pluralist-democratic society, lost its authority after the Revolution and the Civil War. Instead of being a decisive factor and having a leadership role *vis-à-vis* the 'people', they were degraded to the status of 'bourgeois specialist'. They were supposed to carry out their functions, but not speak publicly. The 'red' intelligentsia that came into power, and the new upwardly mobile (*vydvizhentsy*), reinforced the secular–religious style of the regime, already evident in the doctrinaire manner of the first generation of Bolsheviks. This explains the steady shift to the monopolization of public discourse, and the techniques of 're-education' and 're-forging' of non-class strata. The fact that the pressure of public avowal destroyed the identities of bourgeois professionals and fellow-trvellers as well as of the later revolutionary zealots, lay in the logic of the system. It not only wanted to 'accumulate' absolute power for its own sake, but it also wanted the power to radically change society. Therefore identities had to be broken – even if only to simulate socialism.

Notes

1. Translated from the German by Rekha Kamath.
2. Klaus von Beyme, 'Intellektuelle, Intelligenz', in *Sowjetsystem und Demokratische Gesellschaft*, III (Freiburg, 1969) pp. 186–208.
3. Aleksandr Blok, *Rossiia i intelligentsiia (1907–18)* (Petrograd, 1918) p. 68:

   > Burzhua – pochva pod nogami opredelennaia, kak u svin'i – navoz: sem'ia, kapital, sluzhebnoe polozhenie, orden, chin, Bog na ikone, tsar' na trone. Vytashchi eto – i vse poletit vverkh tormaskami. U intelligenta, kak on vsegda khvalitsia, takoi pochvy nikogda ne bylo. Ego tsennosti neveshchestvenny. Ego tsar' mozhno otniat' tol'ko s golovoi vmeste. Umen'e, znanie, metody, navyki, talanty – imushchestvo kochevoe i krylatoe. My bezdomny, bessemeinye, beschinny, nishchi – chto zhe nam teriat'?

4. Zygmunt Bauman, 'Intellectuals in East Central Europe: Continuity and Change', in *Eastern European Politics and Societies*, I (1987) 162–86, 164–5.
5. Petr Lavrov, *Istoricheskie pis'ma*, in his *Filosofiia i sotsiologiia*, vol. 2 (Moscow, 1965) p. 122.
6. Jörg Baberowski, *Autokratie und Justiz: Zum Verhältnis von Rechtsstaatlichkeit und Rückständigkeit im ausgehenden Zarenreich, 1864–1914* (Frankfurt am Main, 1996) p. 533.
7. Sheila Fitzpatrick, 'The Problem of Class Identity in NEP Society', in Sheila Fitzpatrick *et al.* (eds), *Russia in the Era of NEP* (Bloomington, Ind., 1991) pp. 12–33.

8. Dieter Langewiesche, 'National, Nationalismus, Nationalistaat. Forschungsstand und Forschungsperspektiven', in *Neue Politische Literatur*, XXXX (1995) 190–236.

9. Otto Wilhelm Müller, *Intelligencija: Untersuchungen zur Geschichte eines politischen Schlagwortes* (Frankfurt am Main, 1971).

10. See the critique of Daniel R. Brower, 'The Problem of Russian Intelligentsia', in *Slavic Review*, XXVI (1967) 638–47.

11. P. P. Amelin, *Intelligentsiia i sotsializm* (Leningrad, 1970) pp. 45ff.; S. A. Fediukin, *Partiia i intelligentsiia* (Moscow, 1983).

12. R. V. Ivanov-Razumnik, *Shto takoe intelligentsiia* (Berlin, 1920).

13. Franco Venturi, *Roots of Revolution* (New York, 1960); Isaiah Berlin, *Russian Thinkers* (London, 1978); Alain Besançon, *Les origines intellectuelles du Léninisme* (Paris, 1977) [English: *The Intellectual Origins of Leninism* (London, 1981)]; Claudio Sergio Ingerflom, *Le citoyen impossible: Les racines russes du léninisme* (Paris, 1988); and Richard Pipes, *The Russian Revolution, 1889–1919* (London, 1990). chs 9–11.

14. Nancy M. Frieden, *Russian Physicians in the Era of Reform and Revolution, 1856–1905* (Princeton, NJ, 1981); John F. Hutchinson, *Politics and Public Health in Revolutionary Russia, 1890–1918* (Baltimore, 1990); S. J. Seregny, *Russian Teachers and Peasant Revolution: The Politics of Education in 1905* (Bloomington, Ind., 1989); Manfred Späth, 'Fach- und Standesvereinigungen russischer Ingenieure 1900–1914', in *Forschungen zur Geschichte Osteuropas*, XXXV (1984) pp. 7–466.

15. Karl Schlögel, *Jenseits des Grossen Oktober: Das Laboratorium der Moderne, Petersburg, 1909–1921* (Berlin, 1988); E. W. Clowes, S. D. Kassow and J. L. West (eds), *Between Tsar and People: Educated Society and the Quest for Public Identity in Late Imperial Russia* (Princeton, NJ, 1991).

16. Elise Kimerling Wirtschafter, *Structures of Society: Imperial Russia's 'People of Various Ranks'* (Dekalb, Ill., 1994).

17. A. G. Rashin, 'Gramotnost' i narodnoe obrazovanie v Rossii v XIX i nachale XX v.', in *Istoricheskie Zapiski*, XXXVII (1951) 28–80, 72–8; Nicholas Hans, *History of Russian Educational Policy, 1701–1917* (New York, 1964) pp. 236–43.

18. L. K. Erman, *Intelligentsiia v pervoi russkoi revoliutsii* (Moscow, 1966) pp. 15–16.

19. B. N. Mironov, *Istoriia v tsifrakh* (Leningrad, 1991) pp. 65–87.

20. Ben Eklof, 'Peasant Sloth Reconsidered: Strategies of Education and Learning in Rural Russia Before the Revolution', in *Journal of Social History*, XIV (1981) 355–85, 365; Caspar Ferenczi, 'Funktion und Bedeutung der Presse in Russland vor 1914', in *Jahrbücher für Geschichte Osteuropas*, XXX (1982) 362–98; Jeffrey Brooks, 'Readers and Reading at the End of the Tsarist Era', in W. M. Todd (ed.), *Literature and Society in Imperial Russia, 1800–1914* (Stanford, Cal., 1978) pp. 97–149.

21. Jeffrey Brooks, 'The Breakdown in Production and Distribution of Printed Material, 1917–1927', in A. Gleason et al. (eds), *Bolshevik Culture: Experiment and Order in the Russian Revolution* (Bloomington, Ind., 1985) pp. 151–74.

22. Maureen Perrie, 'The Social Composition and Structure of the Socialist-Revolutionary Party Before 1917', in *Soviet Studies*, XXIV (1972) 223–50;

Manfred Hildermeier, 'Zur Sozialstruktur der Führungsgruppen und zur terroristischen Kampfmethode der Sozialrevolutionären Partei Russlands vor 1917', in *Jahrbücher für Geschichte Osteuropas*, xx (1972) 516–50.

23. Erman, *Intelligentsiaa*, pp. 86–115; Heinz-Dietrich Löwe, 'Die Rolle der russischen Intelligenz in der Revolution von 1905', in *Forschungen zur Geschichte Osteuropas*, xxxii (1983) 229–50.

24. Rex Rexheuser, *Dumawahlen und lokale Gesellschaft: Studien zur Sozialgeschichte der russischen Rechten vor 1917* (Cologne: 1980); V. V. Shelokhaev, *Ideologiia i politicheskaia organizatsiia rossiiskoi liberal'noi burzhuazii, 1907–1914 gg.* (Moscow, 1991); I. V. Narskii, *Russkaia provintsial'naia partiinost'* (Cheliabinsk, 1995); Baberowski, *Autokratie und Justiz*; Dittmar Dahlmann, *Die Provinz wählt. Russlands Konstitutionelle Demokraten und die Dumawahlen, 1906–1912* (Cologne: 1996).

25. W. M. Pintner and D. K. Rowney (eds), *Russian Officialdom: The Bureaucratization of Russian Society from the Seventeenth to the Twentieth Century* (Chapel Hill, NC: 1980); Don K. Rowney, *Transition to Technocracy: The Structural Origins of the Soviet Administrative State* (Ithaca and London, 1989).

26. Robert C. Tucker, 'The Image of Dual Russia', in Cyril E. Black (ed.), *The Transformation of Russian Society: Aspects of Social Change since 1861* (Cambridge, Mass., 1960) pp. 587–605; Dietrich Beyrau, 'Janus in Bastschuhen: Die Bauern in der Russischen Revolution, 1905–1917', in *Geschichte und Gesellschaft*, xxi (1995) 585–603.

27. Benjamin Rigberg, 'The Efficacy of Tsarist Censorship Operation, 1894–1917', in *Jahrbücher für Geschichte Osteuropas*, xiv (1966) 327–45; Benjamin Rigberg, 'Tsarist Censorship Performance, 1894–1905', in ibid. xvii (1969) 59–76; Charles Ruud, *Fighting Words: Imperial Censorship and the Russian Press, 1804–1906* (Toronto, 1982); Daniel Balmuth, *Censorship in Russia, 1865–1905* (Washington, 1979).

28. Silke Spieler, *Autonomie oder Reglementierung: Die russische Universität am Vorabend des Ersten Weltkrieges* (Cologne, 1981) pp. 195–230; Samuel D. Kassow, *Students, Professors and the State in Tsarist Russia* (Berkeley, Cal., 1989) pp. 367–8.

29. P. A. Zaionchkovskii, *Samoderzhavie i russkaia armiia na rubezhe XIX–XX stoletii*, ch. 4 (Moscow, 1973); P. A. Zaionchkovskii, *Pravitel'stvennyi apparat samoderzhavnoi Rossii v XIX v.* (Moscow, 1978) [English in *Soviet Studies in History*, xviii (1979) 11–113].

30. Perrie, 'Social Composition'; Hildermeier, 'Zur Sozialstruktur'; Andreas Kappeler, 'Zur Charakteristik russischer Terroristen, 1878–1887', in *Jahrbücher für Geschichte Osteuropa*, xxvii (1979) 520–47; Robert J. Brym, *The Jewish Intelligentsia and Russian Marxism: A Sociological Study of Intellectual Ideological Divergence* (London, 1978); Späth, 'Fach- und Standesvereinigungen', pp. 381–2; Frieden, *Russian Physicians*, pp. 394–6; Jörg Baberowski, 'Juden und Antisemiten in der russischen Rechtsanwaltschaft, 1864–1917', in *Jahrbücher für Geschichte Osteuropas*, xxxxiii (1995) 493–518; Trude Maurer, *Hochschullehrer im Zarenreich: Ein Beitrag zur Sozial- und Bildungsgeschichte*, doctoral dissertation (Göttingen, 1994) pp. 270–8.

31. Werner E. Mosse, 'Makers of the Soviet Union', in *Slavonic and East European Review*, xxxxvi, (1968) 106, 141–54.

32. Joshua Kunitz, *Russian Literature and the Jew: Sociological Inquiry into the Nature and Origin of Literary Patterns* (New York, 1929).

33. Richard Stites, *The Women's Liberation Movement in Russia: Feminism, Nihilism, and Bolshevism, 1860–1930* (Princeton, NJ, 1978); Bianka Pietrow-Ennker, *Russlands 'neue menschen': Die Frauenemanzipations-Bewegung im 19. Jahrhundert biz zur Oktoberrevolution*, doctoral dissertation (Tübingen, 1994).

34. Klaus von Beyme, *Politische Soziologie im zaristischen Russland* (Wiesbaden, 1965); Alexander Vucinich, *Social Thought in Tsarist Russia: The Quest for a General Science of Society, 1861–1917* (Chicago and London, 1976).

35. David Mandel, 'The Intelligentsia and the Working Class in 1917', in *Critique*, xiv (1981) 67–87; for different aspects see Boris I. Kolonitskii, 'Antibourgeois Propaganda and Anti "Burzhui" Consciousness in 1917', in *Russian Review*, liii (1994) 183–96.

36. V. R. Leikina-Svirskaia, *Russkaia intelligentsiia v 1900–1917 godakh* (Moscow, 1981) pp. 249–54.

37. *Lichnyi sostav RKP (B) v 1920 godu* (Moscow, 1921) p. 12.

38. Christopher Read, *Religion, Revolution, and the Russian Intelligentsia, 1900–1912* (London, 1979); M. Bohachevsky-Chomiak and B. G. Rosenthal (eds), *A Revolution of Spirit: Crisis of Value in Russia, 1890–1918* (Newtonville, Mass: 1982).

39. Gisela Oberländer, *Die Vekhi-Diskussion (1909–1912)* (Cologne, 1965); Jeffrey Brooks, 'Vekhi and the Vekhi-Dispute', in *Survey*, xix (1973) 21–59; V. Proskurina, and V. Alloi, 'K istorii sozdaniia "Vekh"', in *Minuvshee*, xi (1992) 249–91.

40. Alessandro Stanziani, 'Spécialistes, bureaucrates et paysans. Les approvisionnements agricoles pendant la première guerre mondiale, 1914–1917', in *Cahiers du monde russe et soviétique*, xvi (1995) 71–94; idem, 'Politische Elite und Agrarspezialisten in der Sowjetunion der zwanziger Jahre', in Th. Bergmann and G. Schäfer (eds), *Liebling der Partei'. Bucharin, Theoretiker des Sozialismus* (Hamburg, 1989).

41. Pietrow-Ennker, *Russlands 'neue Menschen'*, p. 310.

42. Hubertus F. John, *Patriotic Culture in Russia During World War I* (Ithaca, NY, 1995).

43. Roger Pethybridge, *The Spread of the Russian Revolution: Essays on 1917* (London, 1972), pp. 57–82, 140–75.

44. Peter Kenez, *The Birth of the Propaganda State: Soviet Methods of Mass Mobilization, 1917–1929* (Cambridge, 1985).

45. Blok, *Rossiia*, p. 69.

46. Citations from *Iz glubiny* (1919) (Paris, 1967), 57, 92, 145; D. Mereschkowski [Merezhkovskii] et al., *Das Reich des Antichrist: Russland und der Bolschewismus* (Munich, 1921) p. 12.

47. Terence Emmons (ed.), *Time of Troubles: The Diary of Iu. V. Got'e* (Princeton, NJ, 1988) p. 386.

48. Lenin to Gorky, 15 September 1919, in V. I. Lenin, *Polnoe sobranie sochineii*, 5th edn (Moscow, 1965) (hereafter *PSS*), vol. 51, p. 48.

49. Kendall E. Bailes, *Technology and Society under Lenin and Stalin: Origins of the Soviet Technical Intelligentsia, 1917–1945* (Princeton, NJ, 1978); Schlögel, *Jenseits des Grossen Oktober*, ch. 7.

50. Sheila Fitzpatrick, *The Commissariat of Enlightenment: Soviet Organization of Education and the Arts under Lunacharsky, October 1917–1921* (Cambridge, 1970); Oskar Anweiler and Karl-Heinz Ruffmann (eds), *Kulturopolitik der Sowjetunion* (Stuttgart, 1973), pp. 16–45.
51. *Iz istorii VSNKh* (Moscow, 1958), pp. 235, 256; M. S. Melgunow, *Der Rote Terror in Russland, 1918–1923* (Berlin, 1924), p. 304.
52. V. I. Lenin, 'Otvet na otkrytoe pis'mo spetsialista' (1919), *PSS*, vol. 38, p. 219.
53. V. N. Ipatieff [Ipat'ev], *The Life of a Chemist: Memoirs* (Stanford, Cal., 1946).
54. Vladimir Vernadskii, *Zhizneopisanie: Izbrannye trudy. Vospominaniia sovremennikov. Suzhdeniia potomkov* (Moscow, 1993), p. 277.
55. Hilde Hardeman, *Coming to Terms with the Soviet Regime: The 'Changing Signposts' Movement among Russian Emigrés in the Early Twenties* (Dekalb, Ill., 1994).
56. Vernadskii, *Zhizneopisanie*, p. 290ff; Leo Trotzki [Trotsky], *Literatur und Revolution* (Vienna, 1924) p. 25.
57. Mikhail Agurskii, *Ideologiia natsionalbol'shevizma* (Paris, 1980) p. 212.
58. Lenin, 'O znachenii voinstvuiushchego materializma' (1922), *PSS*, vol. 45, p. 33; idem, 'Predislovie' (1922), ibid, p. 52.
59. Lynn Mally, *Culture of the Future: The Proletkult Movement in Revolutionary Russia* (Berkeley, Cal., 1990).
60. Arlen V. Blium, *Za kulisami 'ministerstva pravdy.' Tainaia istoriia sovetskoi cenzury, 1917–1929* (St Petersburg, 1994); V. S. Izmozik, *Glaze i ushi rezhima: Gosudarstvennyi politicheskii kontrol' za naseleniem Sovetskoi Rossii v 1918–1928 gg* (St Petersburg, 1995).
61. Boris Korsch, *The Permanent Purge of Soviet Libraries* (The Hebrew University of Jerusalem, The Soviet and East European Research Centre, Research Paper No. 50) (Jerusalem, 1983); S. Dzimbinov, 'Epitafiia spetskhranu?', in *Novyi Mir*, v (1990) 243–52.
62. *Pisateli ob iskusstve i o sebe. Sbornik statei* (Moscow, 1924), p. 53.
63. Viacheslav P. Polonskii, 'Na vzgliad redaktora', in *Novyi Mir*, VII (1986) 199–217.
64. Kornei Chukovskii, 'Iz dnevnika (1924–1925)', in *Zvezda*, no. 11 (1990) pp. 130–50, 148: 'Kak kritik ia vynuzhden molchat', ibo kritika u nas teper' rappovskoi, sudiat ne po talantam, a po (part) biletam. Sdelali menia detskim pisatelem. No pozornye istorii s moim detskim knigam … zastavili menia soiti s etoi areny. I vot ia nashel poslednii ugol: shutovskii gazetnyi roman pod prikrytiem chuzoi familii. Kto zastavit menia–perestavshego byt' kritikom, perestavshego byt' poetom – idti v romanisty? Da ia, Kornei Chukovskii, vovse ne romanist, a byvshii kritik, byvshii chelovek'.
65. Lecture by Lebedev-Polianskii in 1931, 'O rukovodstve belletristiki', in Blium, *Za kulisami*, p. 232.
66. Richard Stites, *Revolutionary Dreams: Utopian Vision and Experimental Life in the Russian Revolution* (Oxford, 1989) accentuates the libertarian aspects; the totalitarian ambitions are emphasized in Boris Groys, *Gesamtkunstwerk Stalin: Die gespaltene Kultur in der Sowjetunion* (Munich, 1988); Stefan Plaggenbord, *Menschenbilder und kulturelle Praxis in Sowjetrussland zwischen Oktoberrevolution und Stalinismus*, doctoral dissertation (Freiburg, 1993).
67. Iurii Karabchevskii, *Voskresenie Maiakovskogo* (Munich, 1985).

68. John Barber, 'The Establishment of Intellectual Orthodoxy in the USSR, 1928–1934', in *Past & Present*, no. 83 (1979), 141–64; Ia. G. Rokitianskii, 'Tragicheskaia sud'ba akademika D. B. Riazanova', in *Novaia i Noveishaia Istoriia*, II (1992) 106–48; Michael S. Fox, 'Political Culture, Purges and Proletarianization of the Institute of Red Professors, 1921–1929', in *The Russian Review*, LII (1993) 20–42; L. A. Kozlova, 'Institut Krasnoi Professury (1921–1938 gody): Istoriograficheskii ocherk', in *Sotsiologicheskii Zhurnal*, no. 1 (1994) 96–112; Lutz-Dieter Behrendt, *Das Institut der Roten Professur (IRP) in Moskau (1921–1938) als Kaderschmiede der Parteiintelligenz* (forthcoming).

69. Citations from Karl Eimermacher (ed.), *Dokumente zur sowjetischen Literaturpolitik, 1917–1932* (Stuttgart, 1972) pp. 171, 176.

70. Paraphrases and citations from Eimermacher, *Dokumente*, pp. 104, 105; Trotzki, *Literatur*, pp. 33, 40.

71. Iosif V. Stalin, 'O nekotorykh voprosakh istorii bol'shevizma. Pis'mo v redaktsiiu "Proletarskaia Revoliutsiia"', in idem, *Sochineniia*, vol. XIII (Moscow, 1952) pp. 82–102, 98, 101; 'gniloi liberalizm' [p. 98]; '... fal'sifikatorov nashei partii, sistematicheski sryvaia s nikh maski' [p. 101].

72. Sheila Fitzpatrick (ed.), *Cultural Revolution in Russia, 1928–1931* (Bloomington, 1978).

73. *Sovetskaia literatura na novom etape: Stenogramma pervogo plenuma Orgkomiteta Soiuza Sovetskikh Pisatelei* (29 October–3 November 1932) (Moscow, 1932).

74. F. F. Perchenok, 'Akademiia nauk na "velikom perelome"', in *Zven'ia. Istoricheskii al'manakh*, vyp. 1 (Moscow, 1991), pp. 163–235; M. P. Malysheva and V. S. Poznanskii (eds), 'Partiinoe rukovodstvo AN', in *Vestnik RAN*, vol. 64, no. 11 (1994) pp. 1033–43.

75. Naum Jasny, *Soviet Economists of the Twenties: Names to be Remembered* (Cambridge, 1972); A. P. Efimkin, *Dvazhdy reabilitirovannye: N. D. Kondrat'ev, L. N. Iurovskii* (Moscow, 1991).

76. *Pis'ma I. V. Stalina V. M. Molotovii 1925–1936 gg. Sbornik dokumentov* (Moscow, 1995) pp. 211ff.

77. Fediukin, *Partiia i intelligentsiia*, pp. 75–7.

78. F. D. Asnin and V. M. Alpatov, '"Rossiiskaia natsional'naia partiia" – zloveshchaia vydumka sovetskikh chekistov', in *Vestnik RAN*, vol. 64, no. 10 (1994) pp. 920–30.

79. V. P. Leonov *et al.* (eds), *Akademicheskoe delo 1929–1931 gg.* vyp. 1: *Delo po obvineniiu akademika S. F. Platonov* (St Petersburg, 1993); B. V. Anan'ich, V. M. Paneiakh, 'Prinuditel'noe "soavtorstvo"', in *In memoriam: Istoricheskii sbornik pamiati F. F. Perchenka* (Moscow and St Peterburg, 1995), pp. 87–111.

80. Cf. V. A. Ul'ianovskaia, *Formirovanie nauchnoi intelligentsii v SSSR 1917–1937 gg.* (Moscow, 1966) p. 130ff.

81. Boris Pasternak, *Doktor Zhivago*, vol. 2 (Paris, 1959) p. 560.

8

'Democracy' as Identification: Towards the Study of Political Consciousness during the February Revolution[1]

Boris Ivanovich Kolonitskii

Historians of different persuasions write of the February Revolution of 1917 in Russia as a 'democratic' revolution. Generations of Marxists of varying hue therefore have described it as 'a bourgeois-democratic revolution'.

During 'perestroika' (the reforms of 1985–91 in the Soviet Union) pitting democratic February against Bolshevik October became an important component of the historical sensibility of the anti-Communist movement. The February Revolution was regarded as a dramatic, unsuccessful attempt at the modernization and Westernization of Russia. Some histories and memoirs, both liberal and moderate socialist, said much the same. Kerenskii's account, for example, is of this sort, especially his last memoirs. In his opinion, 'the overwhelming majority of the population of Russia with all its heart wanted democracy.'[2]

Such an approach is justified in many respects. Thus both the legislation of the February Revolution and the functioning of the Provisional Government aimed at democratic, elected institutions, the guarantee of the rights of man, and democratic liberties. 'Democratization' was looked upon as a universal solution to all possible problems. After February, there were attempts to democratize the theatre, the Church and the school (in the latter, there was talk of introducing labour training). The course of the Revolution witnessed a unique experiment at democratizing the army, which Kerenskii himself called 'the freest in the world' (the soldiers of the 12th Army, for instance, were proud of the fact that it was 'the most democratic'). The armed forces now saw elected soldiers' committees with sweeping powers, soldiers chose their commanders at different levels, and even offensive action was on occasion decided by vote.

Democratic ideology and phraseology influenced the language of the Revolution. The term *demokratiia* (democracy), which was second in popularity only to the usages *narod* (people), *svoboda* (freedom) and *sotsializm* (socialism), was incontestably 'politically correct', ideologically fashionable and emotionally compelling. A provincial eparchial conference in Kursk came to the conclusion that the republican democratic dispensation accorded most with God's law. It was suggested that a ship of the line, *Imperator Nikolai II*, adopt the name *Demokratiia*. It was not only ships that changed their names. On 8 (21) April 1917,[3] a wounded soldier indicted a special petition: like many others with that surname, he wished to forsake Romanov, which sounded too 'monarchist' and 'unprepossessing' (some Rasputins and Sukhomlinovs also wanted to change their names). He wrote: 'I consider it insulting to myself in these times to bear the name Romanov, and so I request you to permit me to change Romanov to Demokratov.'[4] If the renaming of warships bears witness to the inclusion of a political term in a new state ideology, then the anthroponymic reaction to the Revolution (the change of surname and the decline in popularity of the name Nikolai, which was most common before February) indicates a particular politicization of private life. In this, for neophytes of political life, the term *demokratiia* had a positive meaning; and we must assume that the soldier Romanov (he was not permitted to change his name), thought that he himself and his family and descendants would take pride in the new name.

In practice, it became necessary for all political forces, from the Bolsheviks to the *kornilovtsy* (supporters of General Kornilov), to include the term *demokratiia* in their own political lexicon. Hence, N. A. Berdiaev called L. G. Kornilov 'an indisputable democrat', and B. V. Savinkov regarded the general 'a genuine democrat and an unswerving republican'.[5] In order to counteract German propaganda in Russia, the British and French missions, in collaboration with Kornilov's entourage, set up a special publishing house in Petrograd, which put out not less than twelve million posters. It was called *Demokraticheskaia Rossiia* ('Democratic Russia'). Evidently it was assumed that there would be demand for printed matter with such a label.[6] On the other side, the leader of the Bolsheviks was perceived by his supporters as 'the leader of democracy'; and in May 1917, soldiers wrote in from the front to a Bolshevik newspaper: 'We send our warmest greetings to the leader of Russian democracy and the defender of our interests, comrade Lenin'. A Bolshevik poet declared:

> I sing of the people's family
> Which as democracy is known
> For its bold struggle naturally
> Against apathy and superstition.[7]

Hence, all along the political spectrum it was considered necessary to be called 'democratic'. The satirist D. N. Semenovskii had every reason to describe the situation thus

> All Rus' today is clothed anew
> In devilish motley masquerade
> The pogromist takes the guise of the Kadet
> And who is there who is not a democrat?[8]

The emotional reaction of Lord Hardinge, the Permanent Secretary at the British Foreign Office, testifies in its own way to the popularity of the term 'democracy' in revolutionary Russia. 'How I hate the word democracy today: if we don't win the war, it will be thanks to the Russian revolution and all this chatter about the democracies of the world', he wrote to James Buchanan, the British Ambassador in Petrograd, on 13 (26) April 1917.[9] Not without reason did he doubt the military capacity of the Russian revolutionary army, even as many of his countrymen were enthused over the united struggle of 'democratic countries' with Prussian militarism and absolutism.

However, Russian revolutionaries not only strove for democratic reforms within their own country, but they also longed to make Russia 'the most democratic' state in the world. 'We will construct not some English or German edifice, but a democratic republic in the full sense of the word', announced Kerenskii in Helsingfors on 15 (28) May. He called Russia 'the freest country in the world' and called her 'the avantgarde of the democratic, socialist movement in Europe', 'the most democratic state in Europe', and announced that Russia 'has come to stand at the forefront of all democratic states'. Russian politicians occasionally infected foreigners with their enthusiasm. After a meeting with Kerenskii, G. Williams, the influential British journalist, wrote, 'If all goes well, Russia may become a freer country than England.'[10]

Kerenskii turned out to be not a little close in his sentiments to his political opponent Lenin, who called post-February Russia 'the freest' of countries. Concerning faith in the miracle of 'the transformation of the half-Asiatic despotism into almost the freest country in the world', the Menshevik-defencist, A. N. Potresov, sarcastically commented, 'As if in fact a backward country, which not long ago excited a mixture of apprehension and pity abroad, a country of atomized peoples, submissive to the Cossack whip, can, in a single leap, not only bridge the gulf which from time immemorial has separated it from the cultural levels of the European West, but can also overtake that West, setting standards of hitherto unheard of democratism, and forms of citizenship unseen before.' P. A. Sorokin called this atmosphere 'Slavophilism inside out'. 'Revolutionary messianism' was characteristic of the radicalized masses and the liberal members of the Provisional Government. 'The spirit of the Russian people is the universal democratic spirit by its very nature. It is ready not only to merge with the democracy of the whole world, and to stand at the head of it, but also ready to develop it on the principles of liberty, equality and fraternity', averred the first prime minister, Prince G. E. Lvov, on whose world-view Slavophils exercised a strong influence.[11]

Russian messianic ideas inherited thereafter by the Bolsheviks were, as is evident, characteristic of some leaders of democratic February. Often, in fact, 'revolutionary-democratic' messianism came close even then to ideas of 'the export of revolution'. Hence Tsereteli, the leader of the Mensheviks and a minister in the Provisional Government, asserted that the purpose of the revolution was 'the final victory of democracy inside the country and beyond its borders'. Kerenskii also expressed similar views in April 1917, and said 'we may play a colossal role in world history if we can make other people follow our path, if we can make our friends and enemies respect freedom. But for this it is necessary that they should see that it is impossible to struggle against the ideas of Russian democracy.'[12]

Certainly, such assertions first of all ideologically justified the necessity to continue the war against 'German militarism' – the 'bulwark of monarchism in Europe'. In their propaganda flysheets, therefore, Russian soldiers called on their opponents to follow their example and overthrow their ruling dynasties. However, allies could also become the target of the export of revolution; for instance, calls to carry out an anti-monarchist revolution in Romania were widely disseminated among Russian soldiers within that country. Russian soldiers also put about anti-Shah and anti-feudal ideas in the north of Persia.

The attempt to be 'the most advanced democracy' may be discerned in legislative practice also. For example, the law on elections to the Constituent Assembly included electoral norms which countries with more developed legal structures had arrived at only after decades.

Finally, the very term *demokratiia* was understood in different ways in 1917. Different treatments of the term were thrown up by all possible kinds of political dictionary, which were meant to ease the assimilation of the language of contemporary politics in mass consciousness (contemporaries spoke of the necessity for an appropiate 'translation' of newspapers and flysheets). In many instances, 'democracy' was treated as 'people's power'.[13] However, these concerned some sociopolitical ideal, not real states; hence the dictionary, put out by the Moscow publishing house *Narodnaia Mysl'*, asserted that the USA and France 'are, all in all, bourgeois republics, and little Switzerland is closer to the model of a democratic republic, though she is still far from being an absolute and complete democracy'. Such a formulation assumed that 'a bourgeois republic' can not be democratic. Often, arming the people to replace the standing army was considered the most important attribute of a democratic republic.[14]

But democracy as 'people's power' was not the only one ascribed to it. P. Volkov, author of a dictionary published by the Moscow publishing house, 'Ideia', rightly noted: 'Now the word "democracy" is used either in the sense of "the rule of the people", "the power of the people", or to mean the broad masses of the people, the whole range of democratic parties or a state, founded on democratic principles.'[15] Hence, in some cases, 'democracy' acted as a synonym for 'people' and, accordingly, 'democrat' was defined as *narodnik* ('populist').[16] Sometimes however, this referred not to all the 'people', but only to the 'democratic strata', 'the labouring classes'. Polemicizing with such a point of view, N. A. Arsen'ev, author of the dictionary put out by D. Ia. Makovskii's publishing house in Moscow, wrote: 'Democracy denotes all the people, the rich and the poor, men and women, and so on. Nowadays, only the poor and needy, that is the workers and peasants, are called the democracy; this is not right.' The authors of the *Dictionary of Political Terms and Political Figures*, for instance, took a contrary position, distinguishing between the terms 'democratic republic' and 'democracy': '*demokratiia* ("democracy") pertains to all those classes of the country which live by their own labour: workers, peasants, functionaries, and intelligentsia.'[17] It is significant that the latter dictionary was put out by an extremely moderate liberal publishing house, the 'Osvobozhdennaia Rossiia', which was set up by the Provisional Committee of the State Duma.

The term 'democracy' was sometimes used in a most specific sense, while on occasion it expressed a certain kind of self-identification. Here, 'democracy' was contrasted with, not 'dictatorship', 'police state' and so on, but 'enfranchised elements', [what the French call the *pays légal*] 'ruling classes', and most often, 'bourgeoisie'. The terms 'democracy' and especially 'revolutionary democracy' often emerged as synonyms for the notions 'democratic strata' ('people'), 'democratic organizations' (the soviets and committees were regarded as such in 1917), and 'democratic forces' (where only socialists regarded themselves democrats). The position of socialists sometimes also influenced liberal publications. Hence, even *Birzhevye Vedomosti* named the Executive Committee of the Soviet of Workers' and Soldiers' Deputies 'the leading organ of democracy'. The identification of 'democracy' with the socialists may be found even in Tsereteli's speech in the Constituent Assembly. He spoke of 'the internecine war of democracy, one part of which nullifies the achievements of the whole of democracy and gives it over, bound hand and foot, to the bourgeoisie'. As is evident, 'democracy' was counterposed to 'bourgeoisie', and the Bolsheviks were unconditionally included by him in the camp of 'democracy'. 'The part of democracy represented by you': thus did Tsereteli address the Bolsheviks.[18]

It is significant that comparable usage may be found not only in the texts of 1917, but also in émigré memoirs, to the extent that such usage was firmly established. Even Tsereteli's memoirs reflect it, although they were written over many years. He used this term in different senses. Sometimes, it is 'socialist' democracy and 'purely bourgeois' democracy. Here, he includes a part of the 'bourgeoisie' in 'democracy'. In other places, he writes of 'the united front' 'of all democratic forces', which is not confined to socialists. At the same time, however, he sometimes counterposes 'democracy' and 'bourgeoisie'. Here, he often regards Bolshevism and 'left maximalism' as opponents of 'democracy', and often, describing the conflict between Bolsheviks and moderate socialists, speaks of 'the internecine struggle within the ranks of democracy', that is he includes Bolsheviks in 'the camp of democracy'.[19] In this case, the memoirist Tsereteli employs the socialist jargon of 1917.

This may be found even in such a convinced supporter of agreement with the 'bourgeoisie' as A. N. Potresov: 'the violent ideology of Lenin is only the concentrated and perhaps exaggerated expression of those ideas and sentiments which in part float in the minds of a significant section of democracy', he wrote in 1917.[20]

For Tsereteli, Potresov and many other moderate socialists of 1917, 'democracy' meant the forces represented in the soviets and committees, socialists of differing persuasion. A similar approach is to be found, for instance, in the constitution of the Democratic Conference of 11–14 September (27 September–5 October) – the representatives of the bourgeoisie were not invited to it. In the localities, in fact, activists did not permit families of the landed gentry to participate in the elections to the new zemstvo – for this would be 'undemocratic'.

In his memoirs, Kerenskii criticized the language of Russian socialists and presented his own as if it were the pure democratic position of the Western type. However, Kerenskii the memoirist often misrepresents Kerenskii the politician of 1917 vintage with his grandly modernized and Westernized self-portrait. Actually, that language was also his language. In his well-known speech of 2 (15) March in the Soviet, he declared: 'I am a representative of democracy and the Provisional Government should look upon me as the spokesman of the demands of democracy and ought to take account especially of those opinions which I will put forward as the representative of democracy, by whose means the old order was overthrown.' In other words, he regarded himself alone as the representative of 'democracy'. In another speech, he proclaimed: 'I can, in the name of the Provisional Government of the country, present the greetings and compliments of all democracy: to the workers, soldiers and peasants.'[21] He presented himself as the 'Minister-Democrat' as if to convey that he did not regard other members of the government – Kadets and other liberals – as 'democrats'. Even in earlier émigré works by Kerenskii, we encounter the opposition of 'bourgeoisie-democracy', and 'Russian bourgeoisie-labour democracy'.[22]

The language of the Russian Revolution also influenced foreigners. For example, the well-known English journalist, A. Rains, also wrote of the schism among socialists as a conflict between Bolsheviks and 'the other part of democracy'. A survey done for the British War Ministry speaks of a compromise between 'bourgeois' and 'democratic' parties in Russia. Even the British Ambassador, James Buchanan, resorted to the concepts 'bourgeoisie' and 'democracy' for his descriptions of contending camps.[23]

Historically, 'democracy', 'democrat', and 'genuine democrat' were used for self-identification and, accordingly, political opponents were, so to speak, excluded from the political process. In this regard, the

Russian Revolution of 1917 was no exception. The special feature, in fact, on this occasion was the setting off of 'democracy' against 'bourgeoisie', suggested by differing strands of socialism. Certainly not all agreed with this approach, and attempts were made to pit democracy against socialism. However, in the political life of Russia, the language of class dominated, and the notion of 'democracy' was included in this language, subject to certain changes. We find an unusual confirmation of this in the report of the British vice-consul in Khar'kov: 'Class hatred is intensified through the misuse of foreign words, such as "bourgeoisie", "proletariat", "democrat", "citizen" and "comrade".'[24]

The socialist usage of 'democracy' penetrated mass consciousness and, here, 'democracy' was identified with 'people' as in 'democracy is us'. However, the latter reworked the concepts of 'democracy' and 'republic' to accord with their own traditional notions of power. Mass consciousness furnished its own interpretations of other concepts as well, which were borrowed from the language of contemporary politics, for example 'socialism', 'bourgeoisie' and so on.

James Buchanan recalled that in the first days of the Revolution, a Russian soldier remarked, 'Yes, we need a republic, but at the head of it there ought to be a good tsar.' To the Ambassador this seemed confirmation of the truth of his own views of the low level of political culture of Russians: 'Russia is not sufficiently mature for a purely democratic form of government', he asserted. We come across mention of similar sentiments in other sources: 'We want a republic ... but with a good tsar', wrote the French diplomat de Roben, concerning the views of Russian soldiers. The American historian and slavist F. Holder, who was present in Petrograd in 1917, also noted: 'They speak of soldiers who say that they want a republic similar to the English one, or a republic with a tsar. One soldier asserted that they should elect a President, and when they asked him whom he would elect, the reply came "the tsar". Judging by much evidence, the soldiers do not understand what is happening, what the revolution means.'[25]

Certainly, one may assume that these authors wrote about the same soldiers. Foreigners mixed with each other and met at receptions where they exchanged anecdotes and political news. However, even in the collections of the Russian military censorship, we come across similar excerpts from soldiers' letters: 'We want a democratic republic and a *tsar'-batiushka* for three years'; or, 'it would be good if they were to give us a republic with a clever tsar'. One of the censors reported: 'Almost every letter from the peasants expresses the desire to see a tsar at the head of Russia. Evidently, monarchy is the sole form of government intelligible to peasant notions.'[26] It is possible that officials of military censorship were conservatively minded and chose examples in accord with their political inclinations. Not all peasants and peasant-soldiers who spoke in March and April about the tsar were convinced monarchists (and as is clear, some soldiers wished to restrict the tsar's term of rule). Rather, notions of 'state' and 'tsardom' were synonymous to them, and it was difficult for them to imagine a state (*gosudarstvo*) without a sovereign (*gosudar'*). It is well known that often soldiers refused to take an oath to the Provisional Government, since the very mention of a 'state' in the text of the oath was regarded as counter-revolutionary propagation of monarchism. The soldiers shouted here 'We do not have a state, rather there is a republic.'[27]

In his memoirs, a Menshevik deputy of the Moscow Soviet of Workers' Deputies gives a striking example of the mixture of anti-monarchist sentiment and monarchist mentality. He describes his speech at a meeting of reserve regiments near Vladimir at the beginning of March 1917:

> In the middle of the field there was a rostrum with two or three soldiers on it and a crowd of thousands around it. The place was thick with people. I was speaking, naturally, of war and peace, about land – 'all land to the people' – and of the advantages of a republic over a monarchy. But when I stopped, and when the endless 'hurrahs' and applause ended, a powerful voice spoke out: 'We want you as tsar', which led to a fresh thunder of applause. I declined the throne of the Romanovs and left, oppressed with the thought how easy it was for any adventurer or demagogue to assume authority over these naive and simple people.[28]

The attitude of the 'educated Westernizer' -socialist, who had mastered the language of contemporary politics, to the 'dark' uneducated peasant-soldiers, who did not understand 'the correct' language of democratic socialists, is interesting in this case. However, this is also striking evidence of the fact that the supporters of democracy and 'the people' often spoke in different political languages. The use of the same words – 'democracy', 'republic', 'tsar', 'socialism' and so on – conjured up an illusion of mutual understanding.[29]

To the masses initially, the notions of 'democratic republic' (which could appear as a synonym for 'new life', or 'the bright future') and 'the good tsar' could effortlessly coexist. However, this evidently applied only to the first months of the Revolution. The 'Rasputiniade' and the destruction of the symbols of Empire, and mass anti-monarchist propaganda – all these led to a taboo on the words 'tsar' and 'monarchy' to the almost total exclusion of them from the political lexicon (although in the autumn of 1917 it is possible to notice some revival of monarchist sympathies, which was expressed, for example, in various peasant resolutions). Even an attempt to distribute brochures on the English constitution led to agitation in one of the regiments, for the mere mention of the term 'constitutional monarchy' was received as vile monarchist propaganda. However, mass consciousness, having ceased to use some of the concepts of 'the language of monarchy', retained a monarchist mentality. Democratic ideology could now be superimposed onto a traditional authoritarian and patriarchal culture; and the place of the tsar, the ruler, was now assumed by 'genuine champions of freedom', and 'real leaders of democracy'.

The main 'leader of democracy' became Kerenskii, the most popular leader of February. In 1917, a real cult of 'the leader of the people' took shape (in fact this precise term was used), substantially anticipating comparable cults of the Soviet period. Resolutions called him 'the genuine leader of Russian democracy', 'the symbol of democracy', and so on. In the formation of the Kerenskii cult, the Russian intelligentsia played a not inconsiderable role. Here, the very name of the leader became an extremely important political marker, and people called Kerenskii the 'minister-democrat', 'the symbol of democracy':[30] 'For us Kerenskii is not a minister, he is not the people's tribune, he has ceased even to be a human being. Kerenskii is a symbol of the revolution', so wrote adherents of the 'people's minister' who subjectively considered themselves the devotees of democracy.[31]

It is possible that Kerenskii was right when he asserted that an absolute majority of Russia's population were supporters of democracy. However, did different supporters of 'democracy' follow completely different ends? As is clear, 'the very word democracy' was understood totally differently. This term in the sources of 1917 demands constant 'translation' by historians (and, it must be admitted, such a translation is not always easy). Here, from a contemporary point of view, the understanding of 'democracy' both by many socialists and run-of-the-mill soldiers and workers was often 'incorrect'. However, such a verdict can hardly be considered historical (and in that case, even the understanding of 'democracy' in the *Politics* of Aristotle is 'incorrect'). The very fact of the simultaneous functioning of various languages of politics objectively made the democratic development of the country difficult.

In 1917, the 'language of class', the language of socialists which dominated in the course of the Revolution, had a strong impact on the 'language of democracy'.[32] On the other hand, the deeply authoritarian and patriarchal tradition often adapted to new fashionable ideological constructs, and often deformed them, endowing them with new meaning. Mass 'democratism' of the 1917 type could be combined with the cult of 'the people's' 'democratic' leader. It should be emphasized that the Bolsheviks deployed some of the ideological structures constituted after February when they constructed their model of 'soviet democracy'. In this sense, their politics represented 'a radical continuation of the past, and not a revolutionary break with it'.[33] We should not of course exaggerate the impact of radical political upheavals on mass consciousness – a dramatic change in political symbolism need not be accompanied by the dissolution of deeply laid mental structures.

Notes

1. Translated from the Russian by Hari Vasudevan.
2. A. Kerensky, *Russia at History's Turning Point* (New York, 1965) p. 326.
3. Dates in brackets are according to the Gregorian calendar. They are thirteen days after those by the Russian Orthodox calendar, which was in use in Russia until 1918. Both dates have been given where necessary.
4. *Russkaia volia*, 1(4) June (1917); *Russkoe slovo*, 21 April (4 May) (1917); Rossiiskii gosudarstvennyi istoricheskii arkhiv [hereafter *RGIA*], *fond* [*f.*]1412, *opis*' [*op.*]16, *delo* [*d.*]532. On the changing of names see A. M. Verner, 'What's in a Name? Of Dog-killers, Jews and Rasputin', *Slavic Review*, LIII (1994) 1046–70.
5. N. A. Berdiaiev, 'O svobode i dostoinstve slova', in *Narodopravstvo*, no. 11(1917) p. 6; House of Lords Record Office, Historical Collection, no. 206: the Stow Hill Papers, DS 2/1 (G).
6. B. I. Kolonitskii, 'Izdatel'stvo "Demokraticheskaia Rossiia", inostrannye missii i okruzhenie L. G. Kornilova in Rossiia 1917 godu', in *Novye podkhody i vzgliady: Sbornik nauchnykh trudov* (St Petersburg, 1994) vyp. 2, pp. 28–31.
7. *Pravda*, 11, 19 May (1917).
8. *Russkaia stikhotvornaia satira 1908–1917-kh godov* (Leningrad, 1974) p. 568.
9. Cambridge University Library, Hardinge Papers, vol. 31, p. 311.
10. *A. F. Kerenskii ob armii i voine* (Odessa, 1917) pp. 10, 32; *Rech' A. F. Kerenskogo, voennogo i morskogo ministra, tovarishcha predsedatelia Petrogradskogo Soveta rabochikh i soldatskikh deputatov, proiznesennaia im 29 aprelia, v soveshchanii delegatov fronta* (Moscow, 1917) p. 3; H. Pitcher, *Witnesses of the Russian Revolution* (London, 1994) p. 61.

11. A. N. Potresov, *Posmertnyi sbornik proizvedenii* (Paris, 1937) p. 230; *Volia naroda* 25 September (1917); *Rech'*, 27 April (10 May) (1917).

12. I. G. Tsereteli, *Vospominaniia o Fevral'skoi revoliutsii* (Paris, 1963) *kn.* 1, p. 147. See also p. 119; *Rechi A. F. Kerenskogo* (Kiev, 1917) p. 8.

13. See *Narodnyi slovar'* (Prague, 1917) p. 11; *Narodnyi tolkovyi slovar'* (Prague, 1917) p. 8; *Politicheskii slovar': Obshchestvennoe izlozhenie inostrannykh i drugikh slov, voshedshikh v russkii iazyk* (Prague, 1917) p. 8, etc.

14. Pr. Zvenigorodtsev (ed.), *Politicheskii slovar'* (Moscow, 1917) col. 16; *Tolkovatel' neponiatnykh slov v gazetakh i knigakh* (Odessa, 1917) p. 8.

15. P. Volkov, *Revoliutsionnyi katekhizis (Karmannaia politicheskaia entsiklopediia)* (Moscow, 1917) p. 7.

16. *Politicheskii slovar'* (Piriatin, 1917) p. 14.

17. N. A. Arsen'ev, *Kratkii politicheskii slovar' dlia vsekh* (Moscow, 1917) p. 9; *Tolkovnik politicheskikh slov i politicheskikh slov i politicheskikh deiatelei* (Prague, 1917) p. 22.

18. *Birzhevye vedomosti* 22 April (5 May) (1917); *Pervyi den' Vserossiiskogo uchreditel'nogo sobraniia* (Prague, 1918) pp. 36, 45.

19. Tsereteli, *Vospominaniia o fevral'skoi revoliutsii, kn.* 1, pp. 61, 121; *kn.* 2, pp. 194, 394, 402.

20. Potresov, *Posmertnyi sbornik proizvedenii*, p. 229; Potresov associated Bolshevism with 'revolutionary democracy' even in 1926; see S. Ivanovich, *A. N. Potresov, Opyt kul'turno-psikhologicheskogo portreta* (Paris, 1938) p. 211.

21. A. Kerensky, *Russia as History's Turning Point*, p. 411; *Petrogradskii Sovet rabochikh i soldatskikh deputatov v 1917 godu: Protokoly, stenogrammy i otchety, rezoliutsii, postanovleniia obshchikh sobranii, sobranii sektsii, zasedanii Ispolnitel'nogo komiteta i fraktsii 27 fevralia–25 oktiabria 1917 goda* (St Petersburg, 1993) pp. 77–8.

22. *Vserossiiskoe soveshchanie Sovetov rabochikh i soldatskikh deputatov: Stenograficheskii otchet* (Moscow and Leningrad, 1927) p. 68; A. F. Kerenskii, *Izdaleka: Sbornik statei, 1920–21* (Paris, 1922) pp. 93, 164, 165.

23. Pitcher, *Witnesses*, p. 177; Public Record Office [hereafter PRO], War Office, 158/964; G. Buchanan, *My Mission to Russia and other Diplomatic Memories*, vol. 2 (London, 1923) p. 128.

24. PRO, Foreign Office, 371, 3015, N 225904, 250.

25. Buchanan, vol. 2, pp. 86, 114; see also pp. 111, 128, 216–17; L. de Robien, *The Diary of a Diplomat in Russia, 1917–1918* (London, 1969) p. 24; *War, Revolution and Peace in Russia: The Passages of Frank Golder, 1914–1927* (Stanford, Cal., 1992) p. 46.

26. Rossiiskii Gosudarstvennyi Voenno-Istoricheskii Arkhiv, f. 2003, *op.* 1, *d.* 1494, *l.* 14; Manuscript Division, Russian National Library (formerly the Saltykov–Shchedrin Public Library), *f.* 152, *d.* 98, *l.* 34.

27. D. P. Os'kin, *Zapiski praporshchika* (Moscow, 1931) pp. 110–11.

28. St Antony's College (Oxford), Russian and East European Centre, G. Katkov's Papers, *Moskovskii Sovet rabochikh deputatov, 1917–1922*, p. 10.

29. Significant is the testimony of the well-known historian N. I. Kareev. He spent the summer in the country, where the local blacksmith said to him: 'I want ... our republic to be socialist.' In the end, it appeared that the blacksmith was the owner of a *khutor* and had broken off from the commune, and stood for the guarantee of private ownership and was against the presi-

dential form of government – see N. I. Kareev, *Prozhitoe i perezhitoe* (Leningrad, 1990) p. 268.

30. Gosudarstvennyi Arkhiv Rossiiskoi Federatsii, *f*. 1778, *op*. 1, *d*. 83, *l*. 92; *d*. 85, *l*. 7; *d*. 90, *l*. 50. On the cult of Kerenskii, see A. G. Golikov, *Fenomen Kerenskogo, Otechestvennaia Istoriia*, no. 5 (1992). Regarding the relationship between Kerenskii and the intelligentsia, see B. I. Kolonitskii, 'A. F. Kerenskii i Merezhkovskie', *Literaturnoe obozrenie*, no. 3 (1991).

31. Gosudarstvennyi muzei politicheskoi istorii Rossii (Sankt-Peterburg), *f*. 2, no. 10964. See also A. Kulegin and V. Bobrov, 'Istoriia bez kupiur', in *Sovetskie muzei*, no. 3 (1990) 5–6.

32. On the 'language of class', see D. P. Koenker, 'Moscow in 1917: the View from Below', in D. H. Kaiser (ed.), *The Workers in Russia, 1917: The View from Below* (Cambridge, 1987) pp. 91–2.

33. W. Rosenberg has come to the same conclusion through the study of another problem on the basis of other sources – see 'Sozdanie novogo gosudarstva v 1917: Predstavleniia i deistvitel'nost' in *Anatomiia revoliutsii: 1917 god v Rossii: Massy, partii, vlast'* (St Petersburg, 1994) p. 97.

9
All Power to the Parish? The Problems and Politics of Church Reform in Late Imperial Russia

Gregory L. Freeze

By the late nineteenth century, the agenda for reform in the Russian Orthodox Church had come to encompass a broad array of issues – its relationship to the state, re-establishment of the patriarchate, liberalization of divorce, vernacularization of services, and a plethora of other problems. In the view of many, however, the most critical issues concerned the parish – that nuclear unit of the Church beset with far-reaching difficulties and problems. As lay and clerical contemporaries argued, in modern times the parish had suffered a corrosive decline in its identity, role and authority, especially in two vital matters: disposition of church funds and appointment of the local priest.[1] The issue of parish funds was most sensitive, especially in the mass of poor parishes, which were forced to divert scarce resources to finance diocesan administration and the ecclesiastical schools that served primarily the clergy's own progeny. As a result, the parish ceased to be the nucleus of community life or even to hold the status of a juridical entity (*iuridicheskoe litso*); it could not take up modern social functions (for example, open almshouses or parish schools) and sometimes even had difficulty maintaining the local church and providing traditional religious services.

By the late nineteenth century, many contemporaries – in the government, educated lay society, and the Church itself – had come to believe that the rebirth of Orthodoxy depended largely on revitalizing the parish to make it more meaningful and important in the everyday lives of the laity. In that fundamental sense, parish reform was central to the Church's attempt to revive Orthodoxy and to steel the faithful against the inroads of secularization and proselytization by other confessions. Such reform, however, raised a host of thorny issues, made all the more difficult since parish reform involved not only the Church and canon law, but also the laity and secular state. Ultimately, the parish question was a test of reformability in late Imperial Russia, whether this regime was capable of designing, promulgating and implementing reform.

This essay will explore the 'parish question' in late Imperial Russia – surprisingly, an issue that, despite its significance, has been virtually ignored in the scholarly literature.[2] Drawing upon a large corpus of printed and archival materials,[3] this study seeks to elucidate the politics of parish reform and to explain why here, as in so many other spheres, the old order proved unable to enact and implement effective reform, even on an issue where there was an apparent consensus. It suggests that many factors played a role in thwarting reform, such as the structural problems of late Imperial Russia, such as the abiding ambiguity in Church–state relations and the destructive instrumentalization of political issues in the Duma monarchy. But, *au fond*, it seeks to demonstrate that the fundamental problem was not the method but the substance of a reform involving the transfer of power to the laity. And here the key point is the interactive process between Petersburg architects of reform and social realities at the base: most clergymen – liberal priests, not just reactionary bishops – recognized that parish empowerment carried enormous risk and danger. It was not so much canon, hidebound conservatism or egotistical self-interest, as fear of the 'dark masses' that impelled ranking prelates to resist widespread calls for 'all power to the parish'. It was, in effect, the same set of attitudes and fears that would impel the liberals in 1917 to defer – indefinitely – the very democratization that they had so long preached and promised. All this was no less true of the Church. As one perceptive observer aptly noted in 1913, the Church 'is terrified that church property be put (through the reborn and liberal proposals for the parish) in the hands of gray rural masses, which is still benighted and of course remote from understanding the true interests of the church'.[4]

The parish question in post-reform Russia

After more than a century of varied attempts to tighten diocesan control over the parish, from the 1850s Church and state authorities began seeking ways to 'de-bureaucratize' the parish in order to create greater opportunities for local initiative. Thus, the 'ecclesiastical Great Reforms' sought to revitalize the parish, primarily to improve the material condition of the clergy, but also to generate popular support and financing for charity and schools. In 1864, these efforts culminated in the formation of parish guardianships or councils (*popechitel'stva*),[5] special committees formed voluntarily by the parish and comprised of the priest and laymen elected by parishioners. It was this council's task to raise new funds to support the local church, clergy, charity and schools.[6] In essence, the council was a device to raise funds from parishioners, without any changes in the status of the parish, such as the restoration of its erstwhile right to select ordinands and to dispose of parish funds. As some critics forewarned, the councils neither aroused popular support nor raised substantial funds; even when zealous bishops or priests induced reluctant parishioners to open a council, the councils failed to generate new resources and mainly took an interest in beautification of the church, not schools, charity or the local clergy. As a result, within a decade, the Synod was considering how to restructure the new institution,[7] clear admission that the councils were of little significance.[8] Although a valiant attempt has recently been made to rehabilitate the guardian councils,[9] in fact most parishes refused to establish a council and, even when they did, the new organ accomplished little indeed.[10]

Increasingly disenchanted with the work of guardian councils, in 1893 the Church finally decided to conduct a full review of the institution and asked diocesan bishops to explain why the councils had proven – after nearly three decades – so unpopular and ineffectual.[11] Most bishops confirmed the Synod's negative assessment of the councils and cited a litany of explanatory factors (including subversive opposition from hostile Old Believers), but most emphasized either the parishioners' poverty or their visceral antipathy towards innovation of any sort.[12] For example, the bishop of Kaluga reported that his diocese had relatively few councils, which he attributed partly to the 'complete lack of cultivated and influential people in rural parishes' to provide salutary leadership, and partly to the fact that 'it is difficult to persuade the simple people to support any innovation, especially one associated with a certain monetary expenditure'.[13] Perhaps the most interesting part of these responses was the suggestion from several bishops that women be admitted to the guardian councils; given their manifest heightened piety and zeal, it only made good sense to tap this extraordinary energy and commitment.[14]

Still earlier, disenchantment with the parish and guardian councils inspired a highly publicized proposal by the Moscow provincial zemstvo to revitalize the entire parish as a community, not just rely upon a committee of zealots. In a resolution of 18 December 1880, the zemstvo contended that the parish had suffered a catastrophic decline in authority and hence in its social cohesion and significance, effectively depriving the local community of serving as an all-class social organization. The zemstvo activists therefore proposed to recognize the parish as an independent juridical entity, to re-establish the parish selection of priests, to confer the right of a parish to acquire property (moveable and immoveable), and to allow the parishioners to control parish finances and other property. This zemstvo programme to revitalize the parish, primarily by restoring self-rule (including lay control over local resources and election of clergy), became the model of liberal reform in the coming decades.[15]

Although the Church brusquely rejected the proposal,[16] it could hardly ignore either the problems facing the parish or the prolific public discourse about them. Nevertheless, the Church hierarchs had a quite different diagnosis of what ailed the parish. Whereas lay commentators primarily sought to expand the parish's secular functions in such matters as charity and educational services (either to make Orthodoxy 'relevant' or to help ameliorate social tensions), the bishops were primarily interested in making the parish 'relevant' to spiritual, not secular, needs. Although one need not overlook the political arch-reactionaries, most were chiefly concerned to ensure that the needs and interests of the Church – and hence the faithful – were satisfied. As a result, they believed it essential: (1) that the parish provide adequate and respectable income for the clergy in order to attract and support qualified priests; (2) that the network of parishes correspond to demographic changes; and (3) that local 'financial abuses' in the parish – misappropriation and unauthorized expenditure of parish funds – be eliminated.

The first task – providing proper material support for the local clergy – had long been a concern, eliciting repeated and ineffective attempts at reform ever since Peter the Great. As bishops and priests emphasized, the priest should be liberated from dependence on gratuities (voluntary payments for various rites) and cultivation of parish church lands; only then, they argued, could the priest concentrate on his spiritual mission. To that traditional argument came a new factor in the late 1870s: given the grim prospects of an impecunious existence, many seminarians – no longer obliged to remain in the clerical estate – fled in droves to secular careers. As a result, after decades of too many qualified candidates, the Church suddenly suffered a precipitous decline in the quantity and quality of candidates, especially in outlying areas, even forcing bishops – for the first time since the early nineteenth century – to ordain candidates who lacked a seminary diploma.

By 1900, for example, such ill-trained candidates comprised a majority of new ordinands in Omsk and Tobol'sk; even in Nizhnii Novgorod diocese, they comprised nearly half of all the new priests.[17] Although the Church reacted by attempting to impede the flight of seminarians, it understood that only an improvement in the clergy's status and economic condition could stem the exodus.[18]

The second issue concerned the number and distribution of parishes – a critical determinant in the Church's capacity to provide religious services, inculcate the faith, and combat the challenge from other confessions, especially sectarianism and the Old Belief. By the late nineteenth century, as the Church was well aware, its parish network suffered from grievous deficiencies. One was the failure to keep pace with sheer population growth: ever since the early eighteenth century, the number of parishes had expanded slowly and sporadically – at any rate, far behind the rate of population growth. As a result, the ratio of parishioners to priest had nearly doubled over the ninety years before the First World War, rising from 1,008:1 in 1824 to 1,921:1 in 1914.[19] Especially in so liturgical a confession as Orthodoxy, where the time devoted to the performance of rites was so great, this increase made it exceedingly difficult to carry out old, let alone new, duties.

Paradoxically, the shortages were most acute in the most backward and the most advanced areas of the Empire. On the one hand, the Church had relatively few parishes in northern Russia and Siberia, where low population density and modest resources caused sprawling parishes, some encompassing hundreds of square miles.[20] Noting the problem of such far-flung parishes, the Duma complained in 1914 that 'now it is not enough for a pastor just to perform rites, for he must also be concerned about [his parishioners'] souls: it is necessary to preach to the adults; to organize trustee councils, temperance societies, and missionary circles; to lead popular readings; to manage library and book sales; and to teach religion in the schools that are increasing every year'.[21] These parishes were also the most vulnerable to the proselytizing sectarians and Old Believers. On the other hand, the new urban areas also had a weak, overextended parish infrastructure. As in Western Europe, the Church was unable to keep pace with urban growth and, especially, the influx of migrant labourers to the factories. A special commission in St Petersburg, for example, noted the abnormality of excessively large parishes (some with as many as 30,000 parishioners); under such circumstances, for example, the priest – who had to administer confession to one thousand people per day on the eve of Easter – could do nothing more than perform perfunctory rites.[22]

Priests also complained that service in an urban parish was particularly taxing; given the anomie, complexity and transient residency of seasonal labourers, it was all but impossible to bond with parishioners from such diverse social, geographic and ethnic backgrounds.[23] Such problems affected not only the capitals but cities throughout the Central Industrial Region that experienced high rates of migration and demographic change.[24]

Moreover, in the view of many observers, the parish – regardless of locale – no longer constituted a cohesive, closely-knit community. The situation was somewhat better in the countryside, where membership was based on a territorial definition (that is, a parish included all the inhabitants from certain villages and hamlets); yet even here the surge in geographic mobility inexorably eroded parish ties and identity. Conditions were incalculably worse in the city, where parish boundaries were virtually nonexistent, with parishioners being dispersed throughout the city.[25] Revealingly, by 1905 the Church had yet to establish a system to record and fix membership for urban parishes, even in the capital itself.[26] Finally, apart from social realities, the parish even lacked legal status: deemed to be part of the ecclesiastical domain (*dukhovnoe vedomstvo*), it was not a juridical entity (*iuridicheskoe litso*) in state law and hence could neither sue nor be sued, neither buy nor sell property, nor otherwise act as a legal agent.[27]

Many bishops grew increasingly anxious about a third problem: the parish's growing restiveness – a pronounced and striking determination to assert local interests against the Church hierarchy. Though disorganized, extra-legal and underinstitutionalized, the parish was anything but pliant and meek. On the contrary, especially in the decades after the Great Reforms, the Church encountered unmistakable signs of mounting resistance and, especially, a determination to assert local control over parish finances. That attitude was most apparent in the behaviour of the church elder (*tserkovnyi starosta*) – a layman elected by follow parishioners to serve as church treasurer and often castigated for his cavalier, even illegal, use of church funds.[28] Parish disgruntlement focused mainly on diocesan assessments to finance Church administration and ecclesiastical schools.[29] Since these schools admitted mainly the children of the clergy (and imposed fees and quotas on offspring from other social groups), it is hardly surprising that parishioners resented the diversion of scarce funds to support these schools.[30] According to some reports, diocesan authorities were expropriating the lion's share of parish funds, even as much as 94 per cent in one diocese.[31] All this impelled rebellious parishioners – to the indignation of Church authorities – to use parish funds as they saw fit, even for purposes utterly unrelated to church needs, such as granting interest-bearing loans, paying arrears and dues to the state, and providing subventions for zemstvo (not parish) schools.[32] Likewise, parishioners who had contractually agreed to provide parish levies (to support, for example, additional clergy) later reneged, either reducing or altogether abrogating payments.[33] Parishioners also asserted their rights *vis-à-vis* the local clergy, filing an endless stream of petitions to protest against excessive clerical gratuities or to demand the removal of an unpopular priest.[34] Contentious laity also challenged decisions to reassign them to another parish; while such decisions had the laudable goal of equalizing parish size (and hence finances), they were often at variance with geography and parishioner wish.[35] To combat such recalcitrance, in 1887 the Minister of the Interior distributed a circular to provincial governors forbidding the intervention of peasant assemblies in such ecclesiastical affairs.[36] Imperious demands like this had scant effect, reinforcing the prelates' fear of schemes to expand parish authority and autonomy.

The parish clergy and 'clerical intelligentsia' (faculty in seminaries and academies) held more liberal views, but were often ambivalent if not sceptical of plans for parish empowerment. Some, to be sure, did give unqualified support for the rights of parishioners; an article in the Novgorod diocesan gazette, for example, argued that the parish could effectively address social ills only if the parish was designed as an all-class institution and only if its former prerogatives and power were restored.[37] But even those who voiced support for parish rights (including the power to select local clergy) had reservations. Thus, an essay in the liberal journal of the St Petersburg Ecclesiastical Academy argued that only the 'electoral principle' (*vybornoe nachalo*) could combat the caste-like isolation of the clergy, and re-establish close priest–parishioner relations. Nonetheless, the author admitted serious obstacles to such reform – above all, fear that the uneducated peasants were unqualified to choose and that indeed they might surrender to the temptations of bribes and other irregularities.[38] More sceptical still was an author in the liberal ecclesiastical journal, *Bogoslovskii vestnik*, who emphasized that the parishioners were not prepared for a more active role and that revitalization would be difficult indeed.[39] Underlying such sentiments was the ubiquitous, deeply embedded image of the 'dark people' (*temnyi narod*); as in the secular domain, the Church and even its liberal wing feared that the people were too backward and easily corrupted, as yet unfit to assume a role – ironically – that it had freely played until the end of the eighteenth century.

By the turn of the century, the parish question had come to attract increasing attention in conservative, liberal and even radical revolutionary lay circles.[40] Virtually all concurred that the 'contemporary parish life' was characterized by 'decline, weakness, and inertia'.[41] The dominating figure in the public discussions, A. A. Papkov, chronicled the decline of the parish since Peter the Great and urged the restoration of its former role and power.[42] His writings struck a resonant cord, not only among conservative Slavophiles (yearning to return to pre-Petrine *Gemeinschaft*), but also among liberals and zemstvo activists seeking to extend the zemstvo from the district level (as established in the Great Reforms) to the grass roots. A prominent exponent of the latter view was K. Rovinskii, who proposed to make the parish 'a small zemstvo unit' (*melkaia zemskaia edinitsa*) – an all-class unit of self-government with powers of self-taxation and the charge to satisfy secular and religious needs.[43] Like most clergy, these lay observers dismissed the guardian councils as moribund and proposed to replace them with a new system of parish soviets (*prikhodskie sovety*).[44] Above all, most commentators agreed that the main objective must be parish empowerment, particularly with respect to church finances; so long as the Church siphoned off the bulk of parish revenues for diocesan and seminary needs, it was hardly feasible for the parish to attend to pressing local needs.[45]

These discussions filled the contemporary press and aroused growing interest in government circles. Evidence of official interest came in the imperial manifesto of 26 March 1903, which not only cited the need to improve the condition of the clergy, but also referred to the problem of the parish and guardian councils.[46] The unpopular, but politically astute Minister of the Interior, Viacheslav Plehve, also spoke about the need to 'raise the significance of the Church' and especially the role of the parish.[47] His former arch adversary, Sergei Witte, also regarded the parish as a unique opportunity to unite all estates in addressing local needs.[48]

Although these press discussions did not lead to concrete measures, they put parish reform high on the agenda and formulated the main programmatic conceptions that would prevail during the Revolution of 1905–7 and its aftermath.

Parish reform and the Revolution of 1905–7

The outbreak of revolution in 1905 unleashed not only unprecedented turbulence all across Russia, but also a broad-based reform movement in the Church itself. The immediate impulse was the regime's concessions on religious tolerance and to violate the Church's own interests, most dramatically in the manifesto of 17 April 1905. For the Church, that manifesto was its own equivalent of a 'Bloody Sunday', a clear sign of the regime's willingness to place *raison d'état* over the special interests of Orthodoxy. Explicitly citing the 'changed status of non-Orthodox confessions' and Old Believers in the impending manifesto, the Synod adopted a formal resolution on the need for sweeping reform, not only in such matters as re-establishment of the patriarchate,[49] but also through measures to promote the religious-moral, charitable and educational functions of the parish.[50]

Proposals for parish reform, moreover, continued to elicit a broad consensus. In the Church, support was strongest among the small but highly visible movement of 'renovationists' (*obnovlentsy*).[51] Even more categorical demands came from secular liberals in the Constitutional Democratic Party, which insisted that the parish be recognized as an autonomous juridical entity and that it be armed with all the attendant prerogatives, including control over parish funds and the choice of clergy.[52] Conservative and right-wing parties – for different reasons – also called for parish reform, chiefly because they hoped that a revitalized parish could help defend the existing order.[53] Proponents of reform also included powerful bureaucrats like Witte. Believing that the Church must be fundamentally reformed to compete with other confessions in a new age of religious tolerance, Witte insisted that this revitalization required that the parish be given full legal status, including power over local church revenues.[54]

Such prescriptions, however, were at marked variance with the views of Church authorities. That became apparent when the Synod, waiting for Nicholas II to convoke a Church Council,[55] decided to poll episcopal opinion about the question of ecclesiastical reform.[56] As the bishops' detailed replies made clear, most favoured *some* kind of parish reform, with only a small minority expressing opposition to any change,[57] but only a few prelates expressed support for the liberal programme of parish autonomy and empowerment.[58] For example, the bishop of Minsk favoured measures to revive parish activity, but categorically opposed parish election of priests, not only because it was uncanonical (a violation of episcopal authority and duty), but also because it seemed likely to provoke conflicts and fraudulent 'elections'.[59] Another prelate warned that parishioners were unlikely to use their new power wisely: 'If they manifest their participation in parish life at all, it is to struggle against the clergy and to defend the church elder whenever the clergy begins to restrain the latter's arbitrary expenditure of church sums.'[60]

The revolutionary tumult only intensified such fears, making parishioners increasingly importunate and assertive. They not only intensified criticism of priests for 'solicitation'[61] but even disputed the right of Church authorities to siphon off parish funds to finance diocesan administration and ecclesiastical schools. One rural parish, for example, categorically forbade diocesan authorities to take funds from their church treasury, a policy it denounced as patently illegal.[62] Another parish, claiming that diocesan levies left their local church without operating funds, declared it to be 'unjust for our hard-earned kopecks, donated to the church, be sent beyond the parish boundary to the capital and to diocesan authorities', and demanded that these funds be strictly limited to local use, such as 'education of the people and providing charity for the poor and sick.'[63] Similarly, a parish in Vladimir diocese – citing the urgent need for church repairs – resolved to ban diocesan levies and to reserve its meagre funds exclusively for local needs.[64] Such public sentiments impelled a diocesan assembly of parish clergy in Kazan to warn in September 1905 that the parish 'is more and more clearly beginning to realize the abnormality of the situation, whereby the parishioner makes candle donations or other monetary contributions to maintain and improve his church, but these are sent somewhere else and for some unknown needs and demands'.[65] Two months later, an assembly of parish representatives in Voronezh resolved that it is 'undesirable for the churches to participate in expenditures to maintain church administration and ecclesiastical schools', and demanded that the parish be given the right 'of a juridical entity, including the authority to control the church, charity, education, and the appointment of local clergy'.[66] A radical flysheet from Vologda also denounced the use of parish funds to finance ecclesiastical schools for the clergy's sons; castigating priests for failing to support the agrarian revolution, it declared that 'the majority of priests are on the side of the government – so let the government [pay to] educate future priests'.[67]

The parish clergy – who were in fact far more liberal than the radical flysheet suggested[68] – none the less felt highly ambivalent about this parish revolution. To be sure, some priests – whether from genuine conviction or fear of their parishioners – expressed enthusiastic support for far-reaching parish reform.[69] Some clergy voiced support for parish control over church resources[70] and even lay nomination of clerical appointees (to be sure, with the final authority residing with the bishop).[71] But many clergy, even those liberal on social questions, were more cautious, sharing the bishops' fear that parish power would invite rampant fiscal abuses and the appointment of uneducated – hence cheaper – candidates. Although clerical liberals favoured some parish participation (through the nomination of candidates),[72] most priests warned that the people were 'not yet ready' to assume this responsibility.[73] For example, the diocesan assembly of parish clergy in Ekaterinoslav – while a fervent supporter of parish reform – none the less adopted the following resolution: 'Given the low level of development in the contemporary rural population and the hostile attitude toward the church and clergy on the part of certain strata of educated society, the question of the election of the clergy by the parishioners is without practical significance at the present time.'[74]

Amidst revolutionary tumult inside and outside the Church, the Synod proposed on 18 November 1905 to establish parish soviets to mobilize parish activists and to represent the interests of rank-and-file believers. As the background documentation makes clear, the Synod was alarmed by the failure of the October manifesto to restore calm, and concluded that now – more than ever – the clergy must intercede to re-establish law and order.[75] Although the Synod made the soviet voluntary, it strongly encouraged local clergy to induce their flock to establish and support the new institution. Citing 'today's unruly and anarchist times', the Synod promulgated vague guidelines indicating that the parish was to hold an annual assembly of all heads of household; that this assembly was to elect a parish soviet, and that such soviets were only to be created through voluntary action. At bottom was the desire to mobilize parish activists for a broader mission that included not only religious-moral questions, but also 'charitable and educational matters'.[76] But the Synod's decree had little effect, as most bishops and parish clergy did little – or could do little – to promote the new parish soviets.[77]

The parish question subsequently became part of plans to convene a national church council (*pomestnyi sobor*). No doubt dismayed by the emperor's reluctance to convoke a church council (ostensibly because of the revolutionary tumult),[78] on 14 January 1906 the Synod created a special 'Pre-conciliar Commission' (*Predsobornoe prisutstvie*), with the charge of preparing suitable proposals for an eventual church council.[79] After first compiling and extracting the episcopal replies,[80] the Commission created several subcommissions to deal with various issues, including a 'Fourth Section' (IV *otdel*) on the parish question.[81]

Members included a ranking prelate, several prominent theologians and publicists, and some lay figures known 'for their devotion to the Orthodox Church and their knowledge of theological-historical literature and current parish church life'.[82] By December 1906 the Commission reviewed proposals from the various subcommissions and suspended operations.[83]

After thirty sessions and much internal wrangling, the Fourth Section finally adopted a draft statute for parish reform. It plainly bore the heady imprint of the revolution.[84] Although it paid homage to canon law (reaffirming that the parish was a unit of the diocese and hence subject to episcopal authority), this draft made a distinction between 'Church' and 'parish', with a corresponding division of property and authority. That was most apparent in the controversial issue of parish finances; while safeguarding institutional 'Church' rights, the draft empowered the parish to impose levies and to maintain a separate parish treasury under exclusive local control. With respect to the appointment of clergy, this draft stopped short of re-establishing parish election of priests, but ruled that the bishop – should he spurn such a parish nominee – must give 'a reply, with an explanation for his rejection'. This draft also proffered a broad definition of parish competence, including responsibility to improve church services and singing, establish parish schools, maintain the local church, provide charity, and offer religious-moral guidance and control for the community. This draft also included elaborate rules for the convocation of a plenary parish assembly (all household heads over the age of twenty-five except those convicted of secular or religious offences, and those who declined to provide material support for the church). Following the Synod, it ignored the guardian council and made the parish soviet – comprised of the local clergy, the church elder and elected parish representatives – the chief executive organ.[85]

These proposals elicited intense controversy in Church circles and determined opposition from a broad phalanx of ecclesiastical conservatives. Above all, some prelates opposed *any* parish control over church finances and a role in the selection of clergy. Not without reason, the bishops were obviously reluctant to empower parishioners – especially in view of their revolutionary mood and ominous signs of dechristianization and anticlericalism. Such sentiments had clearly pervaded discussions in the Fourth Section; as its chairman noted, 'some deem all the conclusions of the Section as fruitless and even harmful, ... and came to conclude that no kind of parish reform should be implemented'.[86]

The parish question in the Duma monarchy

The politics of reform after 1906 became still more complex, involving not only the Church and some future Church Council, but increasingly the Duma and the government. This intrusion, without doubt, only reinforced episcopal conservatism and the tendency to move rightward in their notion of parish reform. Amidst a stream of weak procurators and mounting influence of right-wing circles,[87] the ranking prelates wanted to reassert the Church's rights and interests (above all, by re-establishing the patriarchate and convening a Church Council),[88] and rejected the liberal, democratizing and laicizing proposals that had prevailed during the revolution. The reform countenanced in 1905–6 was now unthinkable for the episcopal elite.[89] At the opposing end of the spectrum was the Duma: even the conservative Dumas created by the Stolypin *coup d'état* of 3 June 1907 were determined to impose change upon a recalcitrant Church, particularly in the matter of parish reform. P. A. Stolypin's political ally, the moderate right leadership in the Octobrist Party, made parish reform a clear priority.[90] Indeed, Stolypin himself saw parish reform as an integral element in his programme to bolster the grass-roots infrastructure of the new state.

Initially, at least, Church authorities claimed a continuing commitment to parish reform. Thus, in early 1907, in response to an earlier resolution by the Council of Ministers (approved by the emperor on 17 October 1906), the Synod established a special commission to prepare a new draft statute for parish reform.[91] At least nominally, the Synod concurred about 'the timeliness for a review of the existing legislation that determines the organization of the Orthodox parish'.[92] The Commission, predictably chaired by a ranking prelate,[93] contained high-ranking lay officials in ecclesiastical administration (including the chief procurator and his assistants), two prominent layman (Papkov and F. D. Samarin, also members of the State Council), two prominent professors, and representatives from the Ministry of Education and Ministry of the Interior. The Commission moved slowly, with acrimonious disputes[94] and its discussions were shrouded in secrecy; fuelling rumours that reform had once again been stalled.[95]

Nevertheless, the Parish Commission did finally adopt a text, substantially modifying the more liberal provisions of the draft by the Fourth Section.[96] Thus, the Commission emphasized that the parish was an ecclesiastical, not secular, institution; it was totally subordinate 'to the bishop,' and indeed acquired 'life only through the bishop'. Significantly, the Commission attempted to make the parish more inclusive, not only by proposing that participation in the parish assembly not only be lowered to the age of twenty-one, but also by explicitly providing for the admission of women who were heads of households or held some office in the parish.[97] But the Commission was far more conservative with respect to empowerment. Thus, although it accorded the laity a role in the selection of clergy (with the bishop 'taking into account the attention and petition of parishioners'), it unambiguously left final discretion to the bishop, who was under no obligation to issue 'explanations' for spurning a parish recommendation. As the Commission's journals show, its members feared lay pressure: they warned that a bishop would find it difficult – however valid his objections – to reject a candidate who had been unanimously elected by the parish.[98] Indicative of the prevailing sentiment was the Commission's decision to adopt special rules to protect the priest – *ex officio* chairman of the parish assembly – from the 'crowd'.[99] Although the Commission authorized the parish to raise additional funds (through self-taxation) and to manage directly these new resources, it staunchly defended the Church's control over the traditional sources of parish income.[100]

When the Church finally sent its proposal to the Council of Ministers in September 1908, it did not agree to allow the government, much less the Duma, to legislate on ecclesiastical matters.[101] On the contrary, the Chief Procurator – speaking on behalf of the Synod – declared that most of the draft proposals needed no secular confirmation, since these articles were purportedly a reiteration of earlier Synodal decrees. For example, he cited the articles on the parish's right to recommend candidates; modest as it was, this proposal was not something new, but merely 'restoration of an earlier order'. Apart from a handful of articles (dealing with church property and the parish's status as a juridical entity), which did require action by the State Duma and State Council, the Chief Procurator insisted that most of the text – like the Consistory Charter of 1841 – needed only the emperor's confirmation to take effect.

This proposal, which the Chief Procurator ultimately withdrew, provoked a firestorm of criticism, not only from episcopal conservatives[102] and various ministers (chiefly for violating basic principles of state law). It led to Prime Minister Stolypin himself expressing his profound dissatisfaction with the pace and direction of reform. In a long and important memorandum to the Chief Procurator on 3 October 1909, Stolypin rejected the claim of ranking churchmen that the fundamental problem was state policy – especially its embrace of religious tolerance in 1905 – and instead put full responsibility on the Church itself.

Rejecting strident episcopal claims that religious tolerance (especially in the wake of the manifestoes of 17 April 1905) had spawned massive defections from the Church, Stolypin argued that this law simply formalized what had already existed, and that it merely allowed the confessions to do openly what they had earlier been forced to disseminate clandestinely. More important, Stolypin emphasized the extraordinary initiative and zeal of the other confessions, not only among Old Believers and sectarians, but also the Lutherans in the Baltics and Catholics in the western provinces. And that heightened activity, he argued, was due primarily to their parish organization and initiative. For example, 'almost every Catholic church established fraternities devoted to religious-moral goals and to developing Roman Catholic propaganda', with the parallel establishment of charitable societies.

That activism, declared Stolypin, stood in striking contrast to the Orthodox Church. In his view, the Church was disadvantaged not by state tutelage, law or policy, but by the weakness of its parish infrastructure. Above all, the lay parishioners had virtually no power or function in this system, with catastrophic consequences for the vitality of the parish itself: 'The exclusion of the laity from managing parish affairs made them indifferent to the Church; it left them with the status of temporary visitors to a church, crushing any initiative and activity.' Diocesan exploitation of parish funds, however justified, had major ramifications for the parish and its role: 'The assessment of parish revenues through various types of collections to satisfy diocesan (or even general empire-wide) needs, not local needs, has led to the impoverishment of the parish and its complete helplessness as a social entity.' The result, declared Stolypin, was a parish with neither means nor meaning: 'In many churches of Russia, the most essential needs are not met; they do not provide charity (which, if it does exist, is usually outside the church); virtually nowhere does the parish exist as a social organization; public education, religious enlightenment, or even religious development occur outside the church, which could give it secure foundations.' It was therefore essential, he argued, that the Church undertake fundamental parish reform:

> The recreation of a parish, so appropriate to the spirit of our Church and the spirit of the people, not only will not diminish the stature of the Church, but will unquestionably strengthen its authority. The inclusion of laity in the administration of church property, without doubt, will attract the better elements to the church, unite the parish clergy and believers, give the Church a lively social

significance, unify – behind the lofty idea of serving the interests of the Church – all believers, and juxtapose the Orthodox parish, as a solid unit, against all alien organizations, tendencies, and influences.

In a word, parish empowerment – like the agrarian reforms – would ensure a proper place for the 'better elements' and thereby strengthen the Church and its role in society.[103]

Responding on behalf of the Synod, the Chief Procurator vigorously dissented from such views.[104] He reiterated the Church's view that the massive defection from Orthodoxy *was* a direct consequence of the 17 April 1905 manifesto, which had unleashed 'an explosive growth of Catholicism, Lutheranism, sectarianism', and had thereby facilitated some 200,000 cases of apostasy in 1905–7. The Chief Procurator also warned that some of the sectarian movements posed a threat not only to Orthodoxy but to the state itself.[105] As for parish reform, the Chief Procurator cited the Synod's past efforts and reassured Stolypin that 'the parish question will be subjected to final discussions in the near future'. However, he put Stolypin on notice that the hierarchs had no interest in liberal demands for parish autonomy: 'From the perspective of the church order, it is difficult to speak of "self-rule" of the parish in the precise sense of that word', since canon law clearly makes the parish subordinate to the bishop. Hence it was at once uncanonical and dangerous to permit the parish election of local clergy.

All these exasperating delays finally impelled the Duma to take the initiative and prepare its own formula for parish reform. Thus, in June 1910, some 147 deputies – led by the Octobrist Kamenskii – prepared a proposal to establish the parish as a juridical entity with full control over local resources.[106] In response, the Synod testily spurned this proposal, declaring that only the bishop had authority over church funds, that parishioners 'have no right to change the designation for church property'. Apart from fears that such powers might enable a parish to defect (with all its property) to the Old Belief or a sect, the Synod insisted that canon law does not recognize either the principle of 'parish self-government' or its right to elect parish clergy.[107] The Synod submitted a new version of the parish reform statute, but this text – which proved even more conservative than the previous one – had to be withdrawn within a few months.[108]

By the winter of 1911–12, consonant with the general deterioration in political stability, tensions between the Duma and Church reached a fever pitch. Confronted by another Duma proposal,[109] which the

Synod unceremoniously dismissed as 'unacceptable',[110] but fearful of budgetary reprisals, the Synod hastily instructed the Chief Procurator to revise and resubmit the Church's proposal for a parish statute.[111] Although the Chief Procurator submitted yet another draft to the Council of Ministers in March 1912, this version was even less acceptable than its predecessors, granting the parish neither the status of a juridical entity nor a mechanism for lay participation in the management of local church finances.[112] As the prospects for parish reform – like the convocation of a church council – faded,[113] the Duma became increasingly hostile towards the Church leadership and aggressively pressed its own vision of reform. Thus, in 1913 alone, various Duma factions submitted no less than four proposals for parish reform, all seeking to empower the parish, sometimes even granting the right to elect priests.[114] On 9 September 1913, the Duma sent the Chief Procurator an inventory of its wishes with respect to the Church and, apart from 'the most rapid possible convocation of a national church council', it specifically condemned the diversion of parish funds to support seminaries and urged that the church conduct 'detailed statistical research on the economic condition of the parish'.[115]

Although tactful Chief Procurators sought to defuse Duma opposition (with bland reassurances of imminent reform), the Church had no intention of granting the parish the status and rights envisioned by liberal and moderate reformers. Apart from the rabid arch-conservatives like Antonii (Khrapovitskii) of Volhynia, who rejected any Duma reform as *ipso facto* uncanonical,[116] the Synod adamantly rejected the principle of parish autonomy, at most agreeing to extend the range of parish responsibilities and mission. Indeed, the Church moved rightward in its conception of parish reform. Thus, in yet another revised draft submitted to the Council of Ministers on 30 April 1913, the Synod made few concessions, only granting the parishioners the right to nominate, not elect, the local clergy.[117] The difference between the 1912 draft (prepared by P. P. Izvol'skii)[118] and the 1913 text (revised by the new procurator, V. K. Sabler) was the latter's clear attempt to excoriate any suggestion that the parishioners had a decisive role in selecting local clergy. That change, as the conservative press reported, was at least partly due to an increase in parish petitions asking for the removal and replacement of their current clergy.[119] As hierarchs said privately and the press reported publicly, the Church authorities were becoming ever more fearful of giving the 'dark masses' autonomy and control over the local purse and priest.[120] While one should not underestimate the bishops' genuine respect for tradition and canon, they were no doubt even more concerned about the capacity of the 'dark people' – especially in so turbulent an age – to exercise their authority wisely.

Indeed, such anxiety steadily increased as parishioners became ever more aggressive in asserting their authority, especially on the two key issues – local finances and the parish clergy. For example, in late 1908 the Church faced a veritable revolt in Kazan, where a rebellious church elder organized a meeting that agreed on the 'extreme necessity' of 'freeing the churches from levies for central and consistory administration', and unanimously resolved that 'the church revenues of rural parishes be exempted from obligatory levies'.[121] As a priest in Poltava complained: 'The lack of control over church elders is the cause of the impecunious condition of the diocese. Each church elder has the enormous support of those parishioners who elected him; the parish clergy are completely powerless to combat them.'[122] Such conflicts were especially likely whenever the local clergy endeavoured to raise additional issues for such worthwhile causes as education and charity. Thus, the bishop of Ekaterinoslav complained that 'today's church elders do not understand any of this, and regard it all as the inventions of the local priest, and do everything in their power to oppose the initiatives of priests'.[123] Moreover, wilful parishes sent an endless stream of complaints against hated and allegedly extortionist clergy.[124] As Metropolitan Flavian of Kiev wrote to the Chief Procurator in June 1913: 'Recently, there has been an increase in the frequency of petitions filed by authorized representatives of peasant communities to remove one or another member of the parish staff for alleged illegal actions.'[125] The deterioration in parish–priest relations was, understandably, a cause of growing concern. Revealingly, one prewar diocesan report warned that 'the paternal and patriarchal relations of the clergy to the flock have significantly changed during the last ten years because of the impact of the new living conditions. The years of trouble (1905–7) have not passed without effect; the flock itself is not what it once was.'[126]

As reform stalled, figures like A. A. Papkov – a fervent believer and leading protagonist of reform since the turn of the century – grew increasingly pessimistic and impatient. He published, for example, a devastating account of the current condition of the parish, showing that after five decades half the parishes had yet to establish a trustee council, and that – even when established – these councils had produced little funding, especially for the local charity or even for charity and education.[127] By 1914 Papkov plainly despaired that the Church would ever embark on reform and began to voice hopes that the state or laity would assume the initiative.[128] Later, Papkov urged society to take the initiative by using the Synodal decree of 1905 to establish parish soviets and thereby initiate reform from below.[129] In acerbic notes to Nicholas II, another activist underlined the superior communal organization of other confessions and castigated the Synod for flouting the emperor's instruction of 1906 to undertake parish reform.[130] Despite such private denunciations and public debate, reform seemed no nearer in 1914 than it had before the revolution of 1905.

War and reform

Although the Synod continued to feign an interest in parish reform,[131] the outbreak of war in 1914 not only put the reform issue on hold but, by 1916, gave the Synod an opportunity to declare an official moratorium on action until the end of hostilities. In fact, ranking prelates not only wanted to defer, but to derail reform altogether. That became clear in January 1916, when the presiding member of the Synod, Metropolitan Pitirim, published an article in *Novoe vremia* candidly revealing the Synod's aversion to parish reform. He also openly denounced government proposals, emanating from P. A. Stolypin, to allow the parish to elect priests and control parish finances, as flatly contradictory to canon law and *ipso facto* unacceptable.[132]

First, however, the Synod chose to lay the groundwork for a formal freeze on parish reform – through the time-honoured tactic of diocesan opinion.[133] The responses, as the Synod clearly anticipated, confirmed its aversion to reform that went too far and too soon, in conferring power and perquisites on the parish. To be sure, a few dioceses still insisted upon a liberal vision of parish reform; a group in Minsk, for example, affirmed the need to separate Church from parish funds and even to allow parish nomination of clerical candidates (with final authority, however, resting with the bishop).[134] But most reports categorically rejected liberal plans to grant the laity control over parish finances and, especially, the local clergy. Thus, one assembly of clergy and laity emphasized 'the total unacceptability of the so-called elected clergy',[135] and a council of superintendents in Moscow rejected attempts by the State Duma to superimpose the secular principle of democratic elections to require the popular election of clergy: 'The election of the pastor by the parishioners, without question, is mandated neither by the canons nor the spirit of the Orthodox Church, and it is, at the same time, extremely dangerous for church life in practical terms.'[136] Even more outspoken was the declaration by the Fraternity of St Vladimir (Kiev), which urged the Chief Procurator to withdraw the draft proposal for a parish reform, since the Duma had already decided to establish the election of clergy and parish control over local funds. It also invoked the crisis of war as grounds to procrastinate: 'We have lived for centuries without this reform, so we can live for another two or three years without it.'[137]

Still more direct was the response of laymen and clergy in Vladimir, which hastily dispatched a telegram to authorities in St Petersburg. The central task, they declared, was not institutional and legal reform, but religious revival: 'The renewal of parish life should consist solely in an improvement in the performance of church services, church singing, in tireless preaching by the clergy, and in the development of charitable and educational institutions in the parish church.' It specifically opposed the more radical attempts to reconfigure the parish, especially on the basis of proposals from the State Duma: 'Granting the laity the right to elect the members of the parish clergy and to control church funds and property, is regarded by the assembly as ruinous for the good order of the Church.' It therefore recommended that this church legislation be removed from the purview of the 'non-confessional State Duma'.[138]

Predictably, on 29 April 1916 the Synod decided to withdraw the parish proposal from further consideration by the State Duma. It did not, to be sure, altogether renounce the need for parish reform. Rather, it claimed that the wartime experience, and the situation likely to ensue after the end of hostilities, would create new conditions and resources that could only be considered at some later point.[139] Although it still held out some hints of potential reform (for example, establishing a special committee on parish welfare in September 1916),[140] nothing concrete came of such proposals, and the *ancien régime* came to its inglorious end without the long-awaited, long-promised reform.

All power to the parish

It required revolution to make reform: only in the wake of the February Revolution, with the conservatives purged from the Synod and even diocesan hierarchy, did the Orthodox Church finally and belatedly embark on parish reform.[141] Within a few weeks, diocesan assemblies – often bolstered by a substantial lay participation – passed far-reaching resolutions, including demands for parish reform. Thus, in Vladimir diocese, where a conservative assembly had a few months before dismissed the need for parish reform, a diocesan assembly of clergy and laity emphasized that the Orthodox parish is an ecclesiastical 'juridical entity', that the parish assembly should include all laity over the age of eighteen (regardless of sex), and that clerical appointment could only be made through parish recommendations and consent. It also proposed to establish a parish soviet to manage parish funds, and once alternative funds could be found, to terminate parish assessments for diocesan needs.[142] In Kherson, a diocesan assembly of clergy and laity resolved that all church positions, from top to bottom, should be filled through elections.[143] In Perm, a commission similarly affirmed the parish's role in clerical appointments: if the bishop were to find a parish candidate unworthy, it was incumbent upon him to 'explain' why.[144] The Synod itself, with the conservatives purged and its membership reconstituted, issued 'temporary regulations' on the parish on 17 June 1917. Jettisoning the rhetoric about hierarchical and episcopal rights, it devised a mechanism for the parish election of priests, to be sure, with a formal confirmation by the local bishop.[145] The 'All-Russian Congress of Clergy and Laity', meeting in Moscow the same month, approved a resolution giving the parish total control over local resources.[146]

If the revolution drove the Church towards hasty and radical reform, it also unleashed growing concerns about the consequences of lay power. Shortly after the February Revolution, a diocesan assembly in Riazan complained that 'parishioners are refusing to pay gratuities for rites'.[147] In some areas, moreover, land-hungry peasants were also seizing the plot of parish church land traditionally given for use by the local clergy.[148] Thus, as the Synod complained that same June, many parishes had arbitrarily decided to deny payments of funds to support Church needs outside the parish. While implicitly conceding the depth of popular opposition, the Synod nonetheless explained that – until some alternative source of funding became available – it was essential that the parish provide support for the essential educational, charitable and administrative services at the diocesan level.[149] Moreover, as many clergy soon discovered, 'parish power' included an assertiveness with respect not only to the appointment of new clergy, but also the status, income or even tenure of those presently serving in a parish. One rotaprint from the summer of 1917 declared that the new era of freedom had subjected the clergy to 'denigration' by the people, and that priests 'are insulted, expelled, and even killed'.[150]

Events in Vladimir illustrate graphically how parish assertiveness mushroomed in the months following the February Revolution. Thus, within a month of the February Revolution, the bishop of Vladimir reported receiving petitions from various parishioners to appoint or relocate local clergy.[151] A few weeks later he issued a general communication 'to my flock', reporting that numerous priests from all across the diocese had complained that 'the parishioners insult and oppress them, and in some cases, even allow themselves to use force: they arrest them and expel them from their parishes'.[152] Indeed, within a few months, the diocesan gazette was reporting that 'many of our colleagues have already been deprived of their priestly positions, and many – although still in the parish – suffer unjust insults and humiliation at the hands of parishioners, with the fear that they, along with their large families, will be left homeless and without a crust of bread'. In response, clergy in one district even agreed to form a pastoral 'union' to defend their common interests.[153] A few months later, amidst the parish control over local affairs, the diocesan gazette published a mournful essay, describing how clergy now had to 'bribe' the parishioners for support – merely an inversion of bribes to superiors in the past, and not a whit less inimical to their spiritual authority.[154]

Ironically, the Bolshevik Revolution would usher in the final stage of 'all power to the parish'. With the Decree on the Separation of Church and State in January 1918, the new regime effectively sought to deny the Church formal juridical status and to disestablish its various administrative and other institutional organs; simultaneously, the Bolsheviks confiscated buildings, seized money and other assets, sequestered its printing presses, and essentially attempted to destroy the Church as a national institution. At the same time, to satisfy the religious needs of the population, it allowed each parish to lease and assume responsibility for local churches and their contents; while that parish was specifically denied the status of a juridical entity, in effect the Bolsheviks accorded it de facto status as such, giving the parish the sole power to act in the name of the Church and its interests. Over the coming years, at least until the massive assault on the parish itself during the 'Great Turn' and the 1930s, the parish became the fundamental, determining institution of the Church.[155]

Conclusion

This case study of the 'parish question' suggests several broader conclusions. First, in this as in so many issues, the interests and behaviour of Church and state diverged sharply; the battle over parish reform was but another source of mutual disenchantment and distrust.[156] Second, the pattern of *reforme manquée*, so characteristic of the expiring old regime, extended as well to the domain of the Church and, indeed, even in an issue that elicited a broad consensus about the imperative and urgent need for change. The abortive reform in the parish, in essence, tends to confirm the 'pessimist' view of the *ancien régime*, whether of its autocratic variant or of the Duma monarchy of its final decade. Third, it was not just 'politics' but the magnitude of the problem that made reform so difficult, divisive and elusive. Above all, the Church – like the state – suffered from underinstitutionalization in its very infrastructure; how to regulate yet encourage initiative, how to define authority and rights, and how to interface these lower units were abiding and seemingly unsolvable problems. At bottom, Church bishops, like secular liberals, faced the awful conundrum of empowering the people (to 'unleash vital forces' from below), without either the conviction that the 'dark people' would wisely use this power or the institutional and social means to maintain indirect control. Finally, in a fundamental sense, the October Revolution – by default, not design – served to complete the parish revolution under way since the mid-nineteenth century. The long-term continuities explain, here as in many other respects, why the Bolshevik regime, so fragile and weak in its early years, was able to survive: not merely through the use of force and repression, but far more through an opportunistic acquiescence in popular expectations.

Notes

1. 'Church' denotes the institution, 'church' the local parish unit. 'Ecclesiastical schools' (elementary *dukhovnye uchilishcha*, secondary *seminarii*, and university-level *akademii*) should not be confused with 'parish schools' (*prikhodskie shkoly*), which were established from the mid-nineteenth century to provide elementary instruction for the laity.
2. The neglect has many causes, but especially the traditional inclination to ignore the Church in modern Russian history, and the failure to move beyond politics in the capitals and to explore provincial and local infrastructures. See, for example, the following: E. D. Chermenskii, *IV Gosudarstvennaia Duma i sverzhenie tsarizma v Rossii* (Moscow, 1976), and A. Ia. Avrekh, *Raspad tret'eiunskoi sistemy* (Moscow, 1985). A preliminary attempt at least to address these issues is to be found in P. N. Zyrianov, *Pravoslavnaia tserkov' v bor'be s revoliutsiei* (Moscow, 1984). Exceptions include Vladimir Rozhkov, *Tserkovnye voprosy v Gosudarstvennoi Dume* (Rome, 1975) and E. V. Fominykh, *Proekty*

tserkovnykh preobrazovanii v nachale XX v., doctoral dissertation (Leningrad, 1987) pp. 94–108.

3. This study is based, first and foremost, on a systematic study of the pertinent archival materials, chiefly those found in Rossiiskii gosudarstvennyi istoricheskii arkhiv (hereafter RGIA), St Petersburg, with supplementary materials drawn from an array of other repositories. The conventional notation system for Russian archives is used here: *fond (f.)*, *opis' (op.)*, *god (g.)*, *st. (stol)*, *otd. (otdel)*, *razdel (razd.)*, *delo (d.)*, *list, listy (l. ll.)*, and *oborot (ob.)* But substantial use has also been made of the voluminous materials in the secular and ecclesiastical press, assisted by a number of synoptic reviews: A. G. Boldovskii, *Vozrozhdenie prikhoda (obzor mnenii pechati)* (St Petersburg, 1903); I. V. Preobrazhenskii, *Periodicheskaia pechat' po voprosu o prikhodskoi reforme* (St Petersburg, 1908); P. A. Ivanov, *Reforma prikhoda* (Tomsk, 1914); M. Sviderskii, *Vopros o tserkovnom prikhode v Predsobornom prisutstvii i v russkoi literature XX v.* (Kiev, 1913); M. I. Chel'tsov, 'K voprosu o reforme nashego prikhoda', *Pravoslavnyi sobesednik* (1915) vol. 1, pp. 473–82.

4. B. Tsarskii, 'Prikhodskii vopros', *Novoe vremia*, no. 13470 (11 September 1913).

5. To avoid confusion, the term 'guardian council' designates *popechitel'stvo*, while 'parish soviet' refers to the *prikhodskoi sovet* proposed by the Synod in 1905 (see below).

6. See Gregory L. Freeze, *The Russian Parish Clergy in the Nineteenth Century* (Princeton, NJ, 1983) pt 2, and the literature cited therein.

7. For the text of its 1874 resolution, see RGIA, *f.* 796, *op.* 174, *g.* 1893, *d.* 1292, *l.* 1 *ob.* Even earlier, in 1869, the Church made clear its disillusionment: given the failure of the trustee councils, authorities embarked on a radical scheme to merge small parishes into larger, more economic, units; however, when confronted by a firestorm of popular opposition, it eventually abandoned this attempt and, *nolens, volens*, had to renew hopes in creating a more effective system of trustee councils. See Freeze, *Parish Clergy*, pp. 363–83.

8. For typical critical assessments, see: I. Lebedev, *Tserkovno-prikhodskie popechitel'stva* (Chernigov, 1901), and P. Miroliubov, 'K voprosu o pravoslavnom prikhode', *Tserkovnye vedomosti*, no. 13 (1907) 584–93.

9. Glennys Young, '"Into Church Matters": Lay Identity, Russian Parish Life, and Popular Politics in Late Imperial and Early Soviet Russia, 1864–1925', *Russian History*, XXIII (1996) 367–84; Vera Shevzov, *Popular Orthodoxy in Late Imperial Russia*, doctoral dissertation (Yale University, 1994) pp. 107–25. The former is based on official reports by the chief procurator only; the latter is limited to a single diocese distinguished by a more creditable performance of the councils and makes no use of the general archival materials in RGIA on the council issue.

10. By 1914, for example, only 19,332 trustee councils had been established among the 40,000 churches; as earlier, they spent nearly three-quarters of their meagre funds on church beautification and repairs, not support for the clergy, schools or charity. As one observer noted, the councils generated only about 3.5 kopecks per capita (with only 'one-eighth kopeck per capita' for schools and charity). See the discussion and references in

G. L. Freeze, 'Counter-reformation in Russian Orthodoxy: Popular Response to Religious Innovation, 1922–1925', *Slavic Review*, LIV (Summer 1995) 328.

11. To be sure, some parishes – mainly under the influence of an activist priest – did try to become more engaged in charitable work; in 1883, one parish in Vladimir, for example, specifically established a 'parish charitable society' to provide aid for orphans and the poor. See RGIA, *f.* 797, *op.* 52, *otd.* 2, *st.* 3, *d.* 52. In another parish, a wealthy parishioner donated 6,000 roubles to establish a poor house, *ibid.*, *op.* 62, *otd.* 2, *st.* 3, *d.* 254).

12. For typical responses, see the episcopal reports from Nizhnii Novgorod, ibid., *ll.* 54–8, Podolia *ll.* 61–8, and Tambov *ll.* 102–5.

13. RGIA, *f.* 796, *op.* 174, *g.* 1893, *d.* 1292, *l.* 41.

14. RGIA, *f.* 796, *op.* 174, *g.* 1893, *d.* 1292, *ll.* 176–83, 184–93, 196, 238, 263.

15. See the summation in RGIA, *f.* 796, *op.* 164, *g.* 1883, *d.* 1144, *ll.* 2–12, 14–37 *ob.*; RGIA, *f.* 797, *op.* 53, *otd.* 2, *st.* 3, *d.* 187, *ll.* 1–19. The proposal elicited wide publicity in the central press, including a liberal church tri-weekly (for example, 'Tolki o pravakh prikhoda', *Tserkovno-obshchestvennyi vestnik*, 29 May 1881, no. 64, pp. 1–2), and even in the diocesan press; see 'Tserkov' russkaia v 1880g.', *Kievskie eparkhial'nye vedomosti*, no. 1 (1881) 3–4. The proposal by the Moscow zemstvo was the most famous, but not the only attempt by a zemstvo to initiate parish reform: in January 1881, the provincial zemstvo in Voronezh followed suit, proposing to give parishioners the right to elect clergy and to establish a parish tithe to replace the traditional gratuities used to support the local priest. See RGIA, *f.* 796, *op.* 162, *g.* 1881, *d.* 2218, *l.* 1 (chief procurator to the Synod, 29 January 1881).

16. In a formal resolution not even adopted until four (!) years after the Moscow zemstvo advanced its proposal, the Synod objected to this violation of its provenance and denied that the parish was in need of such radical reform. See RGIA, *f.* 796, *op.* 164, *g.* 1883, *d.* 1144, *ll.* 14–37 *ob.*; *f.* 804, *op.* 1, *razriad* 1, *d.* 175, *ll.* 56–9 *ob.*

17. RGIA, *f.* 796, *op.* 181, *g.* 1900, *d.* 3482, *ll.* 8 *ob.* 9, 12, 14.

18. As recently demonstrated in an exhaustive analysis of documents from priests' sons who migrated to non-ecclesiastical careers, many in fact were not implacable radicals and even exhibited a marked fondness for their clerical estate. See Laurie Manchester, *Russian Orthodox Clergymen's Sons in Late Imperial Secular Society*, doctoral diss. (Columbia University, 1995).

19. RGIA, *f.* 797, *op.* 96, *d.* 5, *ll.* 1 *ob.*-2; *Vsepoddanneishii otchet ober-prokurora Sv. Sinoda po vedomstvu pravoslavnogo ispovedaniia za 1914 g.* (St Petersburg, 1916) appendix.

20. See, for example, the annual report of 1913 from Vologda, where industrialization had not caused significant problems in cities, but some rural areas had too few churches, RGIA, *f.* 796, *op.* 442, *d.* 2570, *ll.* 22–3. This problem even afflicted areas like St Petersburg diocese. Hence, even here the metropolitan complained about a shortage of parishes in rural areas, where the laity – especially during the rainy seasons of the spring and fall – physically had no opportunity to reach the nearest church. See his annual report (*otchet*) for 1903 in RGIA, *f.* 796, *op.* 442, *d.* 1986, *l.* 39.

21. RGIA, *f.* 796, *op.* 189, *d.* 2229/*b*, *ll.* 173–4.

22. 'Izvestiia i zametki', *Tserkovnyi vestnik*, no. 45 (4 November 1904) 1,438.
23. For typical complaints about the difficulty of ministering to urban parishioners, see the following: G., 'Pervye shagi gorodskogo pastyria', *Tserkovnyi vestnik*, no. 3 (20 January 1905) 68–71; M. Kal'nev, 'O postanovke missionerskogo dela v gorodskikh prikhodakh', *Zhurnaly i protokoly zasedanii Vysochaishe uchrezhdennogo predsobornogo prisutstviia*, vol. 2 (St Petersburg, 1906–9) p. 359.
24. For the problems of a parish in Pokrovskii district of Vladimir diocese, with more than 40,000 worker parishioners, see the account in a local newspaper, *Vladimirskii krai*, no. 29 (8 December 1906) 4. See also the candid comments in a pastoral meeting: 'Pastyrskoe sobranie dukhovenstva gubernskogo goroda Vladimira', *Vladimirskie eparkhial'nye vedomosti*, no. 11 (1901) 175, and the description in 'Letopis' tserkovnoi i obshchestvennoi zhizni', *Tserkovnyi vestnik*, no. 16 (20 April 1906) 516.
25. For a description of the 'territorial confusion' in the urban parishes in Vladimir and Tula dioceses, see: 'Pastyrskoe sobranie dukhovenstva gubernskogo goroda Vladimira', *Vladimirskie eparkhial'nye vedomosti*, no. 11 (1906) 175; RGIA, *f.* 796, *op.* 172, *g.* 1891, *d.* 968, *ll.* 1–2 *ob.* For an abortive attempt by the Synod to deal with the problem in 1890, see *Vsepoddanneishii otchet ober-prokurora Sv. Sinoda po vedomstvu pravoslavnogo ispovedaniia za 1890–91* (St Petersburg, 1893) 41–2.
26. On the eve of the 1905 Revolution, for example, a commission of reform-minded clergy in St Petersburg, meeting under the aegis of Metropolitan Antonii (Vadkovskii), emphasized the need to register parishioners and establish order in the parish. See 'Izvestiia i zametki', *Tserkovnyi vestnik*, no. 42 (14 October 1904) 1,340–41.
27. Thus, lacking the status of a juridical entity, the parish could only purchase or sell real estate with the approval of the bishop, Synod and ultimately the emperor himself. See, for example, the file concerning Savva Morozov's purchase of 9 dessiatines from a parish in RGIA, *f.* 796, *op.* 175, *g.* 1894, *d.* 1771.
28. Although already becoming more common in the eighteenth century, this office became obligatory after the reform of ecclesiastical schools in 1808; see Freeze, *Parish Clergy*, p. 112. On the problem of malfeasance by elders, see the Synodal file from 1880 – establishing a special commission to design tighter auditing over church funds – in RGIA, *f.* 796, *op.* 161, *g.* 1880, *d.* 1837, *ll.* 1–4. By far the majority of church elders came from the peasantry and, in urban areas, the merchants; rarely were they ordinary townspeople or privileged elites. For example, the list of church elders for Vladimir diocese in 1875 included the following distribution: peasants (631), merchants (65), townspeople (23), civil servants (14, landowners (12), retired soldiers (6), factory foremen (2), honoured citizen (6). This total for 759 parishes is not inclusive, but clearly reveals the peasantry's preponderance, first and foremost in rural areas. 'Eparkhial'nym nachal'stvom utverzhdeny v dolzhnosti tserkovnykh starost', *Vladimirskie eparkhial'nye vedomosti*, no. 11 (1875) 507–24; no. 12, pp. 552–60; no. 13, pp. 605–8; no. 15, pp. 692–3.
29. In 1900–1, clerical youths comprised 80 per cent of the seminaries; by 1914, for example, clerical quotient had increased to 83 per cent of the

students. See: RGIA, *f. 796, op. 183, d. 835, l. 20 ob.*; *Vsepoddanneishii otchet … 1914 g.*, appendix, 70–1.

30. The main barrier was a 10 per cent quota, often ignored in the breach, especially in outlying areas with a weaker Orthodox establishment. In such cases, the Synod – begrudgingly – had to admit the recruitment and ordination of outsiders. In 1900, upon learning that nonclerical youths comprised 23 per cent of the whole system of ecclesiastical schools, the Synod complained that nonclerical sons 'lack a disposition to serve the Church in the clerical rank, but rather only wish to study so as to obtain advantages in performing their obligatory military service'. RGIA, *f. 796, op. 179, g. 1898, d. 415, l. 10* (Synodal resolution of 12 March 1900). As a result, Church authorities maintained close vigilance on the social make-up of the ecclesiastical schools. See, for example, the reports and inquiries on nonclerical progeny in RGIA, *f. 796, op. 183, g. 1902, d. 253,* and *op. 185, g. 1904, d. 178.*

31. The proportions varied, running as high as 94 per cent in Ufa diocese, but less in others (for example, 80 per cent in Tobol'sk diocese and 85 per cent in Kazan diocese). *Voprosy prikhodskoi, staroobriadcheskoi, veroispovednoi* (St Petersburg, 1910) p. 7.

32. RGIA, *f. 796, op. 174, g. 1893, d. 1292.* For Synodal demands on strict controls (including limits on the amount of parish cash on hand), see also RGIA, *f. 796, op. 183, d. 4375, l. 6.*

33. For a complaint about the typical inclination to default, after initial compliance, see the report from the bishop of Ufa, summarized in a memorandum from the chief procurator to the Synod on 11 October 1892. As the chief procurator emphasized, such violations of contractual agreements are 'almost ubiquitous'. The Synod directed bishops to seek enforcement of such contracts, but to avoid involving state authorities and resorting to coercion. (RGIA, *f. 796, op. 173, g. 1892, d. 1295, ll. 1–11*).

34. Most often the parishioners sought to expel an unpopular priest, usually on the basis of accusations that he extorted excessive fees for mandatory rites. Typical was a petition from a parish in Voronezh diocese (1900) and Vladimir diocese (1901), accusing a priest of extortion, in RGIA, *f. 796, op. 181, g. 1900, d. 2064, ll. 1–13; op. 182, g. 1901, d. 3820, ll. 1–8.* Such files abound in the central archives, as appeals against the failure of the bishop to act; see, for example, the files involving parishes in Astrakhan (1885), Vladimir (1887), Riazan (1888), Kostroma (1890), Nizhnii Novgorod (1891), Kaluga (1891), Chernigov (1897), Riazan (1900), Vladimir (1901), Vladimir (1905), in RGIA, *f. 796, op. 166, g. 1885, d. 1428; op. 168, g. 1887, d. 2051, ll. 1–50; op. 169, g. 1888, d. 2138; op. 171, g. 1890, d. 2284; op. 172, g. 1891, d. 2476; op. 172, g. 1891, d. 2451; op. 178, g. 1897, d. 3392; op. 181, d. 2765; op. 182, d. 3919; op. 186, d. 5656.* Such cases also attracted attention in the secular press; see, for example, the report in *Vladimirskaia gazeta*, no. 12 (10 December 1902), 2. Despite such complaints, conviction and punishment for extortion was rare; of the 3,417 clergy convicted for misdeeds, only 181 involved extortion; by far the greatest involved inebriation (1910), RGIA, *f. 834, op. 4, d. 945, l. 34.* In some cases, contrariwise, the parishioners demanded the return of a priest whom the bishop had forcibly relocated, normally for

committing various misdeeds. See, for example, the files from Orel in 1882 (*op.* 163, *g.* 1882, *d.* 2272), Kursk in 1885 (*op.* 166, *g.* 1885, *d.* 2048), Riazan in 1890 (*op.* 171, *g.* 1890, *d.* 2290), and Vladimir in 1895 (*op.* 176, *d.* 3172).

35. In a typical case, parishioners from one parish won an appeal to the Synod for reassignment to another, closer parish church after the local bishop had rejected their request (for fear that the change would 'lead to the total ruination' of their current church). See RGIA, *f.* 7696, *op.* 182, *g.* 1901, *d.* 1265, *ll.* 1–7. For a typical dispute over the establishment of a new parish (with adverse economic consequences for the neighbouring church), see RGIA, *f.* 796, *op.* 184, *g.* 1903, *d.* 2303.

36. RGIA, *f.* 796, *op.* 168, *g.* 1887, *d.* 2014, *l.* 2–2 *ob.* (MVD circular of 21 March 1887).

37. 'O proshlom i nastoiashchem polozhenii pravoslavnoi tserkovnoi obshchiny ili prikhoda', *Vladimirskie eparkhial'nye vedomosti*, no. 10 (1902) 336–45.

38. M. Novoselov, 'K voprosu o vybornom dukhovenstve', *Tserkovnyi vestnik*, no. 13 (15 March 1904) 398–400.

39. *Bogoslovskii vestnik*, no. 10 (1902).

40. The left focused mainly on their demand for 'a separation of the Church from the state and the school from the Church' (as in the Russian Social Democratic programme from 1903). But some in the revolutionary left cited the parish issue. For example, the Lithuanian Social Democrats demanded 'recognition of religion as a private matter, abolition of subsidies from the state treasury', as well as to regard the parish as a 'private society, which conducts its affairs entirely independently', *Programma politicheskikh partii Rossii* (Moscow, 1995) pp. 82, 22; see also 55, 64, 76, 133, 189, 202, 216.

41. Boldovskii, *Vozrozhdenie prikhoda*, p. 25.

42. After his initial idealized portrait of the medieval Russian parish (*Drevnerusskii prikhod*, 1897), Papkov published numerous articles in the daily press and journals as well as widely received volumes. For an early statement of his main views, see *Nachalo vozrozhdeniia tserkovno-prikhodskoi zhizni v Rossii* (Moscow, 1900).

43. *Novoe vremia*, no. 9726 (27 April 1903). See also: ibid., 1902, no. 9289; 1903, no. 9701; K. Odarenko, *Prikhod i bratstvo* (St Petersburg, 1899); I. P. Kupchinov, *Prikhod kak melkaia zemskaia edinitsa* (Moscow, 1905); S. D. Babushkin, *Tserkovno-prikhodskaia obshchina i zemskii sobor* (Kazan, 1905).

44. 'Zemsko-prikhodskaia organizatsiia', *Novoe vremia*, no. 9726 (2 April 1903).

45. For example, see the comments in 'Dokladnaia zapiska o neobkhodimosti prikhoda', in Rozhkov, *Tserkovnye voprosy*, pp. 281–2.

46. For details, see B. V. Anan'ich, 'O tekste manifesta 26 fevralia 1903 g.', *Vspomogatel'nye istoricheskie distsipliny*, XV (1983) 156–70.

47. 'Dnevnik A. P Kuropatkina', *Krasnyi arkhiv*, II (1922) 43.

48. S Iu. Witte, *Zapiska po krest'ianskomu delu* (St Petersburg, 1904) p. 7.

49. RGIA, *f.* 796, *op.* 205, *d.* 248, *ll.* 2 *ob.* 3 (Synodal resolution of 22 March 1905).

50. Synodal resolution of 18 March 1905 in RGIA, *f.* 796, *op.* 186, *d.* 657, *tom* 1, *l.* 32.

51. For the prominent and early renovationist statement, see Gruppa Petersburgskikh sviashchennikov, *K tserkovnomu soboru* (St Petersburg, 1906) p. 8.
52. *Vestnik narodnoi svobody* (January 1907) 30; N. Ognev, *Na poroge reform russkoi tserkvi i dukhovenstva* (St Petersburg, 1907) pp. 21–3.
53. Thus, an assembly of conservative noblemen explicitly sought to use the parish for purposes of 'ameliorating class conflict among various estates and in the establishment of a stable order in the countryside'. Their vision of parish reform included the formation of new parish councils, recognition of parish control over local funds, and even conferral of auxiliary police powers to support local state authorities. See Kruzhok dvorian vernykh prisiage, *Otchet s'ezda 22–25 aprelia 1906 goda s prilozheniiami* (Moscow, 1906) *prilozhenie 3*.
54. For Witte's memorandum, followed by a response from the Church and later the Chief Procurator K. P. Pobedonostsev, see A. R., *Istoricheskaia zapiska o sud'bakh pravoslavnoi tserkvi* (Moscow, 1912).
55. In September 1904, Nicholas II had averred his interest in convoking such a council: 'The thought of an all-Russian Church Council has long been nestled in my soul. For many questions involving our church life, the discussion of these by a national church council could lead to peace and tranquillity.' RGIA, *f.* 1579, *op.* 1, *d.* 35, *l.* 22 (letter to Pobedonostsev).
56. Synodal resolution of 13 July 1905, RGIA, *f.* 796, *op.* 186, *g.* 1905, *d.* 657, *tom* 1, *l.* 64.
57. The most outspoken was, predictably, Archbishop Antonii (Khrapovitskii) of Volhynia, who castigated parish reform as 'absurd and ridiculous' [*Otzyvy eparkhial'nykh arkhiereev po voprosu o tserkovnoi reforme*, 3 vols, vol. I (St Petersburg, 1906), p. 125]. See also Miroliubov, 'K voprosu', pp. 589–90.
58. The full replies are in *Otzyvy*. For a summary account of episcopal views on the parish question, see the Synod's synopsis of replies in *O blagoustroenii prikhoda. Svod mnenii eparkhial'nykh preosviashchennykh* (St Petersburg, 1906). For a general overview of episcopal opinion, see J. Meyendorff, 'Russian Bishops and Church Reform in 1905', in T. G. Stavrou and R. L. Nichols (eds), *Russian Orthodoxy under the Old Régime* (Minneapolis, 1978) pp. 70–182.
59. *Otzyvy*, I, 35–6.
60. *Otzyvy*, I, 225–6.
61. A typical complaint, sent from 'a peasant' to the Preconciliar Council on 10 December 1906, complained about the clergy's avarice and demand for ever larger gratuities (RGIA, *f.* 796, *op.* 186, *d.* 657, *tom* 3, *l.* 155.
62. 'Selo Lykovo', *Kliaz'ma*, no. 23 (25 January 1906): 3. Such resolutions could also bear an anti-clerical overtone; for example, see a resolution by another parish to reduce the gratuities paid to priests (in Gosudarstvennyi arkhiv Vladimirskoi oblast [hereafter GAVO], *f.* 556, *op.* 111, *d.* 1111, *l.* 387).
63. RGIA, *f.* 796, *op.* 186, *g.* 1905, *d.* 657, *tom* 4, *ll.* 53–3 ob.
64. RGIA, *f.* 796, *op.* 187, *d.* 781, *ll.* 3–4 ob. (resolution of 17 December 1905).
65. 'Zhurnaly zasedanii Kazanskogo eparkhial'nogo s'ezda', *Izvestiia po Kazanskoi eparkhii*, no. 43 (15 November 1905) 1277.
66. RGIA, *f.* 796, *op.* 186, *d.* 657, *tom* 2, *l.* 159 ob.
67. Hectograph flysheet (copy in the Helsinki Slavica Library, 117 kot 5).

68. Contrary to the traditional historiographic image of reactionary priests, prevalent not only in Soviet but also Western historiography, many in the parish clergy – sometimes working majorities in an entire diocese – leaned to the liberal, even left, wing of the political spectrum. Indicative of the spirit was a telegram from the clergy of Voronezh to the State Duma, sent on 21 June 1906: 'Instead of obscurantism and oppression, give us light and freedom! Take heart! Behind you and your truth is God Himself and the people! Long live popular freedom, and may the holy church of Christ grow strong and prosper!' Gosudarstvennyi Arkhiv Rossiiskoi Federatsii (GARF), *f.* 102, *DP OO, op.* 236(2), *d.* 750, *l.* 2; see also the documents in G. L. Freeze (ed.), *From Supplication to Revolution* (New York, 1988) pp. 234–8. For a more general discussion, see G. L. Freeze, 'Church and Politics in Late Imperial Russia: Crisis and Radicalization of the Orthodox Clergy', forthcoming in Anna Geifman (ed.), *Russia under the Last Tsar: Opposition and Subversion, 1894–1917* (Oxford, 2000), pp. 269–97.

69. Thus a pastoral assembly in Voronezh, attended by some 100 priests, emphasized that 'the renewal of parish church life is possible only through the realization of the manifesto of 17 October, through a change in social-economic life of the clergy, and through the autonomy of the parish community', *Tserkovno-obshchestvennaia zhizn'*, no. 20 (24 February 1906) 374.

70. See the resolution of a clerical assembly in Omsk (August 1905) in 'Letopis' tserkovnoi i obshchestvennoi zhizni', *Tserkovnyi vestnik*, no. 38 (22 September 1905) 1206.

71. For example, the diocesan assembly of clergy and laity in Mogilev resolved that the parish should have the right to nominate candidates, subject to episcopal approval; should he reject their candidate as unqualified, he is obliged to explain why, *Protokol postanovlenii i zhurnaly eparkhial'nogo sobraniia dukhovenstva i mirian Mogilevskoi eparkhii 19–21 sentiabria 1906 g.* (Mogilev, 1907) p. 2.

72. See, for example, Z., 'K voprosu o polozhenii dukhovenstva v reformirovannom prikhode', *Tserkovno-obshchestvennyi vestnik*, no. 3 (7 January 1906) 79–85.

73. See, for example, the resolution by the clerical assembly of Smolensk diocese in 1906 ('Zapiska deputatov eparkhial'nogo s'ezda dukhovenstva v fevr. 1906 g.', *Smolenskie eparkhial'nye vedomosti*, no. 5 (1906) *prilozhenie*, 223). Such attitudes, however, could change under the impact of revolution and popular pressure. For example, in discussions held in the early autumn of 1905, an assembly of clergy in Vladimir concluded that parish election of clergy enjoyed historical roots, but observed that this custom presupposed 'a high religious-moral development in the Church community' – a precondition hardly to be found at the present moment. See 'Sobranie v dome Ego Preosviashchenstva', *Vladimirskie eparkhial'nye vedomosti*, no. 20, 1905, p. 595. However, an official diocesan gathering of clergy agreed, at a meeting on 30 November 1905, that parishioners should be accorded the right to select the members of their parish staff (GAVO, *f.* 556, *op.* 1, *d.* 4423, *l.* 9 ob.)

74. At most, this assembly was willing to allow the parish to nominate candidates, but left final disposition entirely to the discretion of the bishop, RGIA, *f.* 796, *op.* 186, *g.* 1906, *d.* 657, *l.* 305.

75. RGIA, *f.* 797, *op.* 75, *otd.* 2, *st.* 3, *d.* 75, *ll.* 202–3.

76. For a convenient text of the decree, widely published in the contemporary Church and secular press, see P. E. Immekus, *Die Russisch-Orthodoxe Landpfarrei zu Beginn de XIX Jahrhunderts* (Würzburg, 1978), pp. 4–5.

77. For the Synod's complaint that 'diocesan authorities reacted to this initiative in a formal way', see RGIA, *f.* 796, *op.* 189, *d.* 2229/*b*, *l.* 252.

78. Although Nicholas declared on 17 December 1905 that the 'proper ordering of the Russian Church is a matter of necessity', he had no intention of summoning a Council – at least for the time being. For his reassurances to the leading prelates, see RGIA, *f.* 796, *op.* 186, *d.* 657, *tom* 1, *l.* 108.

79. Synodal resolution of 14 January 1906 (RGIA, *f.* 796, *op.* 186, *d.* 657, *tom* 3, *l.* 136).

80. RGIA, *f.* 796, *op.* 186, *d.* 657, *tom* 1, *l.* 190.

81. Synodal resolution of 7 March 1906 (RGIA, *f.* 796, *op.* 186, *g.* 657, *tom* 1, *l.* 214).

82. The instruction from the emperor to include Kireev, D. Khomiakov, F. Samarin, Kn. Evgenii Trubetskoi, and Nikolai Aksakov, as reported by the chief procurator to the Synod on 28 February 1906 (RGIA, *f.* 796, *op.* 186, *d.* 657, *tom* 1, *l.* 170). Nevertheless, the exclusively clerical and elite profile of the Commission elicited criticism; as one anonymous memorandum of November 1906 complained, the Commission should have included 'at least one peasant and one rural priest form each district', rather than all the 'the people who, though highly educated, are remote from both provincial life and the people'. RGIA, *f.* 796, *op.* 186, *d.* 657, *tom* 3, *l.* 95.

83. For the general resolutions, adopted in plenary sessions in November and December 1906, see RGIA, *f.* 796, *op.* 186, *d.* 657, *tom* 2, *ll.* 250–1 *ob.*

84. RGIA, *f.* 796, *op.* 186, *d.* 657, *tom* 4, *ll.* 28–47.

85. RGIA, *f.* 796, *op.* 186, *g.* 1905, *d.* 657, *t.* 2, *ll.* 273–4 *ob.* The plenary meeting of the Commission did not make a full-scale review of the Fourth Section's proposal, but did agree to its definition of 'parish' and the need to distinguish between property belonging to the parish, the clergy and the Church, RGIA, *f.* 796, *op.* 186, *d.* 657, *tom* 2, *l.* 251 *ob.*; P. Hauptmann and G. Stricker, *Die Orthodoxe Kirche in Rußland* (Göttingen, 1988), p. 599.

86. *Zhurnaly*, III, 351–2.

87. For details, see Fominykh, 'Proekty', pp. 41–59.

88. The emperor, in response to Church entreaties, made pro forma commitments to summon a Council, but avoided setting a date. See, for example, his decision in April 1907, summarized in Zyrianov, *Pravoslavnaia tserkov'*, p. 194. See also the complaints in 'Iz dnevnika L. Tikhomirova', *Krasnyi arkhiv*, 6/73 (1935) p. 175.

89. An arch-conservative like Antonii (Khrapovitskii) even came to oppose convening a council, for fear that it would adopt uncanonical, liberal reform. See his letter to Izvol'skii in April 1907 in RGIA, *f.* 1569, *op.* 1, *d.* 34, *ll.* 20–4. Similarly, a conservative canonist, I. Berdnikov, warned that if the coming Church council 'will be guided by the spirit of our time, then it will finally destroy the good that still exists among us', RGIA, *f.* 796, *op.* 186, *g.* 1905, *d.* 657, *t.* 1, *l.* 97.

90. During the budget discussions of 1908, the Octobrists added this phrase to the text of the Duma resolution. Gosudarstvennaia duma, 3 sozyv, 1

sessiia, *Stenograficheskii otchet*, 3:1385. For the Octobrist report of late 1907, with demands for a Church Council and reform, see: E. P Kovalevskii, *Narodnoe obrazovanie i tserkovnoe dostoianie* (St Petersburg, 1912) p. 12; *Voprosy very i tserkvi v III Dume* (St Petersburg, 191); *Tserkovnye voprosy na dumskoi kafedre* (Petrograd, 1915) 11–23; *Veroispovednye i tserkovnye voprosy v Gosudarstvennoi Dume III sozyva* (Moscow, 1909) p. 18.

91. For the establishment of this special commission, see RGIA, *f. 796, op.* 186, *g.* 1905, *d.* 657, *tom* 3, *ll.* 202–4 *ob.; f.* 797, *op.* 2, *st.* 3, *d.* 110/*b, l.* 1–1 *ob.* (Chief Procurator to the Synod, 27 February 1907).

92. RGIA, *f.* 796, *op.* 189, *d.* 2229/*b, l.* 210.

93. RGIA, *f.* 796, *op.* 186, *d.* 657, *tom* 4, *l.* 51 (Synodal resolution, 4 October 1907).

94. The protocols of its meetings show strong disagreements on the composition, definition and powers of the parish.

95. *Rossiia*, 23 October 1907.

96. The commission submitted the text of its draft statute on 11 January 1908; the full text is to be found in RGIA, *f.* 796, *op.* 186, *d.* 657, *tom* 4, *ll.* 70–3 *ob.* After some minor revisions, the Chief Procurator transmitted the proposal to the Council of Ministers on 10 October 1908. See *f.* 1405, *op.* 531, *d.* 636, *l.* 11.

97. The desire to involve women, deemed to exhibit greater piety and zeal, became increasingly pronounced. As a Commission protocol (2 October 1907) explained, 'it is extremely desirable and highly useful to involve women, especially the mothers of families, in parish assemblies, where issues of Christian charity and education will be decided'. RGIA, *f.* 796, *op.* 186, *d.* 657, *tom* 4, *l.* 198.

98. RGIA, *f.* 796, *op.* 186, *d.* 657, *tom* 4, *l.* 158.

99. RGIA, *f.* 796, *op.* 186, *d.* 657, *tom* 4, *l.* 206.

100. RGIA, *f.* 796, *op.* 186, *d.* 657, *t.* 4.

101. See RGIA, *f.* 797, *op.* 77, *otd.* 2, *st.* 3, *d.* 100/*v,* l. 8–8 *ob.*

102. Thus, Archbishop Antonii (Khrapovitskii) ridiculed fantasies of a parish revival, warned against the 'dangerous transfer of republican principles into the parish', and – alluding to the parish soviet – dismissed the 'silly Papkov parish collegium' (RGIA, *f.* 1569, *op.* 1, *d.* 34, *ll.* 22, 24). At a congress in the fall of 1909, the Union of Russian People rejected radical parish reform and expressed support only for measures to expand its educational and charitable roles. See *Kolokol* (14 October 1909).

103. RGIA, *f.* 797, *op.* 77, *otd.* 2, *st.* 3, *d.* 110/*v, ll.* 35–42.

104. RGIA, *f.* 797, *op.* 77, *otd.* 2, *st.* 3, *d.* 110/*v, ll.* 43–59.

105. Sectarians like the Stundists, wrote the Chief Procurator, 'consider the equality of property necessary, dream of communal ownership of property, of equal distribution of all valuables, deny any authority, beginning with tsarist authority, reject oaths, despise military service, and avoid the authority of courts established by the state' (ibid.).

106. RGIA, *f.* 797, *op.* 77, *otd.* 2, *st.* 3. *d.* 11/*b, ll.* 63–8.

107. RGIA, *f.* 1405, *op.* 531, *d.* 536, *l.* 44–6.

108. Thus, parish nomination of candidates was only a possibility, not a norm; full authority to decide rested with the bishop, 'who takes into account any petitions from parishioners, if such are presented'. RGIA, *f.* 797, *op.* 77,

otd. 2, *st.* 3, *d.* 110/*b*, *ll.* 95–9 *ob.* The text was approved by the Synod on 24 November 1910; the Chief Procurator transmitted the proposal to the Council of Ministers on 31 December 1910. To dispel conservative nostalgia for the medieval parish, the Church also submitted P. N. Zhukovich's 'Nekotorye cherty istoricheskoi tserkovno-prikhodskoi zhizni na Rusi' (ibid., *ll.* 128–81). The proposal was withdrawn in June 1911.

109. For the proposal of fifty-one Duma members on 23 November 1911, see RGIA, *f.* 797, *op.* 77, *otd.* 2, *st.* 3. *d.* 110/*b*, *ll.* 193–208.

110. RGIA, *f.* 796, *op.* 189, *d.* 2229/*b*, l. 3–3 *ob.*

111. RGIA, *f.* 1405, *op.* 551, *d.* 537, *l.* 93. As the Duma's criticism escalated (amidst discussions of the Church budget subsidies), on 29 February 1912 the Synod suddenly decided to establish a 'Preconciliar Conference' (*Predsobornoe soveshchanie*), comprised exclusively of bishops, in order to channel reform in a highly conservative direction. RGIA, *f.* 796, *op.* 205, *d.* 269; *f.* 669, *op.* 1, *d.* 4, *l.* 18. The absence of Academy professors and lay theologians elicited sharp criticism from reform-minded circles; see, for example, A. Osetskii, *Pomestnyi sobor* (Petrograd, 1917) p. 8.

112. RGIA, *f.* 797, *op.* 77, *otd.* 2, *st.* 3, *d.* 11/*b*, *ll.* 218–23 *ob.*; *f.* 1405, *op.* 531, *d.* 536, *ll.* 95–9. The Chief Procurator transmitted the proposal to the Council of Ministers on 8 March 1912.

113. Amidst revelations about the Rasputin spectacle (which came into full public view in the first months of 1912), Nicholas informed the Chief Procurator outright that, 'I have come to the final conclusion that, at present, it is impossible to predetermine the time for convoking the National Church Council', and instructed him not to raise this issue with ranking ministers. RGIA, *f.* 1569, *op.* 1, *d.* 72, *l.* 2 (Nicholas to Sabler, 2 March 1912).

114. *Prikhodskii vopros v IV-oi Gosudarstvennoi Dume*, (St Petersburg, 1914). For the proposal of thirty-four deputies (granting the status of juridical entity, power of self-taxation and right to elect parish clergy), see RGIA, *f.* 796, *op.* 189, *d.* 2229/*b*, *ll.* 173–4.

115. RGIA, *f.* 797, *op.* 83, *otd.* 1, *st.* 1, *d.* 136, *ll.* 3–67 ('Svod pozhelanii komissii Gosudarstvennoi Dumy').

116. Rozhkov, *Tserkovnye voprosy*, pp. 289–90.

117. 'Tserkovnye dela', *Novoe vremia*, no. 13333 (23 April 1913).

118. RGIA, *f.* 797, *op.* 77, *otd.* 2, *st.* 3, *d.* 110/*v*, *ll.* 216–17 *ob.*

119. 'Vecherniaia khronika', *Novoe vremia*, no. 13557 (7 December 1913).

120. B. Tsarevskii, 'Prikhodskii vopros', *Novoe vremia*, no. 13470 (11 September 1913).

121. I. S. Iakimov, *Kak ia byl tserkovnym starostoi* (Kazan, 1909) p. 32.

122. 1914 letter in RGIA, *f.* 796, *op.* 198, *otd.* 2, *st.* 1, *d.* 876, *l.* 30.

123. RGIA, *f.* 796, *op.* 442, *d.* 2577, *ll.* 4–5.

124. For typical complaints and demands for the removal of local clergy, see the cases involving priests in Viatka in 1909 (RGIA, *f.* 796, *op.* 190, *ch.* 1, *otd.* 1, *st.* 2, *d.* 342), Vladimir in 1910 (*op.* 191, *ch.* 2, *otd.* 5, *st.* 2, *d.* 189), and Moscow and Chernigov in 1913 (*op.* 197, *otd.* 5, *st.* 1, *dd.* 166, 299).

125. RGIA, *f.* 797, *op.* 83, *otd.* 3, *st.* 5, *d.* 182a, *l.* 1 (letter of 26 June 1913).

126. RGIA, *f.* 796, *op.* 442, *d.* 2570, *l.* 29.

127. A. A. Papkov, 'Za tserkovnoi stenoi', *Novoe vremia*, no. 13628 (17 February 1914).

128. A. A. Papkov, 'Gosudarstvennaia pomoshch' v prikhodskom dele', *Novoe vremia*, no. 13599 (20 January 1914).
129. A. A. Papkov, 'Iavochnyi poriadok dlia osushchestvleniia prikhodskoi reformy', *Novoe vremia*, no. 13621 (11 February 1914).
130. RGIA, *f.* 797, *op.* 84, *otd.* 2, *st.* 3, *d.* 396, *l.* 53 (letter of 25 May 1915) and *f.* 796, *op.* 189, *d.* 2296/*b*, *l.* 235.
131. As before, the Synod still had to deflect proposals from the Synod, including the draft of thirty-two deputies in May 1914; for its rejection of the proposal, see RGIA, *f.* 796, *op.* 189, *d.* 2229/*b*, *ll.* 178–83. For the Church's own proposal to the Council of Ministers (approved 25 April 1914 by the Council of Ministers and submitted on 8 June 1914 to the Duma), see RGIA, *f.* 796, *op.* 84, *otd.* 2, *st.* 3, *d.* 396, *ll.* 1–1 *ob.*, 6–26.
132. Mitr. Pitirim, 'Ob ustroenii pravoslavnogo prikhoda', *Novoe vremia*, 19 January 1916. The other members of the Synod were, however, not grateful for such candour; four days later, responding to private criticism, Pitirim explained that he was unaware of any impropriety in publishing the piece, denied actually being the author of the text, and. apologized to the other members of the Synod for his indiscretion. He asked, and received, the Synod's 'forgiveness' for his actions. RGIA, *f.* 796, *op.* 445, *d.* 223, *ll.* 139–40.
133. For Synod resolutions of early 1916, emphasizing the deleterious impact of such factors as serfdom and alcoholism on parish life, see: RGIA, *f.* 796, *op.* 189, *d.* 2229/*b*, *ll.* 260–1 and *op.* 445, *d.* 223, *ll.* 1–2.
134. RGIA, *f.* 796, *op.* 445, *d.* 223, *ll.* 16–17. Liberal sentiments were also apparent on other issues, such as the right of women to participate in plenary assemblies of the parish; see the recommendation from an assembly in Vologda in RGIA, *f.* 796, *op.* 445, *d.* 223, *ll.* 30–1.
135. RGIA, *f.* 796, *op.* 445, *d.* 223, *ll.* 19–20.
136. RGIA, *f.* 796, *op.* 445, *d.* 223, *ll.* 9–14 *ob.*
137. Typically, although this assembly agreed that the parish might make recommendations, the bishop could appoint a candidate on his own authority, with no need to make any explanations to the parishioners for his decision. RGIA, *f.* 796, *op.* 445, *d.* 223, *ll.* 7–8.
138. RGIA, *f.* 796, *op.* 189, *d.* 2229/*b*, *l.* 271.
139. RGIA, *f.* 797, *op.* 84, *otd.* 2, *st.* 3, *d.* 396, *l.* 121–121[???] *ob.*
140. RGIA, *f.* 796, *op.* 445, *d.* 218, *ll.* 1–7.
141. Ironically, a small booklet by B. V. Titlinov (*Vopros o prikhodskoi reforme v tsarstvovanie Aleksandra II* (Petrograd, 1917, declaring parish reform to be the key issue of the day, was approved by the censorship on 24 February 1917 – amidst the first days of the February Revolution.
142. 'Zhurnal Vladimirskogo eparkhial'nogo s'ezda dukhovenstva i mirian', *Vladimirskie eparkhial'nye vedomosti*, no. 21/21 (1917) 218.
143. Otdel rukopisei, Rossiiskaia gosudarstvennaia biblioteka (hereafter OR RGB), *f.* 60, *op.* 1, *papka* 3, *d.* 3, *l.* 17 (19–26 April 1917 assembly).
144. RGIA, *f.* 796, *op.* 445, *d.* 223, *ll.* 90–1.
145. *Vremennoe polozhenie o pravoslavnom prikhode* (Petrograd, 1917); also published under the same title in the main central ecclesiastical journal, *Tserkovnye vedomosti*, no. 28 (1 July): 193–9.
146. OR RGB, *f.* 60, *op.* 14, *d.* 13, *ll.* 9 *ob.*-10.

147. OR RGB, *f.* 10, *op.* 1, *papka* 4, *d.* 2, *l.* 8 (diocesan assembly of 22–3 March 1917).
148. OR RGB, *f.* 60, *op.* 1, *papka* 10, *d.* 2.
149. 'Ukaz Sv. Prav. Sinoda', *Vladimirskie eparkhial'nye vedomosti*, no. 26 (8 July 1917) 249.
150. Otdel rukopisei, Rossiiskaia gosudarstvennaia biblioteka, *f.* 60, *op.* 1, *papka* 60, *d.* 14, *l.* 3 ('K vserossiiskomu s'ezdu dukhovenstva').
151. 'Predlozhenie Ego Vysokokopreosviashchenstva', *Vladimirskie eparkhial'nye vedomosti*, no. 13 (30 March 1917) 167.
152. Aleksei, 'K moei pastve', *Vladimirskie eparkhial'nye vedomosti*, no. 15 (1917) 184.
153. 'Vozzvanie pastyrei Pokrovskogo uezda Vladimirskoi gubernii', *Vladimirskie eparkhial'nye vedomosti*, no. 24/25 (30 June 1917), 246; 'Ustav pastyrskogo pokrovskogo soiuza', ibid., no. 26 (1917) 254–6; A. Gloriozov, 'Pastyrskii soiuz', ibid., 24/25 (30 June), 245–6.
154. 'Kak eto pechal'no', *Vladimirskie eparkhial'nye vedomosti*, no. 23 (1917) 238.
155. See G. L. Freeze, 'From Institutional to Popular Secularization: Stalinist Campaigns against Parish Orthodoxy in the 1930s', forthcoming in: Manfred Hildermeier (ed.), *Schriften des Historischen Kollegs; Kolloquien* (Munich: Oldenburg Verlag, 1998).
156. See G. L. Freeze, 'Handmaiden of the State? The Orthodox Church in Imperial Russia Reconsidered', *Journal of Ecclesiastical History*, XXXVI (1985) 82–102.

10
The Poetics of Eurasia: Velimir Khlebnikov between Empire and Revolution

Harsha Ram

Velimir Khlebnikov

The great futurist poet Velimir Khlebnikov (1885–1922), more renowned than read today, was a key protagonist in the artistic and political revolt that was the Russian avant-garde. Known to connoisseurs of Russian literature as one of the principal innovators of Russian poetic language, Velimir Khlebnikov was also hailed during his own life, if only by his fellow futurists, as the King of Time. For Khlebnikov's written legacy embraces more than his literary production: in his collected works, alongside some of the most startling verse in the Russian language, we find page upon page of mathematical formulae, algebraic equations that are presented to us as the foundations of a precise science of history.

This twin legacy – of poetry and of what might be called a speculative theory of historical time – is more than a remarkable if aberrant episode in Russian letters. It represents a major poet's abstracted but engaged meditation upon his own historical moment, that saw the profound crisis of the Russian Empire revealed in war and resolved, however tentatively, in revolution.

Khlebnikov's life and work dramatizes the great dilemmas of a nation caught between empire and revolution, dilemmas that the poet was to live in geographical terms no less than in history. Khlebnikov was born in the Kalmyk steppe, near the Caspian Sea. It is this southern Volga region, where the Russian, Iranian and Turanian worlds have met and mingled over centuries, that serves as a key to the poet's personal geography. The former Tatar capitals of Astrakhan, the 'most naked and ontological of all Russian cities, a caravanserai',[1] and Kazan, where the mathematician Lobachevskii had taught and where

Khlebnikov himself studied, both served as points of reference that drew Khlebnikov's world southward, away from the established cultural centres of St Petersburg and Moscow.

Khlebnikov's life was largely lived along this north–south axis that we know as the Russian equivalent of the more familiar European dichotomy of east and west. The culminating moment in this trajectory was Khlebnikov's journey, in the summer of 1921, over the Caucasus to Baku and thence across the Caspian to northern Iran. Khlebnikov's experience of Azerbaijan and Iran provided the basis for his last great outpouring of verse and theoretical speculation, which resonate as part of an essential widening of Russia's political and aesthetic horizons.[2]

Khlebnikov's life and work can be read as a major literary milestone within a wider cultural tendency. Since dubbed Eurasianism, this tendency has consistently attempted to interpret Russian history as geographical destiny, and to tilt Russia's geopolitical orientation and cultural allegiances towards Eurasia – in polemical opposition to European hegemony, to be sure, but also to the inevitable dichotomization of east and west. Khlebnikov's writings provide us with a historical poetics and even an epistemology of Eurasia as a historical space and a literary construct. The pages to come will seek to sketch out the salient features of this poetics, in its startling novelty, its inevitable embeddedness in Russia's literary tradition, and in its unique resolution of the historical crisis of 1917.

Eurasia and panmongolism

Russian nineteenth-century literature, we might recall, had privileged the Caucasus and Transcaucasia in its literary renderings of empire. The great Caucasian poems of Pushkin and Lermontov dramatized Russian imperial policy towards its southern peripheries, which culminated in the protracted war waged by Russian forces in Chechnia and Dagestan throughout the early and mid-nineteenth century. This Caucasian tradition can be said to end with Tolstoi's great, if belated, masterpiece *Haji Murat* (completed in 1904): at the cusp of the new century, the broader tensions of great power competition in Central Asia, India and the Far East – Kipling's 'Great Game' – had begun to impinge on Russian culture.

The complex of anxieties engendered in Russia by geopolitical rivalries spanning the entire Eurasian landmass, implicating Russia, Britain, Japan, China and Ottoman Turkey, found a ready literary idiom with the appearance of the philosopher Vladimir Solov'ëv's celebrated 'A Short Story of the Anti-Christ' ('Kratkaia povest' ob Antikhriste') in 1900, where it was christened *panmongolism*.[3] In Solov'ëv's immensely influential formulation, the ancient memory of the thirteenth-century Mongol invasions of the Eurasian steppe was recapitulated as an imminent threat to Russia and humanity and a harbinger of the Antichrist. Written in response to the Chinese Boxer rebellion and acquiring a prophetic timeliness after the Russo-Japanese War of 1905, Solov'ëv's panmongolism engendered a cultural idiom that collapsed the political present of Russian imperial policy into a remote past (the Tatar yoke) and an impending future (the Apocalypse). It transformed the dense particularities of Central Asia, Ottoman Turkey and the Far East into a loosely defined Eurasian continent that could be evoked as a traumatic geography, within which ancient historical resentments, fears of racial miscegenation and millenarian expectations of imminent revolution could coexist in a nervous interrogation of Russia's own location in space and time.

Solov'ëv's panmongolian vision, part orientalism and part eschatology, was destined to reverberate through the works of an entire generation of Russian writers known as symbolists. In Aleksandr Blok's astonishing poem 'The Scythians' ('*Skify*', 1918) a crucial shift in this paradigm occurs: the east–west axis of Solov'ëvian millenarianism is deflected in its direction and meaning. The Apocalypse, which for Solov'ëv was an *external* threat to Christian Russia, is here internalized as Russia's own geographical and racial burden: 'Like obedient lackeys, we / Held the shield between two hostile races / the Mongols and Europe!' In absorbing the shock of the Mongol invasion, Blok's Russia has *itself* been orientalized and thus addresses the west as Asiatic: 'Yes, we are Scythian!' Blok cries, 'yes we are Asian, / with slanted and avaricious eyes!'[4] It is important to note the spatial fluidity in what is otherwise a crudely racializing idiom: in panmongolism east and west function as apparent racial or civilizational absolutes that are nevertheless always collapsing inward: they are *not* in fact dichotomies but perspectival thresholds through which Russia will measure her national and imperial destiny.

In its subtler 'Scythian' formulations, panmongolism emerged as the first and most influential literary formulation of what would shortly be known as 'the Eurasian debate' in early twentieth-century Russian culture. Inevitably, then, panmongolism was to serve as a powerful polemical precedent for Khlebnikov's own musings on Orient and empire.

As perhaps no Russian before him, Khlebnikov came to deplore the 'artifical narrowness of Russian literature'. In a programmatic article of 1913, 'Expanding the Boundaries of Russian Literature' ('O rasshirenii predelov russkoi slovesnosti'), the poet observes:

> [Russian literature] has not known the influence of Persia and the Mongols, although the Mongolo-Finns preceded the Russians in possession of their land. ... Of the borderlands it has celebrated only the Caucasus, but not the Urals or Siberia. ... Nor is there a creation or achievement that might express the spirit of the continent [*materika*] and the soul of the vanquished natives, like Longfellow's *Hiawatha*. Such a work transmits the breath of life, as it were, from the vanquished to the victor.[5]

This geographical *ars poetica* is precious in revealing Khlebnikov's basic philological strategy: to widen Russian literature systematically towards the geographical and ethnic confines of its own imperial borders. Khlebnikov contemplates the Russian imperial adventure in its full temporal and spatial range. The vast steppe regions, the southern Volga, Transcaucasia and Central Asia proper are relived in their prolonged and continent-wide encounter with Russian culture, an encounter whose history the poet will trace back beyond the Petrine reforms, into a prehistory that predates even the carefully nursed memory of the Tatar yoke.

Khlebnikov's philology, then, is inseparable from territory: its struggle for cultural breadth directly follows the logic of Russian expansion without seeking to absolve or abstract its own linguistic discoveries from the colonial encounters that occasioned them. The poet's work, it is worth emphasizing, seeks neither to celebrate empire nor simply to denounce it. Khlebnikov's guiding spirit is never crudely chauvinistic or Great Russian but rather 'continent-wide' [*materikovym*].

Khlebnikov's Eurasianism, however, was more than a geographical reorientation or a cultural polemic. The poet's great ambition was to synthesize the salient tendencies of Russian imperial culture into a poetic vision that would also constitute a critique of the *cognitive* basis of historical knowledge. In the remainder of this paper, I propose to address this imbrication of the poetic and the historical in Khlebnikov's work in two stages: (1) with reference to his programmatic manifestos, where the poet's literary and political categories are most clearly complementary, and (2) by elucidating those elements of his theory of time and of the linguistic sign that, I would suggest, constitute nothing less than an epistemology of empire. In all instances, the Eurasian land mass will emerge as Khlebnikov's organizing principle, bringing together a specific if mobile geographical matrix and an increasingly abstract elaboration of history.

Khlebnikov's futurist manifestos

In the shrilly irreverent manifestos of the futurist movement, such as 'The Trumpet of the Martians' ('Truba marsian', 1916), 'Lalia Rides a Tiger' ('Lialia na tigre', 1916) and 'An Appeal by the Presidents of Planet Earth' ('Vozzvanie predsedatelei zemnogo shara', 1917), the distinction, fundamental to all avant-garde movements, between tradition and innovation is expressed as a deepening gap between *space* (the stasis of received truths) and *time* (the dynamism of the new). The unit through which this gap is asserted is the political state, along with the idiom, heard frequently enough during the Great War, of competing nationalisms.

The futurists' youth rebellion against the cultural establishment is proclaimed in an act of political secession that unilaterally establishes the 'independent state of time (devoid of space) [*nezavisimoe gosudarstvo vremeni (lishennoe prostranstva)*].'[6] A generational conflict becomes a struggle between nations – nations, moreover, that are different precisely as time differs from space: 'We have founded the state of time, ... leaving to the states of space the chance to reconcile themselves to its existence by leaving it alone, or by engaging it in a bitter struggle.'[7] What does Khlebnikov's state of time look like?

> We have studied the soil of the continent of time, and found it fertile. But firm hands from *back there* have grabbed us and are preventing us from carrying out our splendid betrayal of space. Has there ever been anything more intoxicating than this betrayal? ... We summon you to a land where trees can talk, where there are scholarly associations that look like waves, where there are springtime armies of love, *where time blooms* like a *bird-cherry tree* and moves like a piston, where a superman [*zachelovek*] in a carpenter's apron saws the ages [*vremena*] into boards and treats tomorrow as might a turner of wood.[8]

The rhetoric of militant vanguards is always richly contradictory and Khlebnikov's is no exception. The futurists' declared hypostasis of time must initially deflate the importance of space, including one of the most potent forms of spatialization available – the nation state. Yet space is attacked in the very idiom of territorial integrity that is the political precondition of national sovereignty: the unit of Khlebnikovian time thus paradoxically remains geographical, more specifically, *territorial*. The visionary core of his temporal unit is in fact a form of spatial autonomy, an artisanal utopia where craftsmen manipulate – and spatialize – time as artistic form. There is no temporal sequentiality here, just contiguous raw matter to be moulded at will.

The terms of the celebrated dispute between the Italian futurist Filippo Marinetti and his Russian futurist counterparts now appear clearer. Behind the rather puerile conflict that flared up in 1914 over artisitic primacy – which futurism, and hence which country, Italy or Russia, came first? – lies a profound divergence in each movement's conceptualization of time and space. Where the Italian futurists asserted time as *velocità*, the accelerating speed of Western modernity, Khlebnikov responded characteristically by interpreting their claim as an act of European territorial aggression. In an open letter to Marinetti, co-authored with Benedikt Lifshits, we read:

> Today the Italian colony on the Neva and certain natives are falling at the feet of Marinetti for personal reasons, betraying Russian art just as it takes its first step on the road to freedom and honour. They are making Asia bend its noble neck beneath Europe's yoke. ... Foreigner, remember what country you have come to![9]

If Khlebnikov consistently asserts visionary time as a form of spatial autonomy, his attack on Marinetti reveals here the location of his own utopia. *Pure time is here territorialized as Asia*, a continent awakening to its inviolable right to self-determination. The toponym 'Asia' here clearly embraces Russia also: it is only Russia's *role* in Asia, as against her place in it, that remains in question. A powerful answer was provided by the Bolshevik Revolution, by which the Soviet Union would assume a position of leadership in Eurasia and the world. Leadership, we should note, is a troubling synecdoche: while remaining part of a greater whole, the leader speaks for its entirety, assuming a totalizing function that exceeds his actual physical limits.

In 1918 Khlebnikov wrote a series of declarations that amounted to a sweeping act of global decolonization. One such manifesto, 'An Indo-Russian Union' ('Indo-russkii soiuz'), has been published in Russian but is as yet little known. A striking index of the poet's broadly political sympathies, the text merits the attention of a wider readership (the full

Russian text and its translation can be found as an appendix to this chapter):

(1) The Society's goal to defend the shores of Asia from pirates and to create a single maritime frontier.

(2) We know that the bell that sounds for Russia's freedom will not touch European ears.

(3) As with distinct social classes, nation states are divided into oppressor states and enslaved states. ...

(5) Among the enslaved states are the great nations of the Continent of ASSU (China, India, Persia, Russia, Siam, Afghanistan). The islands are oppressors, the continents are enslaved. ...

(7) From the ashes of the Great War a single Asia has been born. ...

(9) This union has been created by the will of Fate in Astrakhan, a city uniting three worlds – the Aryan, the Indian and the Caspian, the triangle of Christ, the Buddha, Muhammad. ...

> We speak as the first Asians to take cognizance of their insular unity.

> May every citizen of our island pass from the Yellow Sea to the Baltic, from the White Sea to the Indian Ocean, unimpeded by any border.

> May the tattooed patterns of nation states be effaced from Asia's body by the will of Asians.

> The dependent territories of Asia are uniting to form one island.

> We, the citizens of the new world, liberated and united by Asia, parade triumphantly before you. ...

Nations, follow us![10]

In Khlebnikov's political manifestos of 1918 the poet's ideology clearly evolves beyond the nationalist cultural vanguardism of his pre-revolutionary years, in loose tandem with Bolshevik and Comintern debates on what came to be called the 'national question'. If the October Revolution seemed a possible materialization of Khlebnikov's utopia, its concrete result was, like Khlebnikov's own rhetoric, a powerful paradox: Leninism combined a trenchant critique of European and Great Russian imperialism with a ruthless impulse towards territorial reconsolidation and the reconfiguration of the imperial nation state in a new guise.[11]

Somewhat like the double-edged premise of the Bolshevik Revolution, Khlebnikov's political discourse is startling both in its disturbing conventionality and remarkable novelty. Deeply embedded in the rhetoric of imperial rivalry that marks both his theory of history and his polemical encounters with other schools of art, the poet's manifestos reproduce the familiar spiral of aggressive triumphalism that typifies both imperialist ambition and nationalist response. In these manifestos, as in the early declarations of the Bolshevik leaders, a political geography, liberated and renamed, is finally reunified and subordinated to a new social order that re-enters the geopolitical game on different terms. As with Bolshevism, then, there is a sense in which Khlebnikov's internationalism is crucially circumscribed – by the imperative of territorial unity, the strategic geographical interests of the new republic, and by the ideology of vanguard party leadership itself. Much like Soviet Russia, then, Khlebnikov's utopia is above all a state, united and inviolable, in which power devolves exclusively to the artist as to the party: playfully crowned 'Chairman of the Globe' and 'King of Time', Khlebnikov remains, even in his utopia, its prophet and revolutionary leader.

If Khlebnikov's debt to Leninism is evident, so too is the startling boldness of his revolutionary manifestos, which by no means adhere passively to Bolshevik orthodoxy. Speaking in the name of Asia rather than Russia or Soviet communism, Khlebnikov's manifestos go well beyond the gestural solidarity of the Bolsheviks towards Russia's Asian neighbours. They confront the terror of revolutionary cataclysm and cultural hybridity, which the Russian modernists had called panmongolism, and embrace it as a utopian destiny. To be sure, this embrace is also the realization, in a radically different guise, of tsarist Russia's long-standing if self-deluding ambition to conquer Persia and India. Yet in inverting Russia's Europeanizing civilizational mission and making Asia her cultural focus, Khlebnikov's vision finally seems what might be called *critically* imperial. Asia is less russified than Russia is made Asiatic and it is in this shift of emphasis that we must culturally situate Khlebnikov's Eurasian or pan-Asian sentiment.

Theorizing imperial history

The greatest novelty of Khlebnikov's Eurasianism, however, does not lie in the political sympathies it evinces. It is to be found in the scientific discoveries made in the 'laboratory of time' which, in Khlebnikov's mind, was to govern revolutionary Asia as its 'Supreme Soviet'.

Khlebnikov's attempts at formulating a theory of time were as obsessive as they were prolonged. In a proleptic epitaph (written at the age of nineteen!) the poet asks to be remembered for having 'found the true classification for the sciences', 'connect [ing] time to space', and 'creat [ing] a geometry of numbers'.[12] In 1911 he writes to the painter Matiushin: 'I spend all my time working on numbers [or dates: *chislami*] and the fate of nations as dependent variables of numbers [*chisel*], and have made some progress.'[13]

By 1912 progress had indeed been made: Khlebnikov's dialogue 'Teacher and Pupil' ('Uchitel' i uchenik') was his first published formulation of the laws governing the flow of history. The lines that follow, at least in Khlebnikov's later estimation, contain nothing less than a prediction of the October Revolution:

> *Pupil*: ... I have sought the rules that dictate the destiny of nations. ... I assert ... that 1383 years separate the fall of states and the loss of liberty. ... I have found in general that time z separates such events where $z = (365 + 48y)x$, where y may have a negative or positive value ... if $y = 2$, and $x = 3$, then $z = (365 + 48 \times 2)3 = 1383$. The fall of states is divided by this period of time. ... The Polovtsy conquered the Russian steppe in 1093, 1383 years after the fall of Samnium in the year 290. And in the year 534 the kingdom of the Vandals was conquered; should we not expect the fall of a state in 1917?
>
> *Teacher*: This is a real art. But how did you achieve it?
>
> *Pupil*: The clear stars of the South awoke the Chaldean in me. On the day of Ivan Kupalo I found my fern[14] – the law that governs the fall of states. I know about the mind of continents that is quite unlike the mind of islanders. The son of proud Asia cannot be reconciled with the peninsular reason of Europeans.[15]

Throughout his life Khlebnikov sought the laws that governed history: to recognize its patterns, he believed, is to anticipate and finally neutralize its upheavals. Khlebnikov measured historical time by calibrating the dates that marked the rise and fall of empires. The above passage not only provides us with a mathematical account of imperial history; it also locates the origin of the poet's theories in a generic 'South' here identified as Asia.

In Khlebnikov's astonishing final poem or 'supersaga' *Zangezi* (1922), an amalgam of prophetic utterances, visionary poetry and quasi-scientific data, the celebrated medieval battle of Kulikovo, which saw the Khan Mamai and his Golden Horde defeated at the hands of Prince Dmitrii of Moscow in 1380, is described as being the result of the equation 2 multiplied by 3 raised to the power of 11:

Волны народов одна за другой
Катились на запад
Готы и гунны, с ними татары.
Через дважды в одинадцатой три
Выросла в шлеме сугробов Москва,
Сказала Востоку: «Ни шагу!»

[Waves of nations one after another
Rolled westward:
Goths and Huns, with them the Tatars.
In two times three to the eleventh power
Moscow rose up in a helmet of snowdrifts
And said to the East: 'Not one more step!']16

Russia's celebrated triumph over the Tatar foe is here drained of any naïvely patriotic resonance. The victory, we are implicitly told, is not due to any inherent Russian superiority, eventually to be anchored in a European identity. It is merely the outcome of a larger mathematical principle of retributive justice, by which the earlier victories of the steppe-dwelling nomads must be finally countered by the Russian people.

The above examples of Khlebnikov's numerical theory of history perhaps suffice for us to note some of its salient features. As a cognitive tool these equations look like a bizarre conversion of fortune-telling into a positivist science. Far from being a singular and fixed law of time, they are at best an endless proliferation of loosely connected formulae applicable only to discrete sets of events, at worst a series of random variations (additions, subtractions, multiplications) of key integers, indices and theorems (2 to the power of n, 3 to the power of n but also 365, 317, 243, 242 and so on) that yoke together events picked equally at random. Infinite theoretical modifications prevent the possibility of radical discrepancy, while the principle of event and counter-event is never so absolute or self-evident as not to make the juxtaposition of any two or more given moments seem finally arbitrary and their formulations somewhat *ad hoc*.

Clearly, Khlebnikov's theory of number commands our attention not for its accuracy but as a poetics and as a tentative epistemology of time. As such it combines a startling theoretical radicalism with a philosophy of history that is conceptually rather conservative. In the terms of the linguist Roman Jakobson, Khlebnikov's 'axis of selection' (the axis that chooses one or more of many related terms within a given paradigm) is founded on an entirely traditional notion of history as a collection of *events*, empirically datable just as a datum of science is verifiable.[17] According to the logic of this axis, even as complex a problematic as empire or revolution can and should be reduced to a series of designated watersheds – battles, assassinations, the crowning or toppling of a monarch. The *cognitive* value of their dates as historical fact is never questioned. In what sense does the year 1917, for example, inherently signify the Russian Revolution except as a synecdoche?

It is only Khlebnikov's 'axis of combination' (again in Jakobson's terms) that appears truly innovative. The axis of combination (which complements the axis of selection by reorganizing the units chosen into syntagmatic sequences – be they mathematical equations or lines of verse) breaks entirely with the notion of time as a flow of contiguous, successive moments: 'The new way of thinking time brings to the fore the operation of division and asserts that distant points may be more identical than two neighbouring ones ...'[18] The operation of division rearranges scattered points into new correlations, revealing the rhythmic vibrations that are seen to underlie them.

Universally applicable, these patterns of repetition derive *in the first instance from the problematic of nation and empire* and then ramify into an infinite number of series that calculate the rise of individuals, generations, religions and even private emotional states: 'The law of the vibratory movement of a nation-state differs from the law of the movement of an individual soul only in the sense that their times are measured by two neighbouring members of the set S: the unit of 365 plus or minus 48n for nation-states is a year, for an individual soul it is a day.'[19]

If the question of imperial nationhood constitutes the paradigm for all other rhythmic patterns, it is not only because Khlebnikov believes imperialism, as it is commonly understood, to be a powerful influence on the course of history. More importantly, it is because Khlebnikov thinks *time itself imperially*, as a despotism, a 'realm of numbers' (*gosudarstvo chisel*) of which he is king and prophet, dictating the outcome of any given aspect of existence.

The presence of numerical equations in Khlebnikov's verse makes for a unique interference of metalanguage and poetry. Unlike Khlebnikov's theory of letters, which is more readily absorbed into the fabric of his work as assonance and alliteration, his numerical values, even when loosely metrical, create a kind of secondary rhythm. Let us recall Roman Jakobson's definition of the poetic function as that which 'projects the principle of equivalence from the axis of selection into the axis of combination'. Jakobson goes on to distinguish poetry from metalanguage: 'the sequence [or axis of combination] is used to build the equation, whereas in poetry the equation is used to build a sequence'.[20] Where Khlebnikov's theory of number appears as *poetry*, a metalinguistic principle of equation is superimposed onto the poetic function: the abstract patterns of equational laws function to produce both poetic equivalence and historical parallels.

As fantastically random as they may appear as mathematical formulae, these patterns are rhythmically consistent in their way of producing *repetition*, in poetry as in history. One such pattern – indeed for Khlebnikov the decisive one – is the endless struggle between east and west. Khlebnikov will find its traces in any number of distinct conflicts: the perennial wars between the nomadic tribes of Eurasia and the sedentary urban cultures of Europe and the imperial expansion of the great European powers through Asia are all equally found to be the result of a temporal law that effectively *produces* both east and west:

Через степени три
Смена военной зари.
Древнему чету и нечету
Там покоряется меч и тут.
....
Оси событий из чучела мира торчат –
Пу́гала войн проткнувшие прутья.
Проволока мира – число.
Что зто? Истины члены?
Иль пустобрех?
Востока и запада волны
Сменяются степенью трех.

[In the space of powers of three
Shifts the dawn of war.
The ancient [law of] odd and even
here overpowers even the sword.
... The axes of events stick out from the scarecrow of the world –
The piercing branches of the scarecrow of wars.
The wire of the world is number.
What is this? The vessel of truth?

Or idle chatter?
The waves of East and West
Displace each other to the power of three.][21]

Here the figure of 3 to the power of *n* arranges history into rhythmic waves of imperial aggression emanating alternately from east and west. It is worth noting that repetition in Khlebnikov is the condition of difference rather than sameness in time and space, of *shifts* (Khlebnikov himself calls them *smeny* or *sdvigi*) in geographical perspective. East for Poland, Russia becomes the west when repelling an eastern invasion ('Moscow / Said to the East: "Not one more step!"'). Clearly, within the strictly mathematical model of time, east and west are not absolute hypostases but changing perspectives produced by the directional thrust of historical violence. This becomes clear from Khlebnikov's extraordinary reinterpretation of the Russo-Japanese War of 1904–5 in the same section of *Zangezi*:

Вслед за отходом татарских тревог –
Это Русь пошла на восток.
Через два раза в десятой степени три
После взятия Искера,
После суровых очей Ермака,
Отраженных в сибирской реке,
Наступает день битвы Мукдена,
Где много земле отдали удали.
Это всегда так: после трех в степени энной
Наступил отрицательный сдвиг.
Стесселем стал Ермак
Через три в десятой степени дней
И столько же.
Чем Куликово было татарам,
Тем грозный Мукден был для русских.
В очках ученого пророка
Его видал за письменным столом
Владимир Соловьев.

[Following the receding of the Tatar troubles –
It was Russia's turn to go east.
In two times three to the tenth power
After the taking of Isker,
After the austere eyes of Yermak

Were reflected in the Siberian river,
The day arrives for the battle of Mukden,
Where much daring was sacrificed for land.
This is always the case: after three to the nth power
The negative shift set in. / Yermak became Stessel
In days numbering three to the tenth power
    and as many again.
What Kulikovo had been for the Tatars,
Terrible Mukden was for the Russians.
Wearing the glasses of a learned prophet
Seated at his writing desk, Vladimir Solov'ëv
    Saw this.][22]

Despite its pious acknowledgement of Vladimir Solov'ëv, this passage in fact undermines the basic premise of panmongolism and Russian symbolist eschatology as a whole. The Russo-Japanese War, we know, was a watershed for Russian modernism and for Russian imperial consciousness generally. In Khlebnikov's account, Russia's defeat at the hands of the Japanese is seen to put an end to the cycle of Russia's expansion in the Far East: the law of 3 to the power of n days separates the conquest of Siberia by the Cossack explorer Yermak in 1581 from the surrender of Port Arthur by the Russian commander Stessel and the subsequent battle of Mukden in 1905. Khlebnikov's interpretation fundamentally dislodges the panmongolian schema: what for the symbolists was a defeat that replayed the humiliation of the Tatar yoke, definitively linking the Orient to past and impending cataclysms, is now seen as the consequence of Russia's own expansionist policies in Siberia. The apocalyptic threat from the east is no more than the most recent manifestation of an ongoing mathematical principle, in which east and west are equal players, winning and losing in turn.

Khlebnikov's law of time thus functions to ground history in repetition as a differential principle, dictating the confines of empire and the success and failure of revolution. His thinking assumes a rather traditional and positivistic notion of history as a series of datable events, only to reinterpret these data as part of an east–west cycle that moulds events remote in time into consistent spatial patterns of territorial loss and gain.

Khlebnikovian history, however, is not infinite; its final utopian horizon, the moment where time merges with space:

The somewhat happy thought kept occurring to me that in essence neither time nor space exists, but rather two different calculations [*scheta*], two inclines [*skate*] of the same roof, two paths along the same edifice of numbers.

Time and space appear to be the one and the same tree of calculation, but in the one case [time – H. R.] the imaginary squirrel of calculation moves from the branches to the base, and in the other [space] from the base to the branches.[23]

Once the laws of time are revealed, time no longer differs, ontologically speaking, from space. Both rise up as from the soil, vertical abstractions that differ only in the direction of their variables: time is descent, space ascent. All of Khlebnikov's work points towards this utopian moment, where time and space become one. It is the promise of freedom, rationally achieved. It does not end history, like the symbolists' Apocalypse, but grasps its hidden laws, calibrated according to the rhythms of aggression, the cycles of violence that have determined the rise and demise of nations.

This utopia, for Khlebnikov, has a name: Asia. We can now see how Khlebnikov's literary manifestos polemically corroborate his deeper intuitions about the nature of history. In promulgating the laws of time just as his manifestos unite Russia and Asia, Khlebnikov merges absolute historical time with reterritorialized imperial space. *A mathematical abstraction of time corresponds to a liberation of space*, and both coincide to constitute Khlebnikov's Asia.

The crucial, if hidden, significance of Khlebnikov's work within Russia's tradition (and perhaps even for current postcolonial historiography) now becomes clearer. If the Eurasian debate has served to this day as the principal spatial and temporal paradigm by which Russia has represented the historical and cultural possibilities of empire, then Khlebnikov's writings might well be seen as its most self-critical moment.[24] While sharing with other Eurasianists a belief in the geographical ineluctability – and hence unity – of Eurasia, Khlebnikov understood the logic of empire less as a goal to be justified than as a mechanism to be understood and possibly dismantled. By deriving his great speculative and poetic syntheses from the deeper pulse of global violence, Khlebnikov freed Eurasianism from the parochial purpose of mirroring Russian chauvinist anxieties, in order to ponder the very role of time and space as historical conditions and epistemological categories. Just as east and west are produced and dissolved in a bloody cycle that only knowledge can end, so Asia too is less a toponym, a place on the map, than the very possibility of calculating and perhaps overcoming empire.

Appendix: 'An Indo-Russian Union'

Written in Astrakhan in September 1918, Khlebnikov's manifesto 'An Indo-Russian Union' is a strikingly precocious literary adaptation of the internationalist and anti-imperialist sentiment unleashed by the October Revolution, which is here radicalized into a project of pan-Asian liberation. Beyond the familiar conflation, characteristic of the time, of literary and political vanguardism – the artist as revolutionary Party – we find a provocative conceptualization of Asia as a geography, one that anticipates the post-Second World War era of decolonization more than it typifies the Bolshevik Revolution itself.

Not only does the manifesto identify Russia in opposition to Europe as one of the oppressed nations of Asia. One might say that Asia is itself viewed less as a fact of empirical geography than as the performative gesture that maps its contours as if for the first time. In a sense, Asia does not pre-exist the declarative act that liberates it from bondage, raising it from its present condition of fragmentation to a new territorial unity.

This reterritorialization, which constitutes Asia as such, clearly mirrors the physical and discursive transformation, in the aftermath of the Revolution, of the Russian Empire into the Soviet Union. The same dynamic, however, is here extended beyond the old imperial borders of Russia to Asia as a whole, while Khlebnikov's dream is less the Leninist goal of world revolution than a unified Eurasian homeland. Eurasia's heart, moreover, is Astrakhan, and not the traditional Russian urban centres to the north, which had been the privileged locus of tsarist and Soviet culture. Astrakhan and the Caspian Sea region mark the site of an older confluence of civilizational and spiritual legacies.

Inspired in part by the rhetoric of Bolshevik proclamations, Khlebnikov's manifestos are thus also marked by other forms of linguistic and conceptual energy. Their playfully exaggerated claims on behalf of the artist are typical of the European avant-garde, while their cosmic and universalist aspirations, however secular in content, derive their force from the revelatory idiom of religious prophecy (specifically from an oriental – Near Eastern or South Asian – cultural matrix). Finally, Khlebnikov's use of neologisms and graphic marks (e.g., 'Assu' as a toponym signifying 'Asia') marks an ongoing effort to rethink the linguistic and cognitive basis of space and time. This reworking of sign systems corresponds to a new 'organic' vision of human geography, that privileges islands and maritime borders over the artificial territorial divisions of geopolitics. The goal of history is thus to coincide with the natural unity of continents.

The text below, published here in Russian, is based on the handwritten manuscript located in the Moscow archives (RGALI, *fond* 527, *op.* 1, *ed. khr.* 112). Minor emendations have been made to the text for the sake of consistency in punctuation and grammar. The translation provided below may be compared to the earlier English translation by Paul Schmidt in the *Collected Works of Velimir Khlebnikov*, vol. 1, pp. 341–2. A small number of interpretative errors and textual misreadings found in the Schmidt version have been corrected.

Индо-русский союз

(1) О[бществ]о ставит себе целью защиту берегов Азии от морских разбойников и создание единой морской границы.

(2) Мы знаем, что колокол русской свободы не заденет уха европейца.

(3) Как и отдельные классы, государства делятся на государства-угне татели и государства-порабощенные.

(4) Пока во всех государствах пролетарии не взяли власть, государс- тва можно разделить на госуд[арства] пролетари[ев] и госуд[арства] буржуа.

(5) К угнетаемым государствам относятся великие народы материка Ассу (Китай, Индия, Персия, Россия, Сиам, Афганистан). Острова-угнетатели, материки-угнетаемые.

(6) Максимум морских границ, полное отсутсвие сухопутных.

(7) Из пепла великой войны родилась единая Азия.

(8) Мы, облаченные в тяжелые латы положительных наук, спешим на помош нащей общей матери.

(9) В Астрахани, соединяющей три мира – арийский, индийский и кас пийский, треугольника Христа, Будд[ы] и Магомета волею Судьбы образован єтот союз.

(10) Подлинник начертан на листьях лотоса и хранится в чаталгае. Постановлением трех хранителем его назначено Каспийское море. Мы выступаем как первые азиаты, сознающие свое островное единство.

Пусть гражданин нащего острова пройдет от желтого моря до Балтийского, от Белого моря до Индийского океана, не встречая границ.

Пусть татуировка государств будет смыта с тела Азии волей азийцев.

Уделы Азии соединяются в остров.

Мы, граждане нового мира, освобожденные и обЪединенные
Азией, проходим перед вами праздничным шествием.
Удивляются нам.

Девушки, сплетающие венки – кладите их под ноги победителей
будущего.

Терния, которыми поспешат оцарапать ноги, идущие к единству,
мы поспешим обратить в розы.

Нащ путь – к единству Звезд через единство Азии и через свободу
материка к свободе Земного шара.

Мы идем по этому пути не как деятели смерти, а как молодые
Вишну в рубахе рабочего.

Песни и слово – наще волшебное оружие.

Смотрите, Азия только одна, а [у] нее столько женихов – японцы,
англичане, американцы.

Нашим ответом будет натянутый лук Одиссея.

Начиная нашу жизнь, мы вырываем Индию из великобританских
когтей.

Индия – ты свободна.

Трое первых, назвавших себя азиятами, освобождают тебя.

Вспомни заветы Цейлона, так и мы стучимся в твой разум, остров
Ассу.

Мы бросились в глуб веков и собрали подписи Будд[ы], Конфуция
и Толстого.

Народы Азии, думайте больше о своем единстве и оно не оставит
вас.

Мы зажигаем светильник.

Народы Азии посылают лучших сынов поддерживать заженное
пламя.

Мы созываем конгресс угнетенных народов у великих озер.
Великие мысли рождаются около великих озер.

Здесь у самого большого озера в мире родилась мысль о самом
большом острове мира.

(11)   Мы призываем Россию к немедленному соединиению с южным
Китаем для образования мирового тыла великой Швейцарии,
Азии.

Мы приносим в жертву Δ нащи сердца превозглашемому Δ
[треугольни]-ку рас.

Делая єто, мы делаем бессмертными наши имена и вонзаем их в
гриву бегущих столетий.

Народы, следуйте за нами!

12 сент. 1918, 5 ч. 27 м.
Астрахань

An Indo-Russian Union

(1) The Society's goal is to defend the shores of Asia from pirates and to create a single maritime frontier.

(2) We know that the bell that sounds for Russia's freedom will not touch European ears.

(3) As with distinct social classes, nation states are divided into oppressor states and enslaved states.

(4) Until the proletariat assumes power in every state, states can be divided into proletarian states and bourgeois states.

(5) Among the enslaved states are the great nations of the Continent of ASSU (China, India, Persia, Russia, Siam, Afghanistan). The islands are oppressors, the continents are enslaved.

(6) We need to maximize maritime frontiers, while land frontiers must be eliminated.

(7) From the ashes of the Great War a single Asia has been born.

(8) Clothed in the heavy armour of the positive sciences, we rush to the aid of our common mother.

(9) This Union has been created by the will of Fate in Astrakhan, [a city] uniting three worlds – the Aryan, the Indian and the Caspian, the triangle of Christ, the Buddha and Muhammad.

(10) The original text has been inscribed on lotus leaves and is kept in Chatalgai. By a decree of the [above] three, the Caspian Sea is declared to be its guardian.

We speak as the first Asians to take cognizance of their insular unity.

May every citizen of our island pass from the Yellow Sea to the Baltic, from the White Sea to the Indian Ocean, unimpeded by any border.

May the tattooed patterns of nation states be effaced from Asia's body by the will of Asians.

The dependent territories of Asia are uniting to form one island.

We, the citizens of the new world, liberated and united by Asia, parade triumphantly before you. People marvel at us.

Girls, weave wreaths and lay them beneath the feet of those who have conquered the future.

Any thorns placed hastily to scratch our feet as we march towards unity we shall turn quickly into roses.

Our path leads from the unity of Asia to the unity of the Stars, and through the freedom of the continent to the freedom of the entire planet.

We follow this path not as agents of death but like young Vishnus dressed in the shirts of working men.

Songs and words are our magic weapons.

Asia is just one, but look how many suitors she has – the Japanese, the English, the Americans. To this our response shall be the drawn bow of Odysseus.

To being our new life, we snatch India from the clutches of Great Britain. India – you are free.

The first three to call themselves Asian are setting you free.

Remember the behest of Ceylon, so we too knock on the door of your reason, o island of Assu.

We have plunged into the depths of past ages and collected the signatures of the Buddha, Confucius and Tolstoi.

Nations of Asia, ponder your unity more often, and it will not abandon you. We are lighting the lamp.

The nations of Asia are sending the best of their sons to maintain the kindled flame.

We call for a congress of enslaved nations to gather by the great lakes. Great thoughts arise on the shores of great lakes.

Here, by the largest lake in the world, the thought of the largest island arose.

(11) We appeal to Russia to unite immediately with southern China in order to constitute Asia as a universal rearguard, a greater Switzerland.

We sacrifice Δ our hearts to the proclaimed Δ [tri]-angle of races.

In doing this, we immortalize our names and plunge them into the manes of the galloping centuries.

Nations, follow us!

12 September 1918, 5:27 a.m.
Astrakhan

Notes

1. The phrase is D. S. Mirsky's, in 'Khlebnikov', *Versty*, no. 3 (1928) 146.
2. On Khlebnikov's relationship to the Orient or the Russian south, see Iu. M. Loshchits and V. N. Turbin, 'Tema vostoka v tvorchestve V. Khlebnikova', *Narody Azii i Afriki*, no. 4 (1996); A. Kosterin, 'Russkie Dervishi', *Moskva*, no. 9 (1966); V. V. Ivanov, 'Struktura stikhotvoreniia Khlebnikova "Menia pronosiat na slonovykh"', *Trudy po znakovym sistemam*, no. 3 (1967); A. E. Parnis, 'V. Khlebnikov v revoliutsionnom Giliane (novye materialy)', *Narody Azii i Afriki*, no. 5 (1967) 157–64; O. Samorodova, 'Poèt na Kavkaze', *Zvezda*, no. 6 (1972); Solomon Mirsky,

Der Orient im Werk Velimir Khlebnikovs (Munich, 1975); A. E. Parnis, 'Iuzhnoslavianskaia tema Velimira Khlebnikova: Novye materialy k tvorcheskoi biografii poèta', *Zarubezhnye slaviane i russkaia literatura* (Leningrad, 1978); A. Parnis, 'V. Khlebnikov – Sotrudnik "Krasnogo Voina"', *Literaturnoe Obozrenie*, no. 2 (1980); P. Tartakovskii, *Russkie poèty i vostok. Bunin Khlebnikov Esenin* (Tashkent: Izdatel'stvo literatury i iskusstva imeni Gafura Guliama, 1986); P. I. Tartakovskii, 'Drevneiranskaia mifologiia v khudozhestvennoi strukture tvorenii pozdnego Khlebnikova', *Khlebnikovskie chteniia* (St Petersburg: Muzei Anny Akhmatovoi v Fontannom Dome, 1991), pp. 40–9; and Aleksandr Parnis, '"Tuda, tuda, gde Izanagi ..." Nekotorye zametki k teme "Khlebnikov i Iaponiia"', *Iskusstva awangarda: Iazyk mirovogo obshcheniia. Materialy mezhdunarodnoi komferentsii 10–11 dekabria 1992 g.* (Ufa: Muzei sovremennogo iskusstva 'Vostok', 1993).

3. The tale 'Kratkaia povest' ob Antikhriste' is part of a larger text, *Tri razgovora*. For the Russian text, see V. S. Solov'ëv, *Izbrannoe* (Moscow: Sovetskaia Rossiia, 1990) pp. 231–424. An English translation of the story is available in Vladimir Solovyov, *War, Progress and the End of History: Three Conversations Including a Short Story of the Anti-Christ*, trans. Alexander Bakshy (Hudson, NY: Lindisfarne Press, 1990) pp. 159–91. Cf. also the closely related poem by Solov'ëv, 'Panmongolizm', *Stikhotvoreniia*, 6th edn (Moscow: I. N. Kushnerev, 1915) pp. 287–8, a radically simplified variant of the longer prose text. The poem was also used by Blok as an epigraph to his *Skify*. These texts are usefully read in the light of Solov'ëv's ethico-political vision: in relation to the Orient see his 'Tri sily', *Sochineniia v dvukh tomakh*, vol. 1 (Moscow: Pravda, 1989), pp. 19–31, 'Mir Vostoka i Zapada', vol. 2, pp. 602–5 and 'Pis'mo o vostochmom voprose', vol. 2, pp. 636–9. For a genealogy of panmongolism, see Ettore Lo Gatto, '*Panmongolismo* di V. Solov'ëv, *I venienti Unni* di v. Briusov e *Gli Sciti* di A. Blok', *For Roman Jakobson* (The Hague: Mouton, 1956), and Georges Nivat, 'Du "panmongolisme" au "mouvement eurasien", Histoire d'un thème littéraire', *Cahiers du monde russe et soviétique*, III (1996) 460–78. Panmongolism has generally been viewed as the progenitor of the Scythianism of Blok and Ivanov-Razumnik and the émigré Eurasian movement of the 1920s involving N. S. Trubetzkoy, George Vernadsky, D. S. Mirsky and others. See N. S. Trubetzkoy, *The Legacy of Genghis Khan and Other Essays on Russia's Identity*, ed. Anatoly Liberman (Ann Arbor: Michigan Slavic Publications, 1991); D. S. Mirsky 'The Eurasian Movement', *The Slavonic Review*, VI/17 (1927), 311–19; Charles J. Halperin, 'George Vernadsky, Eurasianism, the Mongols, and Russia', *Slavic Review*, Fall (1982) 477–93. With the collapse of the Soviet Union the Eurasian question is being raised once more: cf. D. S. Likhachev, 'Les mythes et i'histoire russe', *Lettres Internationales*, no. 34 (Autumn 1992); and Denis Dragunskii, 'Evraziiskii vybor', *Druzhba narodov*, no. 9 (1992). Two recent and immensely useful summaries in English of nearly two centuries of related intellectual debates are Mark Bassin, 'Russia betwen Europe and Asia: the Ideological Construction of Geographical Space', *Slavic Review*, L/1, (Spring 1991) 1–17, and Madhavan K. Palat, 'Eurasianism as an Ideology for Russia's Future', *Economic and Political Weekly*, XXVII/51 (December 1993) 2799–2809.

4. Blok's poem 'The Scythians' appeared alongside an article by Ivanov-Razumnik in 1918; see Aleksandr Blok, 'Skify', *Sobranie sochinenii v shesti tomakh*, vol. 2 (Leningrad: Khudozhestvennaia literatura, 1971) pp. 253–5. The importance of Solov'ëv's eschatological orientalism for Russian modernism cannot be underestimated, although it was modified by each of those who felt its impact. See Briusov's 'Griadushchie gunny', which appeared as part of the collection *Stephanos* (1905), a text saturated with impressions of the 1905 Revolution; Andrei Belyi, 'Apokalipsis v russkoi peèzii', *Vesy*, no. 4 (April 1905) 11–28, and 'Vladimir Solov'ev. Iz vospominanii', *Arabeski* (Moscow: Musaget, 1911); D. Orlov (ed.), *Aleksandr Blok – Andrei Belyi Perepiska* (Munich: Wilhelm Fink, 1969 [1940]), in particular the letters of 1911, and Blok's article 'Narod i intelligentsiia' where the Battle of Kulikovo is used as an allegory of the Russian intellectual's conflict with his *own* nation.

5. Velimir Khlebnikov, 'O rasshirenii predelov russkoi slovesnosti', *Neizdannye proizvedeniia*, ed. N. Khardzhiev and T. Grits (Moscow: Khudozhestvennaia literatura, 1940) pp. 341–2. An English translation is available as 'Expanding the Boundaries of Russian Literature', *Collected Works of Velimir Khlebnikov*, trans. Paul Schmidt, vol. 1 (Cambridge, Mass.: Harvard University Press, 1987), pp. 253–4. (Where available, the English citation of Khlebnikov's work will henceforth be given in parentheses, after the Russian citation. The translations provided in the text, however, are generally my own.)

6. Velimir Khlebnikov, 'Truba marsian', *Sobranie proizvedenii Velimira Khlebnikova*, ed. N. Stepanov (Leningrad: Izdatel'stvo pisatelei v Leningrade, 1929–53), vol. 5, p. 152 ('The Trumpet of the Martians', *Collected Works*, vol. 1, p. 323).

7. Khlebnikov, 'Lialia na tigre', *Sobranie proizvedenii*, vol. 5, p. 213 ('Lalia Rides a Tiger', *Collected Works*, vol. 1, p. 330).

8. Khlebnikov, 'Truba marsian', *Sobranie proizvedenii*, vol. 5, p. 152 ('The Trumpet of the Martians', *Collected Works*, vol. 1, p. 322).

9. Khlebnikov, 'Na priezd Marinetti v Rossiiu', *Sobranie proizvedenii*, vol. 5, p. 250.

10. Khlebnikov, 'Indo-russkii Soiuz', Russian State Archive for Literature and Art (RGALI), Moscow, *fond* 527, *op.* 1, *ed. khr.* 112. My thanks to Natalia Zlydneva for her help in obtaining the manuscript, and for providing me with its partial transcription. The same text has been translated into English, see 'An Indo-Russian Union', *Collected Works*, vol. 1, pp. 341–2. I provide the full Russian text of the manifesto and a new translation as an appendix to this article. See also Khlebnikov's other manifesto 'Asiaunion', *Collected Works*, vol. 1, p. 343, and A. Parnis, 'V. Khlebnikov-Sotrudnik "Krasnogo voina"', p. 107. I would suggest that Khlebnikov generally uses the term 'Asia' or poetic neologisms such as 'Assu' or 'az' to signify what later historians such as Trubetzkoy termed 'Eurasia'. In both cases Russia's position in this larger entity remains the most vexed question.

11. Marxist debates on colonialism and the national question have been traced by Hélène Carrère d'Encausse and Stuart R. Schram, *Marxism and Asia* (London: Allen Lane, Penguin, 1969). For the history of Central Asia and the Far East during the revolutionary period see Edward Hallet Carr, *The*

Bolshevik Revolution, 1917–1923, vol. 3 (New York: W. W. Norton, 1985) pp. 229–70, 467–548. Lenin's writings on the subject have been gathered in V. I. Lenin, *The National Liberation Movement in the East,* 3rd rev. edn (Moscow: Progress Publishers, 1969) and *Questions of National Policy and Proletarian Internationalism* (Moscow: Progress Publishers, 1969).

12. Khlebnikov, 'Pust' na mogil'noi prochtut', *Neizdannye proizvedeniia,* p. 318 (*Collected Works,* vol. 1, p. 196).

13. Dated April 1911, *Neizdannye proizvedeniia,* p. 360 (*Collected Works,* vol. 1, p. 160): 'Vse vremia ia rabotaiu nad chislami i sud'bami narodov, kak zav-isimymi peremennymi chisel, i sdelal nekotorye shagi.'

14. The fern is a reference to a Russian folk-belief that a magical plant blooms on the eve of the festival of Ivan Kupala (John the Baptist), whose fiery colour reveals the presence of buried treasure. Khlebnikov's treasure is of course the Law of Time.

15. Khlebnikov, 'Uchitel' i uchenik. O slovakh, gorodakh i narodakh', *Sobranie proizvedenii,* vol. 5, pp. 175, 178–9.

16. Khlebnikov, *Zangezi, Sobranie proizvedenii,* vol. 3, p. 349 (*Collected Works,* vol. 2, p. 359). It should be noted that Khlebnikov had an equally complex theory of the letter elaborating a geometrical understanding of space that complemented his mathematical notion of time. Given the obvious relevance of spatial categories to a toponym such as Eurasia, the poet's geometrical theory of the letter is essential for a full understanding of Khlebnikov's poetics. For reasons of economy, however, I choose not to explore this dimension here.

17. Roman Jakobson's notion of the poetic function in terms of the axes of selection and combination is elaborated in 'Linguistics and Poetics', *Language in Literature* (Cambridge, Mass.: Belknap/Harvard University Press, 1987) p. 71.

18. Khlebnikov, 'Nasha osnova', *Sobranie proizvedenii,* vol. 5, pp. 241–2 ('Our Fundamentals', *Collected Works,* vol. 1, pp. 389–90).

19. Khlebnikov, 'Vremia mera mira', *Sobranie proizvedenii,* vol. 5, p. 438.

20. Roman Jakobson, 'Linguistics and Poetics', p. 71.

21. Khlebnikov, *Zangezi, Sobranie proizvedenii,* vol. 3, pp. 351–2 (*Collected Works,* vol. 2, p. 361).

22. Khlebnikov, *Zangezi, Sobranie proizvedenii,* vol. 3, pp. 350–1 (*Collected Works,* vol. 2, p. 360).

23. Khlebnikov, 'Otryvok iz dosok sud'by', *Sobranie proizvedenii,* vol. 5, p. 478.

24. Two very different yet related contemporary figures may be seen as typical representatives of Brezhnev-era Eurasianism: L. N. Gumilev and O. Suleimanov. See Olzhas Suleimanov, *Az i Ia.: Kniga blagonamerennogo chi-tatelia* (Alma-Ata: Izd. Zhazushy, 1975) and L. N. Gumilev, *Ritmy Evrazii: Epokhi i tsivilizatsii* (Moscow: Ekopros, 1993). One could argue that at least Suleimanov adopts elements of a Khlebnikovian poetics: the blurring of the distinction between literature (specifically poetry) and scholarship (specifically linguistics and historiography), whereby the poetic sign becomes a means of raising epistemological questions about knowledge and its disciplinary formations.

Index